WHEN SHADOWS FALL
A Journey Of Faith

Aug, 2001

Christene Bolte-Luthey

Dearest most precious friends Steve and Bonnie,

It is my sincere prayer that you both will be blessed by my thoughts and what God has placed on my heart to share. Thank you for all your love, support and kindness. You are loved and very appreciated. God Bless and keep you always,

Chrissy

Copyright © 2001 by Christene Bolte-Luthey
All rights reserved.
No part of this book may be reproduced, restored in a retrieval system, or transmitted by means, electronic, mechanical, photocopying, recording, or otherwise, without written consent from the author.

ISBN: 0 75963 306 1

This book is printed on acid free paper.

Unless otherwise noted, Scripture quotations are from the Holy Bible, New King James Version (NKJV)

1stBooks - rev. 4/27/01

WHEN SHADOWS FALL
A Journey Of Faith

"All too often we take for granted our briefness of days
Until a personal tragedy or near-fatal incident
Makes us aware of our MORTALITY.
Those who are fortunate, come to the understanding that
LIFE IS BUT A VAPOR, and TIME no doubt is LIMITED.
WHEN SHADOWS FALL, we stand face to face with our humanity.
If we are attentive, we become aware of the separating line
Between God's Love and Forgiveness and His Judgment of sin.
As our heart sees this reality
We suddenly realize the immense need to make peace with our Maker
And discover the only way to do that
Is through a personal relationship with JESUS CHRIST."

Chris Luthey

Contents

Introduction ix

One: **Consider The Storm**
    The Distant Muffled Roar *1*
    Consumed By Darkness *3*
    No Place To Run Or Hide *4*
    Love Beyond Self *5*
    Everything Was Gone *6*

Two: **The Greatest Fear**
    An Image Of Death *9*
    A Portrait Of Life *11*
    The Gulf Between Heaven And Hell *12*
    Humbled By Mercy *13*
    Depart From Me I Never Knew You *14*

Three: **On The Edge Of Eternity**
    Consider Your Mortality *17*
    Death Is Inevitable *18*
    Called To Give An Account *18*
    Washed By The Blood *20*
    What Have We Done For God's Glory? *22*
    Sort Through The Baggage *24*

Four: **Life Is But A Vapor**
    The Brevity Of Life *28*
    Take Courage *29*
    Face To Face With Our Values *31*
    I May Not Have Tomorrow *31*

Five: **The Just Shall Live By Faith**
    Is Christ The Lord Of Your Life *37*
    The Day Has Come To Search Ourselves *39*
    Age Of Rebellion *41*
    Harden Not Your Heart *42*

	Could We Bear His Cross...43	
	Have We Insulted The Spirit Of Grace?...45	
	Love So Pure And True..46	

Six: **Behold The Plumb line** *(Part 1: Law/Wickedness/Death)*
    In The Beginning...49
    What Is Our Motivation...51
    The Wickedness Of Man..59
    The Judgment Of The Ungodly...61
    Consider The Latter End..66
    False Worship And Teachers...67
    Remember Your Ways..70
    Plunged Into Darkness..72
    True Regret...76
    Find A Bible Believing Church..78
    Choose Life Not Death..79

    Behold The Plumb line *(Part 2: Grace/Righteousness/Life)*
    The Depth Of God..92
    God Will Not Be Mocked..92
    If Not For Grace...95
    Time To Change..97
    A Choice Is Required Of You...99

Seven: **Eternity In The Balance**
    Christ The Cornerstone..103
    Christ Our Foundation...107
    All Is Vanity..114
    Fortune And Fame...115
    Where Is Our Treasure...116
    Honesty...117
    The Final Assessment..122

Eight: **When Shadows Fall**
    Yielding To The Master's Hand...132
    Needing The Peace Of God..136
    Faith Comes By Hearing..138
    Only For A Time...143

Constantly And Faithfully *144*
A Faithful Friend *148*
When Shadows Fall *151*
Crisis And Loss *152*
When Suffering Comes *156*
Why Would God Allow This Pain? *174*
Vessels Of Honor *176*

Nine: **A Portrait Of Grace**
Bridges To Victory *199*
Consider The Goal *199*
God's Grace Is Real *200*
Contemplate The Dream *206*
Overcoming Adversity *207*
Only Christ Can Say To The Wounded *210*
Confirm Your Commitment *211*
Condition Yourself *213*

Ten: **Pressing Toward The Goal**
Onward To Victory *218*
Christ Is The Vine *219*
Faith That Conquers *222*
Obedience To God's Will *224*
Food For The Soul *226*
Establish A Relationship *229*
The Challenge *231*
The Character Of Christ *246*
The Great Commission *247*

Eleven: **Poems To Inspire Your Heart**
Our Loving Shepherd (Faith & Hope) *256*
Our Shelter In The Storm (Courage & Strength) *286*
Our Savior, Lord And King (Blessing & Encouragement) *318*
Our Source Of Grace & Peace (Meditations, Devotions & Prayer) *345*

Introduction

When Shadows Fall might be considered to be a book of life and death meditations. It holds many hopeful outcomes for those who read and use it to explore attitudes and emotions that surface as we journey throughout life and its adversities. It is not only to be read; it is to practice and inspire. It is to help discover Biblical Solutions amidst life's difficulties and understand the process by which God uses suffering and loss, to produce within us Christ-like perseverance, character and love.

The Holy Bible says, **"In the world you will have tribulation" [John 16:33]**. This I found is terribly TRUE. Beginning in 1985 in the midst of TORNADO my soul was laid bare, displaying the reality of Heaven's Glory and Hell's torment. Humbled as never before, I realized for the first time in my life, the depth of God's awesome Grace and the measure of His wonderful love. Although it is hard to explain, God made his presence known and the fairness of His Righteous judgment. At that moment, mere words cannot express the range of emotions I sensed inside, beholding the love of Jesus Christ, which I had so carelessly ignored and taken for granted.

God was going to sentence me to my eternal dwelling place, and REGRET was all I that I knew. **"Enter by the narrow gate; for wide is the gate and broad is the way that leads to destruction" [Matt. 7:13]**. Standing there, feeling the weight of my OWN guilt and shame, it was apparent by the horror of this understanding, that the word of God is emphatically true! **"Not everyone who says to me, Lord, Lord shall enter the kingdom of heaven, but he who does the will of my Father in heaven. Many will say to me in that day, Lord, Lord, we have prophesied in your name, cast out demons in your name, and done many wonders in your name. And I will declare to them I never knew you, depart from me, you who practice lawlessness!" [Matt. 7:21-23]**.

In a mysterious way, when this "SHADOW" fell I observed a portrait of eternity that unveiled a glimpse of both heaven and hell. Guilty and ashamed, I realized the sorrow of NOT developing a PERSONAL relationship with the One who had died for me. Jesus Christ. The One who came to pardon my soul from the future judgment of God and spare me from sin's chains? In viewing this portrait of grace, my heart was broken, for it was clearly apparent to me that if you have lived your life apart from Christ, you shall eventually experience the greatest void the soul shall ever feel. Hearing from the Lord and giver of life speak to you, **"depart from me, I never knew you,"** then to be taken and cast away from God's presence for all eternity.

No mind could begin to measure the triumph amidst tragedy my life has known <u>since</u> I have gained the understanding I will share with you throughout these pages. I want to explore with you many things we carelessly take for granted, and the consequences of what we do without thinking. It is my prayer that as you read the pages within you will search your heart and mind for anything that separates YOU from God? Using my personal testimonies only as a means of help, support, and encouragement as you strive toward spiritual growth according to the will of God, that you also may become a new creation in Jesus Christ—being reconciled to your Heavenly Father.

I encourage you along with myself, to learn how to identify with Christ in His suffering. I hope that my testimony will not only be as "salt" which stings, but also "light" that may illuminate any places where darkness may exist in your life. Jesus invites us to **"Follow Him," [Matt. 9:9].** So long as we by the measure of our faith attempt to yield our lives to the Holy Spirit's power, God will accomplish a life-changing transformation in us that will one day reveal a portrait of grace that will remain throughout eternity!

WHEN SHADOWS FALL upon our lives, we often experience shock, anger, fear, grief, depression, loneliness, or pain. It is then we need to know that Jesus Christ has borne the same sufferings on the cross. Learning to live with any painful experience is without a doubt a unique journey that has no one perfect course. Yet the stages of our healing are most helpful if we look to God and allow our affliction to produce character. By learning to be patient, trusting the love of our Heavenly Father, we'll gain a Godly perspective of what suffering may accomplish for God's glory.

<u>From time to time throughout this book I have added</u> **<u>inquiry sheets</u>** <u>where you may write your feelings when pondering a subject, if you so desire?</u> This writing offers the freedom to HONESTLY note your thoughts without fear of criticism or judgment, as you need be the only one looking at its contents? Please make use of these pages; perhaps God will use them to disclose understanding? Each day we going through a process of refining and purifying in which God will allow life's trials to ultimately build within us Christ-like character. ***This maturity takes a lifetime of perseverance so do not despair!***

Even though it seems at times we're walking through "shadows," "valleys" or "fire," believe that you and I are NEVER ALONE! **[Job 23:10]** tells us, **"God knows the way I take."** He has promised to be with us in everything. He will never leave or abandon our side. We must only yield to His will whatever it may be. Permitting us to be molded into that which he has purposed from the beginning of time. As we submit our will and ways to the refining fires of God's soul searching forge and life changing grace, we will come into a deeper relationship with Him and stand with unshakable faith.

This book is intended for everyone, it's life changing contents know no limits. The **Scripture verses** you will find throughout this book are taken from the HOLY BIBLE (New King James Version—NKJV) and **have all been put into BOLD PRINT to help you identify what is the infallible word of GOD**. Please keep the Holy Bible at all times central as you are reading and draw from its infinite wisdom the spiritual nourishment required to grow in the Lord. Be careful and keep your heart open to the Holy Spirit. As we allow God to live and work in our lives we will see opportunities to help others who are brokenhearted or suffering. As we step out in faith to become a vessel of God's healing, we along with Jesus can use our wounds to bring LOVE and HOPE to the weary.

"For now we see in a mirror, dimly, but then face to face. Now I know in part, but then I shall know just as I also am known. And now abide faith, hope, love, these three; but he greatest is love" [1 Corinthians 13:12-13]. I dedicate this book to the will and glory of God my Heavenly Father to whom I owe all gratitude and thanks for the Salvation of my soul and that of my family. Therefore, **"Rejoice if your sorrow leads you to repentance. For you were made sorry in a Godly manner, that you might suffer from us in nothing. For Godly sorrow produces repentance to Salvation not to be regretted, but the sorrow of the world produces death" [2 Cor. 7:9-10]**.

Forgive me if you find throughout the beginning chapters that my message sounds at all tedious, God has placed an intense burden on my heart to express a crucially significant subject to every soul. Trust and believe that every line and verse throughout these pages I have personally asked MYSELF. *I say most sincerely that if these truths are received into even ONE person's heart so that they come to know personally Jesus Christ as* **Savior,** *every "SHADOW" that has "fallen" on my life,—will have been worth it!*

Christene Luthey

WHEN SHADOWS FALL
(A note from Jesus)

WHEN *SHADOWS FALL* and veil your view
FEAR NOT: I walk abreast of you…
When *DARKNESS* envelops the light of day
TRUST in My hand to guide your way…
When *DANGER* brings uncertainty
BELIEVE my word shall set you free…
When *OMINOUS FOG* pursues your peace
REST in My arms for sweet release…
When *SUNLESS SKIES* make dim your heart
Have **FAITH** that we shall never part…
When *DREADFUL STORMS* make hard your life
RECEIVE My Grace to cease your strife…
When *FATAL CLOUDS* bring gloomy tears
COME near to me, I'll dry your tears…
When *HEAVY RAIN* obscures your mind
WALK with ME and HOPE you'll find…

Christene Luthey

One
CONSIDER THE STORM

"In this you greatly rejoice, though now for a season, if need be, you are in heaviness through manifold temptations: That the trial of your faith being much more precious than gold that perishes, though it be tried with fire might be found unto praise and honour and glory at the appearing of Jesus Christ" [1 Peter 1:6].

> A storm no doubt was coming, I heard its muffled roar
> There within the distance, was rain but nothing more.
> I caught the pounding thunder, as lightening cut the sky
> Hail fell around me, but I did not ponder why.
>
> There was no need to worry, "it soon will pass I said,"
> As tantrums always do (I thought) turning then my head,
> To see I'd been deluded, as danger swept the land
> Death was now upon me, I did not understand.
>
> Where would I now run to find, shelter from this pain?
> Regrettably, I knew inside, I'd lived my life in vain.
> Had I considered Death before? Not that I could say.
> I did not take into account, that it would come my way.
>
> It showed no mercy toward my grief, no pity did it show
> But rather mocked quite spitefully, as if you didn't know.
> No time to make my peace with God, He'd closed the golden gate
> It *seemed* that it was over now, no chance to choose my fate?

THE DISTANT MUFFLED ROAR

A storm indeed was brewing, I could hear in the distance the muffled pounding of rolling thunder. Bringing to mind thoughts of a train yard. Making dinner as usual, I proceeded to go about my evening business giving little thought to the storm. Instead, I focused on my precious little angel we called "Dolly," as she began wiggling herself into her rocking chair to watch one of her favorite shows. I had just finished papering her room in delicate yellow roses and like our sweet little girl they added charm and grace to our newly acquired home.

I was just beginning the sixteenth week of my second pregnancy and found my thoughts flooded with visions again of blankets, bottles and booties. It was amazing, Scott and I had just celebrated our third year of marriage, and the ages of twenty-three and twenty-five, it seemed as though we had reached the summit of happiness. We were comfortably settled and ready for the baby. Things could not have been more perfect.

Little time had passed before I realized that the distant muffled roar seemed to be advancing toward the house. The rain at first seemed to be a harmless May shower, but the crushing sound of hail was evidence of unforeseen dangers. Lighting the sky like the flash of a flame, fire bolts forked through the air discharging and displaying with each and every strike, convincing evidence of its supreme authority and wielding power. Anxious and on edge, I watched as the storm continued its outbursts of anger and fury on the landscape, hammering the ground with ice.

As the rain continued pouring out in spasms, I was not capable of understanding the storm's violent advances. Yet each passing second gave birth to new tension. As minutes rolled on, it became harder to disregard the frightening thoughts of danger. I could not believe the horrendous rolling of thunder, which echoed like a kettledrum timpani. It soon became aggravating and was slowly unraveling my nerves. In the living room my little angel seemed utterly undaunted, missing not a beat in the flow of her rocking cadence.

Little by little, an odd stillness returned as the smoke tinted clouds made their thunderous departure. Still scolding the sky both thunder and lightening moved onward, moving on in a leisurely manner, leaving behind only halfhearted outburst of its dawning eruptions.

From the front door of the house I heard a bizarre and frightening murmur, which seemed to be mocking thunder with its ominous tone. It sounded in a way as if in wretched pain. Then, a swelling moan began to take over the landscape like an avalanche of stone. Out-doing thunders menacing bombardment, the atrocious moan seemed to amplify its boisterous murmur as I drew closer to the door. Bound to determine the disturbing mystery, I resolved myself once and for all to identify the mind-boggling sound.

There upon cautiously opening the window and looking through the screen, less than one hundred yards away, a shocking view arose, at which point almost instantaneously the structure of our house began to abruptly shake underneath my feet. Clutching firmly to the frame of the door it was difficult to imagine or believe that the moaning noise was NOT approaching thunder, but rather—a twisting, infuriated monster with a violent demeanor on a rampage with villainous power, raging with force en route for our home!

CONSUMED BY DARKNESS

There for a moment in the archives of my mind, I recalled for a brief second the faint but distant roar I had filed heedlessly in the vault of human neglect. I could not escape the result of carelessly choosing to ignore the admonition in thunder's compulsion to give warning of the approaching riotous beast. Feeling utterly consumed by its ghastly grunting and threatening size, I watched the grayish white mass whirling onward in its dreadful fury. Committed it seemed to utterly fill the sky with darkness. Drawing nearer and nearer with each beat of my heart, it quickly disoriented my sense of direction as it extended and unfolded itself across the ground, until it had ruthlessly enveloped the entire landscape. Even so, I knew that I must run. From that moment on, my only thought was to protect my precious little baby girl.

Turning around, I flew toward her like an eagle sweeping its prey. Clinching her under my arm, I ran toward the bedroom. From the closet I quickly seized a blanket to wrap her in and ran suddenly to the back door. There entered my mind these grievous words, "There's no turning back from here." As my trembling hand opened the door, a rampage of tumult flooded my spirit with a heavy weight of fear, as the power of its progression began surging throughout the depths of my being. All the while adding to the tension was the stress on my mind of the storm's unruly sound, which continued unscrupulously to burden my brain. Accompanying these perilous foes, were demolished shreds of wreckage spinning out of control amidst the sky. Making the decision to escape an extremely treacherous one.

Massive clusters of black and gray pounded the ground around us as I attempted to enclose my "Dolly" in the rain soaked blanket. It felt as though I ran forever amidst the ominous cloud, which seemed to show no mercy for its violence. Instead, it seemed emphatically determined to devour everything in its path. Belching and spewing forth in a projectile manner from its callous darkness, everything it had swallowed.

Christene Bolte-Luthey

NO PLACE TO RUN OR HIDE

There was no place to run or hide. No refuge against the ruins that were spiraling throughout the darkened sky. Still, I continued running, striving desperately to go beyond what seemed to be the edge of this fatal darkness, but I knew deep inside my heart that we were not going to make it there. The odds were against us. I could sense it with every step I took. With the horror of falling short of this wearisome goal came an indescribable heat to my throat, burning like embers you might touch in a fire. My neck began to enlarge, making it nearly impossible to swallow or take in air. As unthinkable as it may seem, my throat began to expand out to my chin, like an inflated balloon. What I discovered at a later time from the doctor was that I had experienced the effects of "atmospheric pressure," (which is the pressure due to the weight of the earth's atmosphere.) Believe me, thoughts of my body breaking open were gripping and true, too true to imagine.

Mangled debris continued to fall on and around us. Mounds of broken glass and twisted metal overwhelmed the landscape. I could not help but cry as we were abruptly forced to the ground by a falling tree. We had unsuccessfully fallen short of our only escape from the horrendous whirlwind. I had disastrously failed to attain the goal, and was physically incapable of outrunning the abominable shadow. There we lay, imagining no possible way of escape beneath the cold, drenched, severed remains of the trees. We had gone as far as we could bodily go. There was nothing more I could do. I had not the power, knowledge or control to cease or defuse the TORNADO, (which was a "level five" meaning that winds were in excess of 100-200 miles an hour.)

Knowing the dreadful wind would soon overtake over us, I began tucking my little girl's tiny frame beneath my body as a means of protection. This was particularly difficult because we were so severely restricted underneath the weight of the fallen rubble. From that moment on I did not have the courage to look around me. Rather, all thoughts were centered on my "Dolly's" ability to receive air. In trying to shelter her the agonizing thought that I could possibly smother her in the process pressed hard on my mind and held a fear of its own.

Unbelievably I do not recall my little sweetheart ever attempting to break free of the cocoon I had woven around her while running. Instead, she remained tranquil and made not the slightest sound as we laid waiting for the twisting storm to go by. As she rested silently below me, like a baby bird nestled under its mother's feathers, I started to pray with all that was in me.

There amidst the deafening thunder and furious roar, we tried our best to contend with the earth as it wrathfully shook us back and forth. It was as though we were being sifted like particles through a massive sieve. As the storm drew nearer with its groaning and growling, it felt as though we were going to be drawn up into the violent mass. For a time that seemed like infinity it was my utmost fear.

LOVE BEYOND SELF

Holding on firmly to my precious baby girl, I pressed my face deep into the waterlogged blanket, mixing my tears with the rain. In that affectionate instant my little girl and I became miraculously united in a way that no language could ever express. In the middle of such a horror-stricken moment, my spirit discerned in a powerful way, what it truly means to love—beyond your self. I understood how it is to have your soul intertwined with another heart. Wondrously woven, if you will, into another life, and all of a sudden I realized the magnificence of God's plan for human existence. In that second I held my baby girl tightly and knew in my mind that DEATH alone could separate us. I determined heart and soul that by no means and under no circumstances other than my own passing, would I let go of her. Even if it meant that I would die. With my heart yearning desperately to "save" her, and the life of our unborn baby, I cried out to God again in prayer pleading to Him from the depths of despair, "Dear God, please keep us safe!"

This desperate longing to keep HER from death flooded my mind with a multitude of thoughts and emotions that would for a brief second set us apart from the menacing storm. It was absolutely clear to me in that instant that we are ALL merely frightened, powerless, frail CHILDREN that are kept ONLY by the GRACE and MERCY OF ALMIGHTY GOD. As I lay entirety defenseless on the ground disarmed by disaster and stripped of human pride, my spirit was broken down. My life, in the blink of an eye had been shown its vulnerability and I realized apart from God there was nothing I could do about it.

Christene Bolte-Luthey

EVERYTHING WAS GONE

Unexpectedly, the thundering bellows were replaced by a solemn stillness that shocked me. Stillness in the air supported the hope that perhaps the tornado had finally passed over and had left us behind as it continued its attack upon the land.

I wanted very much to free my little girl from the weight of my body. I had to be sure she'd been safe and injured and look upon her beautiful face. Throwing off debris I attempted to venture out from beneath the clusters of mangled trees, hoping to find a place where we would receive help.

NOTHING in life prepared me for the dreadful view I beheld upon stepping out from our hiding place. EVERTHING WAS GONE! The tranquil place that once existed were people had lived had tragically been reduced to jagged and twisted rubble. This upsetting scene branded upon the walls of my mind forever, heartache and fear that few hearts will know. As I stood there holding "Dolly" amidst the homes that had been reduced to rubble, I found myself encircled by shattered thoughts and broken dreams in what would have passed for a combat zone.

Never before had I felt so ALONE in my life. Everywhere I turned, electric lines were hurled and strung haphazardly all through the area. The atrocious scene resembled an intricate spider web of demolished wreckage. Gas lines were severed and hissing, permeating the atmosphere with a caustic stench. As I began walking gradually throughout the sea of disaster, I wondered if we would make it all right past the flammable material, but all the while, one riveting thought pressed fearfully on my mind. The horror of not knowing WHO had, or had NOT escaped the vicious storm.

Before long, firemen began arriving upon the pillaged landscape, assisting those in need. As I headed for the top of the hill not far from where our home once rested, help was approaching; it was awful to assess the damage that had been done within a matter of seconds. Laying all around me scattered to the wind, were the slivered remnants our home. All our belongings had vanished and the only thing bearing witness of our existence was a lonely row of mailboxes that had surprisingly remained standing. The picture was depressing and absolutely unbelievable!

CONSIDER THE STORM (Poem Continued)

A tragic day I never thought would set its hand on me,

Destroying all I'd built upon oh so carefully.
Death, you are an evil one, I've seen your awful face,
Whirling shreds of agony all about the place.

You rage with force en route to kill, to only steal away,
Halted only by one prayer, made from the heart today.
I've seen you and your wicked face; I recognize your game,
Now I am your enemy, my life is not the same.

I make this vow and hold it fast to take up Christ's commission
To warn my brethren of your plan, which leads them to perdition.
I'll tell them of the love of Christ, whose love is pure and true
He'll rescue them with his own blood, from the likes of you.

Yes, death, you sought to claim me, but I am living still
And with the time my Father gives, I'll carry out His will.
That others too will realize, the fiendish lies you've planted
And fight in JESUS'S name against, the things we take for granted.

May you be taunted knowing now, that Christ will set-them free,
Armed we'll run the race to win, Claiming VICTORY!

Christene Luthey

"For whatever is born of God overcomes the world. And this is the victory that has overcome the world—our faith. Who is he who overcomes the world, but he who believes that Jesus is the Son of God?" [1 John 5:4-5].

Two
THE GREATEST FEAR

"Not everyone that saith to me, Lord, Lord, shall enter into the kingdom of heaven; But he that doeth the will of my Father which is in heaven. Many will say to me in that day, Lord, Lord, have we not prophesied in thy name? And in thy name have cast out devils? And in thy name done many wonderful works? And then I will profess unto them, I never knew you: Depart from me, ye that work iniquity. [Matthew 7:21-23]

Great are the fears I have known in this life,
Entangled throughout them were sorrow and strife.
Yet one remains constant, consuming my heart
Ever in thoughts of a soul that's apart
From God who redeemed it, from hell and the grave
Who died for its freedom, forever to save.

Woe unto me, If this fear is not
Considered in depth and the price it was bought.
Woe unto me, if for granted I take
The blessed Redeemer, who bled for my sake.
When I find that life was meant from the start
For man to know God and ponder His heart.

But everything life held for me here
Gained favor over the greatest fear
TO STAND IN GOD'S PRESENCE
BEHOLDING HIS FACE
AND NOT KNOW THE PEACE
OF HIS PRECIOUS GRACE.

Hearing then spoken, "Depart now from me"
"For thou art the worker of iniquity."
Yes, great are the fears we face every day
But none can quite fathom
A soul gone astray.
Hopeless and sinking with no hope at all
If it has rejected, God's loving call.

Christene Luthey

AN IMAGE OF DEATH

As I reached the crest of the hill it became apparent that I was beholding another life-altering scene. Within a ragged breath, it seemed that the world and everything in it was instantaneously frozen in time. As I gazed toward the base of the hill, it was as though my heart had ceased beating, as I viewed standing there—my mother and brother who were UNAWARE that there were ANY survivors.

They could NOT see ME at the crown of the entrance to the driveway where I was standing—observing them, for it was entirely impassable from where they stood. The heap of wreckage obscured their view. Everything that had once belonged to us had vanished entirely. The savage storm had gulped and tossed off the sum of our entire life within a matter of minutes. Not a trace of our existence remained. It was as though we had perished in the tornado along with our things, and the terror in my mother's scream said it all!

It was obvious as she became panic-stricken; at this horrible moment she assumed we were dead... Causing me to look at an image of my own death through HER eyes. I was trapped again in a whirlwind of thought as I watched an effigy of death being sewn in my life's portrait. Granting me knowledge regarding my life and its significance, which I had never before considered.

Melting my heart with her tears, my mother's expression of grief stirred my soul and impressed upon my mind a reflection of selfless love that split my heart in two. Little did I realize when the day had first begun, that my well-intentioned life would literally be turned up side down, forcing me toward a genuine understanding of my own mortality. The picture was callous and grim. Yet it was also overflowing with joy and elation. I felt both pain and pleasure as I beheld her affectionate tears, taking hold of my heart in a manner that words cannot begin to describe. The love she demonstrated chilled me to the bone, while her sorrow seemed to shatter my spirit like the splintered pieces of a broken mirror. What prohibited me from calling out to her, I did not know, but I could sense my heart screaming—I'M HERE!

The grave expression that seemed to age and change my mother's face will never leave my heart. In that moment, I had observed a self-denying love that longed completely to surrender her life for another. Within these moments it was clear as I watched her face lose color, that if God would allow, she would have traded, her life for mine. The weight of the world had suddenly landed upon her shoulders as she stood there weeping passionately. Perhaps some may disagree, but I sincerely believe that the days of her life were shortened amidst the despair suffered within that moment, by the wear and tear upon her heart throughout the darkness of it all.

I was in an awful dream, drowning in slow motion as I stood there. The air was thick with the smell of chopped tree remains. You could nearly taste it. The picture drained every ounce of strength from my body. My feet were bare; resembling pincushions speckled with deep puncture wounds, inflicted by the locust tree thorns I had run through in the storm.

While mom was still screaming, overwhelmed with horror and fear, my brother began running as fast as he could to see what was at the top of the hill. Immediately mom was trailing only two strides behind him, impelled to reckon with the unknown. It was then that we saw each other. It was a remarkable sentimental moment filled with love, appreciation and thankfulness. After crying for a brief moment embracing one another, we turned to abandon the ravaged scene.

As soon as I knew that "Dolly" was well, Scott took me to see the doctor. I was very concerned about the visit. Just minutes *before* the tornado one could scarcely tell by looking at me that I was four months pregnant. Now I looked as though I was past due. After a quick examination the doctor told me that I had severely torn every abdominal muscle while running and that the baby's heart beat could not be heard. "There is nothing you can do now but rest," the doctor said. "You've been through a terribly traumatic ordeal, go home and rest." Then I was told to "return tomorrow."

I couldn't believe my ears. What was he saying? I felt as though I was going to die again. He couldn't be serious. This couldn't' be happening. After all we'd just been through, what did he mean, "rest?" I was shocked and immediately speechless with the thought of those unthinkable words.

There was only one thing to do. When I entered my mother's house I ran for the bedroom to PRAY. Falling to my knees I began to earnestly cry out to God again. "Please, Dear Lord," I cried, "If I'm going to lose this baby, then please be merciful and take it from me now." I didn't think that I could bear going through the remaining months and lose the baby *then*. That thought seemed to be more than I could endure. Deep in my heart I knew that the baby was a gift from God, not something I owned or deserved. Again I prayed, "Please have mercy and hear my prayer." I knew that I had to place that tiny life in God's hands because it was out of my control. It was probably one of the hardest things I have ever had to do. Surrendering everything to God's will, then wait for an answer which I knew deep inside would come within a few days. If a heartbeat WAS heard, I was going to trust that all would be well. Yet I knew that I had to leave the entire outcome to God's will. In doing that, I did find peace enough to rest, as I had been told and able to lay hold of the hope I needed to see me through.

Nearly seven days had passed before an answer came. <u>Throughout that time I realized many important things about life and pondered in great depth WHAT God had revealed to me of Himself and eternity on that hill.</u> A heartbeat was heard and I knew that God had wondrously sheltered the life inside me. Of the joy I felt within that moment, mere words cannot begin to make known. In spite of our catastrophe, our baby WAS ALIVE, "Dolly was unharmed and my wounds were healing fine.

A PORTRAIT OF LIFE

Now, to the best of my ability I want to share with you the significance of the things the Spirit of God revealed to me while standing at the top of the entrance to where we lived that day. As I have already stated, an image of death was supernaturally impressed within my portrait of life, in which I discerned the value, purpose and meaning of existence.

In an instant, I became miraculously aware of the many things I had done so carelessly without a second thought. I began to search in my heart and mind, the people and places I had so wrongfully taken for granted. It was there and then that I distinctly understood the true and unforgettable context of REGRET! It was all my heart could feel. I knew that I had reached this defaming destination for a reason whose purpose reached far beyond my wildest dreams. It was belittling, mortifying and devastating. For in the midst of this terrible regret, I beheld my life's pitiful portrait where I could see my soul teetering ignorantly back and forth on the scales of right and wrong. Inadvertently leaning toward treacherous, unwise decisions in the balance of eternity, which rested in the hands of Almighty God's supreme authority. In this I was left standing without excuse and found regrettably that God considered me imperfect on the scales of His Righteousness, Justice and Holy Laws.

God had unveiled my UNAPPROVED soul before my very own eyes. Revealing to me that His word is fixed and forever certain, filling me with an unalterable awareness of TODAY, and an inconceivable sense of gratitude for His mercy, grace, and love. He had applied his awesome power to my life and granted me the wisdom to see His Sovereign right to GIVE, or TAKE life, and do as <u>He wills</u>.

As I stood treasuring this act of kindness, watching Him make each magnificent move by measure of his mercy, this never to be forgotten gift of hope and grace humbled me. Yet with each pass of His life giving brush, I realized an even greater sense of sorrow and regret. This seemed to bring more misery and despair to my heart than I had ever known or felt before. This burden oppressed my heart and mortified my soul. Bringing more horror and anguish to the depths of my being than any mind could dare to fathom. <u>I had TAKEN GOD'S ETERNAL LIFE GIVING GRACE FOR GRANTED, and a heavy shadow of shame had covered me</u>. I also became miserably aware that throughout my life I had only an established a "SURFACE" type of faith, not the deep sorrowful faith that TRULY recognizes and regretfully REPENTS of sin. I understood that simply *admitting* that I was a "sinner" <u>was not enough to be truly "saved."</u>

THE GULF BETWEEN HEAVEN AND HELL

To my surprise, God had an all-embracing purpose behind this particular moment for me (and for you also.) Like many people, I had neglectfully taken LIFE for granted and disregarded eternal consequences. Thus discovering in an agonizing way that too many of us have lost sight of the fact that we are NOT invincible, but rather, human beings subject to death. This is not only factual physically but SPIRITUALLY also. I realized that it is time for <u>all of us</u>, to find purpose and meaning before it is too late.

A portrait of my life had been positioned before me bringing torment to my spirit in an instant, revealing a canvas created by Almighty God that clearly displayed A LINE. This WAS NO ORDINARY LINE. In fact I knew deep within my soul that it was <u>the line that separates ETERNAL LIFE (Heaven's glory) from ETERNAL DEATH (Hell's torment)</u>.

Impressing forever on my mind, Abraham's unalterable words found in the book of Luke, **"And besides all this, between us and you there is a GREAT GULF FIXED, so that those who want to pass from here to you cannot, nor can those from there pass to us" [Luke 16:26]**.

I was humbled beyond words, enlightened by God's grace and mercy throughout these outstanding events. These discoveries were gloriously revealing the astonishing length and breadth of God's unfathomable grace to the core of my soul. I realized that <u>his heart and love for us is much greater than any mind could ever begin to interpret</u>. In feeling His love and tender kindness, my heart was overwhelmed with regret, viewing the portrait again. Within this moment, it seemed that I was being shown every fault; every imperfection, every transgression, sin, error, and trespass that ever pertained to my life.

Along with these was the frightening awareness of my transgressions and guilt before Him. Aware of His Holy presence, I knew that: <u>WITHOUT HIS MERCY, I would be ETERNALLY CONDEMNED</u>. Damned to hell forever for having disregarded His precious word and sacred laws. <u>I at once was filled with dread, and sorrowfully concerned knowing that my life was being weighed in the balance of God's divine judgment and was found extremely lacking.</u> It was terribly clear that I had thoughtlessly taken for granted the greatest gift God could bestow upon man, His precious beloved Son Jesus Christ and His priceless mercy and love.

HUMBLED BY MERCY

This knowledge fixed within my soul the certainty that **we are to PERSONALLY KNOW JESUS CHRIST** (God's sinless Son) <u>who gave His life for the purpose of Payment for the sin debts of those who believe and trust in HIM</u>. (Read: **Matthew 28:19, John 3:17-18, 10:37-38, Romans 5:10, 1 Tim. 2:4, 2 Peter 3:9, Gen. 1:1, Acts 4:12**). I had NOT totally SURRENDERED my HEART with a sincere commitment, nor had I made CHRIST the LORD of my LIFE, and I seriously began to wonder HOW MANY PEOPLE WERE OUT THERE IN THIS WORLD like ME? Who have gone to church their entire life, attended church functions and <u>STILL missed the message</u>? I had a lot of *surface,* "head" knowledge, but <u>had not received it into my HEART or made Christ the LORD of my life</u>…

Here was the matter disclosed, our lives are in vain if we are living apart from Christ Jesus. With this affirmation it was now very clear to me: that there IS ONLY ONE WAY to enter into Heaven's glory, and that is found in God's Holy word, but all too often we pay no heed to it or carelessly take it for granted. **[Matthew 7:13-14] "Enter by the NARROW GATE; for wide is the gate and broad is the way that leads to destruction, and there are many who go in by it. Because narrow is the gate and difficult is the way which leads to LIFE, and there are few who find it."**

DEPART FROM ME I NEVER KNEW YOU

Many of us claim very quickly to be "Christians," but in all honesty and truth, we may NOT be. A TRUE "Christian" is one who has come to the end of his or her self, admitting and repenting of his **sins** and has trusted by faith, Christ's death on the cross as payment for them. This is something we all need to consider. When Christ confronts us with a portrait of our life, to assess its value, if we do not know him we will stand before God trembling in fear of condemnation. I know this for certain. Not one of us can afford to *carelessly assume* we are "saved." If you are taking Salvation for granted and neglecting a personal relationship with Jesus Christ, I humbly urge you to please WAKE UP and stop deceiving yourself.

Going back to the "surface" faith that I spoke of before, reevaluate (if you claim to be a Christian) when you asked Christ Jesus into your heart. Did you do this just because you knew it was the "right" thing to do? Were you with a group of people who had been asked to receive Christ as Lord, and just went along with the crowd? I inquire about this because in pondering these questions I realized that many times this happens when we attend a gathering and get "caught up in the moment." I have known several people who did these things and ended up having the Devil steal the word from their heart shortly after they had given Christ their life, because their MOTIVATION was wrong and Satan knew it. The conviction they felt was not SINCERE and therefore they did not truly believe in Christ as their Savior and actually become the "Born Again" believers spoken about in the word of God.

According to God's word concerning His glorious kingdom, it is emphatically clear that: Strangers to Jesus Christ will not enter the doors of heaven. **"Not everyone who says to me, Lord, Lord, shall enter the kingdom of heaven, but he who does the will of my father in heaven. Many will say to me in that day, Lord, Lord, we have prophesied in** your name, cast out demons in your name, and done many wonders in your name? And I will declare to them, I NEVER KNEW YOU; DEPART FROM ME, you who practice lawlessness" [Matthew 7:21-23]. "Do you not know that to whom you present yourselves slaves to obey, you are that one's slaves whom you obey, whether of SIN leading to DEATH, or of obedience, leading to Righteousness?" [Romans 6:16]. Dear friends may the Holy Spirit call YOU as He has ME out of the darkness and into His light. The light of Truth, honesty, integrity, and obedience to God's will.

LIKE A WHIRLWIND

His coming shall be like a violent wind
Unlike any man's ever known
And trembling beneath Him the earth shall proclaim
The depth of the grace He has shown.
Hearts will then fail laughter will cease
Hatred will reign; there will be no peace
Enemies, all will be to another
For LOVE was the thread, binding one to another.

If we refuse to listen, to heed God's words of woe
And love of the world more than Christ
"Depart" He'll say, "now go."
Though freedom He had bought for all
And victory he had planned

The gift of Love is fruitless when
It's left within his hand.

C. Luthey

"For God so loved the world
that He gave His only Begotten Son,
that whoever believes in Him
should not perish but have everlasting life.
For God did not send His Son into the world to condemn the world,
but that the world through Him might be saved" [John 3:16-17].

Something to ponder in depth, must we face death before we realize the true meaning of LIFE? Must we nearly lose a child before we see the priceless treasures God has bestowed upon us? Must we lose everything before we understand that: Where our heart is, our soul will abide. We are going to spend eternity either with Christ in Glory or in Hell with Satan. This one thing is certain: Eternity is forever… <u>I am sorry to say that it took a terrible tragedy to awaken MY spirit from the deep and careless sleep that it was sinking in. Yet I rejoice today for the lessons these trials have taught me and thank God from the depths of my soul for granting me the blessed opportunity to know and follow Christ.</u>

A Prayer

Dear Lord, please help me trust in Thee,
That through your Son, I'll be set free
Help me listen, help me love, Help me seek Thy face above.
All that this world should show me this day
Please lead me and guide me that I may not stray.
I receive Thy gift of peace, thy freedom too, my soul release.
Let me know thy victory sweet, that I may ever more complete
The journey here on earth until, you call me home, my role fulfill. Amen

**"For by grace you have been saved through faith,
and that not of yourselves;
it is the gift of God, not of works,
lest anyone should boast" [Ephesians 2:8-9].**

Three

ON THE EDGE OF ETERNITY

"But God said to him, 'you fool! This night your soul will be required of you; then who will get what you have prepared for yourself?" This is how it will be with anyone who stores up things for himself but is not rich toward God" [Luke 12:21-22]. "And it is appointed for men to die once, but after this the judgment" [Heb. 9:27].

Let us not consider hell, rebellion and great sin
After stepping through the gates, forever locked within
Let us yonder look to see the "lake of fire" there
And "brimstone" where the soul is plunged, in torture deep to share.

Undergoing torments of, the "second death" ordeal
A never-ending agony, that time shall never heal.
Eternity, apart from God, to think of it is pain
No presence, past, just future, with only tears to gain.

Consider please, before hell's gate, in sorrow you should stand,
The wretched souls of those who chose, to build their lives on sand.
Save your tears, SALVATION waits, to welcome you within
The "sting of death" no longer reigns; CHRIST paid your debt for sin!

GRACE has ransomed those who trust, believing **Christ who said,**
"I am the way, the truth, the life, risen from the dead."
Christene Luthey

CONSIDER YOUR MORTALITY

Like it or not, death approaches each of us, which no doubt disturbs the mind and its tranquility (especially if you have not made peace with God.) Yet it is better to trouble the mind for a moment, than to grieve the soul forever. May I please ask you to examine your own heart in the following question? Will it take a catastrophe in your life to consider life, death, sin and judgment? I inquire because many of us never think of these things until our days are so far spent that barely a word can be uttered from one's lips, and THEN, we seem ready to begin pondering eternity and "wish..."

DEATH IS INEVITABLE

Death should be a subject of the highest importance. In fact it IS inevitable, it should be a universal concern, but it is not. **"All must die,"** God has appointed, **[Hebrews 9:27],** without JESUS CHRIST there is NO security from the grave, regardless of who we are, what we own, or who we know. Our lives exist only by the grace of God, hour-by-hour, moment-by-moment.

We may argue somewhat about death, but none can escape its certainty. Always imposing anxiety and fear upon those who are <u>unprepared and unforgiven</u>. It is a fact that time quickly passes by, and we like flowers—fade. Still, in light of our mortality, though daily before us, it seems to go carelessly unnoticed, and all too often we journey through life, unchanged, and still bearing the weight of our own SIN when Jesus came to pay that debt for us and give us freedom.

There shall be NO EXCUSE for any man or woman as he stands filled with regret before his Creator, striving to no avail to convince the Almighty that his life was spent, "unaware of the reality of death." Be attentive my friend to the fact that all of us shall one day be called to severe account of our thoughts-less ways and deeds if we do not strive to follow Christ Jesus. Oh, how great that audit shall be, as we are individually, justly and strictly examined by the TRUTH of God's Holy word. Without Christ, the **unforgiven sinner** shall remain utterly speechless as he considers that trusting in the things of THIS WORLD, or in himself only led his soul to the blackest regions of despair. How sad it will be for those who have placed their faith in *worldly things*, and not in the sinless hands of Jesus Christ.

CALLED TO GIVE AN ACCOUNT

God have mercy, what shall we profit if our soul is a stranger to the one who gave it life? Consider this, the day will come when you and I shall stand before God and our lives will be brought to account for each allotted moment and shown the tender mercy and grace God bestowed upon us throughout our lives.

Note: Those who shut Jesus Christ out of their lives, can in NO WAY enter through the gates of glory. I tell you the truth. Those of us who choose to live without Christ shall die without him also. Thus we would then be eternally banished from heaven for all time. Yes, banished and forever, chained in the darkened mansions of the damned. Christ Himself said **in [Mark 16:16] "Go into all the world and preach the gospel to every creature. He who believes will be saved; but he who does not believe will be condemned."** Again, in **[2 Thes. 2:9-12] "The coming of the lawless one is according to the working of Satan, all power, signs, and lying wonders, and with all unrighteous deception among those who perish, because they did not receive the love of the truth, that they might be saved."** And again in **[Romans 14:23] "But he who doubts is condemned if he eats because he does not eat from faith; for whatever is not from faith is sin."**

Let us not turn our backs on these truths. Death stands firm to its purpose, and it has but one, to claim victory over your soul and mine, unless we trust Christ with our salvation. There is no hope or peace for any of us if the weight of our sin still rests upon OUR shoulders. I tell you this because I want you to consider today how awful judgment will be for any of us who rely on ourselves for salvation. We cannot save ourselves! Only Christ can pardon your soul and mine from sin and its destination.

It is time to raise our hands, yielding our soul to the only, means of salvation, which is Christ Jesus, as God's word reveals, **[Romans 3:23-26] "All have sinned and fall short of the glory of God being justified freely by His grace through the redemption that is in Christ Jesus, whom God set forth to be a propitiation by His blood, through faith, to demonstrate His righteousness, because in His forbearance God had passed over the sins that were previously committed, to demonstrate at the present time His righteousness, that He might be just and the justifier of the one who has faith in Jesus."**

Again, we need to remember and daily recall that **"there is no creature hidden from His sight, but all things are naked and open to the eyes of Him to whom we must give account" [Heb. 4:13].** Isn't it past time to draw near in faith to Christ if we have not by now? The word of God tells us that He is coming again soon to save those who are eagerly waiting for His return. **"For he will finish the work and cut it short in righteousness,** because the Lord will make a short work upon the earth" **[Romans 9:28]**.

The question is, are we waiting for Him, or are we paying no heed to each and every opportunity we've been given to KNOW Jesus Christ? Have the things of this *world become* more significant to us than "eagerly waiting" on His coming? How much have you or I learned about Jesus Christ in the time we've been granted on this earth? How much about Him have you or I shared with others?

I know what it feels like to have every material thing you own in this world be taken from you. It is a bewildering tragedy. Yet this I also know, to spend your life laboring in vain for things that are passing away and neglecting the most precious gift God has bestowed upon man, is the greatest waste in life you can imagine. We are foolish if we fritter away the days of our lives, knowing that there are so few hours on earth allotted each soul by the grace of God. <u>Lord help us, may we learn how not to misspend the minutes we are given and avoid the devastation of taking our salvation for granted.</u> I pray that each and every one of us will gain knowledge of and appreciate the magnificent lengths Almighty God our blessed heavenly Father has taken to demonstrate His love for you and I. So that we will strive to attain the companionship He has desired with us from the beginning of time.

WASHED BY THE BLOOD

As scenes of my portrait were being laid bare before me, I realized a multitude of instances where I had heedlessly overlooked, or forsaken God's gift of grace in my life. This imposed upon my heart and soul an overwhelming sense of depravity that reduced me again to tears. The weight of my sin and humiliation before a HOLY God depreciated each and every ounce of pride I had held ever held in my heart—Immediately! My portrait would soon reveal <u>whether or not the blood of God's beloved son had washed MY SINS away. Was CHRIST the foundation upon which I had built my life?</u>

The only way to inherit the kingdom of God is to be, **"WASHED, sanctified, justified in the name of the Lord Jesus and by the Spirit of God, who takes away the sin of the world" [John 1:29]**. One must first come to know Godly sorrow if he is to be saved, according to **[2 Cor. 7:10] "For Godly sorrow produces repentance leading to salvation, not to be** regretted; but the sorrow of the world produces death." Time and time again, we are told that, **"The wages of sin is death, but the gift of God is eternal life in Jesus Christ our Lord" [Rom. 6:23].** The *good news* is that, **"In him we have redemption through His blood, the forgiveness of sins, according to the riches of his grace." [Eph. 1:7].** That is what "being washed in the blood of the Lamb" means. It is, **"by grace we have been saved through faith, and not that of ourselves; it is the gift of God, not of works, lest anyone should boast: [Eph. 2:8-9].**

Dear one, have YOU by GRACE been SAVED through FAITH? Remember, neither you nor I can earn salvation by works, nor buy it with all the money in the world. Grace is a gift from God. You can only receive it through faith, having a personal relationship with Christ. I believe that <u>if we forsake this precious blood that was shed for the remission of our sins, we will seal forever our destiny in hell</u>. You see, God in His righteousness <u>cannot and will not</u> have anything to do with SIN in His glorious kingdom. He is bound to his written word forever. Therefore, only those of us who have **truly** placed our complete trust in HIM shall be "saved," and receive our eternal life and rewards in heaven.

Let each and every one of us begin from this day forward if we have not before now, live each day as though we believe with all our heart that the storm of God's judgment is somewhere on the horizon, and will one day knock on our door. I appeal to you; please do not turn away from God's loving words of admonition accept it and begin at the moment building your life on the firm foundation that is Christ Jesus. Then you and I with Christ Jesus as our "cornerstone" will be able to withstand the trials and tribulations of this world.

> In the distance if you listen
> You can hear the muffled roar
> As the storm draws ever closer still
> Heading for YOUR door.
>
> Will YOU be ready friend—to trust?
> The house you're living in?
> Or will you then be "washed away"
> Because you harbor SIN?

It's a question every soul should ask
To cleanse and wash the heart
HAVE I PLACED MY TRUST <u>IN CHRIST</u>?
And done my worldly part?

Knowing that the choice I make
Will seal my destiny
Enveloping me in LOVE or CHAINS
Throughout Eternity...

Christene Luthey

WHAT HAVE WE DONE FOR GOD'S GLORY?

The second thing I knew that God was searching for in my portrait of life was: <u>WHAT I had done for His glory</u>. The question, not only had I trusted Jesus Christ as my personal Savior, but also had I been a faithful servant? Had I lived as a someone God would greet saying, **"Well done, good and faithful servant; you have been faithful over a few things, I will make you ruler over many things. Enter into the joy of your Lord" [Matt. 25:23],** or would my actions and behavior be unfortunately cast out and away from God like the **"unprofitable servant into outer darkness. Where there shall be weeping and gnashing of teeth" [Matt. 25:30]?**

When our time on earth is through or the Son of Man comes again to judge the nations, each and every one of us will be shown a portrait of our life. **"All nations will be gathered before Him, and He will separate them one from another, as a shepherd divides His sheep from the goats. And He will set the sheep on His right hand, but the goats on His left" [Matt. 25:32-33].** To those on His right hand He will say, **"Come you blessed of my father, inherit the kingdom prepared for you from the foundation of the world" [Matt. 25:34].** To those on His left hand He will reply, **"Depart from me, you cursed into the everlasting fire prepared for the Devil and his angels" [Matt. 25:41]. "And these will go away into everlasting punishment, but the righteous into eternal life" [Matt. 25:46].**

"God is a discerner of thoughts and intents of the heart. And there is no creature hidden from His sight, but all things are naked and open to the eyes of Him to whom we must give account" [Heb. 4:11]. I thank God for these truths and I pray YOU WILL ALSO, so that we could hold them in our heart and receive eternal life through Jesus Christ. I know that yielding my heart, and sin debt to the Son of God is the <u>only way</u> I will escape the great Day of Judgment that is coming on this nation. Believe it or not, you may find all of these things written in God's His Holy word so that you too might be spared by the Good news of the gospel of Christ and be saved.

If you look you will see that every word of God points to the dividing LINE that was revealed to me that could have resulted in eternal separation from God. In fact, God's word does more than just point to it; it also discloses the consequences for each side. Here is something we can all think about. Are we ready for God's appraisal of our life? <u>I certainly wasn't **before** I trusted Christ Jesus,</u> and I believe that very few of us will be swift to answer <u>YES</u> to that question. Knowing that our lives apart from Christ Jesus are going to be weighed on the scales of God's divine truth, I think that all of us would have to say that we would be found terribly lacking when it comes to living a life that is worthy of God's approval. That is why we ought to be so thankful for His amazing grace and the wonderful Good News of God's forgiveness through His beloved Son. I know that my life at the time of the tornado was in terribly jeopardy of being forever separated from the love of God. <u>All because I had failed to take God's word into my heart seriously and carelessly took my life and my Salvation for granted</u>. I was guilty of my sin because I had not begged forgiveness and wholly surrendered it to Christ. Could you say today that YOU are guilty of the same?

I pray YOU have gained some awareness of taking things in life for granted from what I've shared of MY lack of knowledge and negligence? I truly believe it is crucial that we all come to know Jesus Christ and gain understanding of God's will, and the way He expects us to live. Have you have ever had an experience that caused YOU to realize your need of a Savior? If not, there is a possibility that you might be living with a false sense of security as to receiving eternal life? I mean, if you have never before pondered these questions, it's likely that you might be taking Salvation for granted also?

I hope it does not take your life being literally turned BEFORE you make peace with God? At the time of the tornado I had honestly never given death any thought. I was barely twenty-five years old, and <u>NEVER</u> took into consideration that **"My soul would be required of me."** No one wants to ponder such topics. Thoughts such as these seem to frighten or make us sad? Yet, we all need to know that contemplating matters as these can be very healthy and actually comforting <u>if we have sought freedom from sin and fear</u>

<u>through forgiveness in Christ</u>. When we have been forgiven we no longer bear the guilt of our sin that makes us afraid to meet God. Instead you can rejoice in knowing that a "mansion" awaits you in heaven. There your soul may rejoice in the Glory of Christ forever!

SORT THROUGH THE BAGGAGE

In a terrifying way, the tornado did for me what I should have been doing all along. Heaving the baggage of sin in my life OVERBOARD! When I began doing so, I found peace within my spirit and began to observe changes in my walk with Christ. I learned the hard way that if we don't "let go" of the things in life that hold no ETERNAL value, we risk sinking with the ship by trying to hold on to this world. Since then I have become seriously aware that <u>TOMORROW is NOT PROMISED to any of us</u>. The hours that we *SPEND—TODAY* may be our last. This is also true for those we know and love. Because of the tornado, I learned that every breath I take is a GIFT from God. I understand that He alone controls each beat of your heart and mine. I recognize that my life consists of the grace He has granted; and my days although in God's hands—are numbered…

I realize that until the moment God summons us to live with Him in glory, we must do our utmost to abide in Him. Seeking His will daily. The more time we spend filling our lives with his word the easier we'll discover it is to sort out—what is, and is not, important. As we go through each day, let us ask ourselves if the things in our life reflect Christ and our walk with Him? If they <u>do not</u>, we must "let them go!" Realizing, that we are living in perilous times. Each day you and I face adversities that will sift and prove what is really valued in our hearts. Reflecting on this we need to, **"Take heed and beware of covetousness, for one's life does not consist of the abundance of the things he possesses" [Luke 12:15].** Let us not be deceived, when we die, we CANNOT take our earthly possessions with us! So let us as Jesus said, **"Lay up for yourselves treasures in heaven, where neither moth nor rust destroy and where thieves do not break in and steal. For where your treasure is, there your heart will be also" [Matthew 6:20-21]**

TOO SOON OUR LIVES ARE SPENT

It shall be far better to have lived without
Than to hold the world's treasures
And find yourself standing
On the wrong side of the gates of heaven.
There is but ONE WAY to receive ETERNAL LIFE
Through Jesus Christ, the Son of God
Therefore choose the NARROW WAY
Listen and REPENT!
Borrowed are our minutes here
Too soon our lives are spent…

C. Luthey

"Then Peter said to them, repent, and let every one of you be baptized in the name of Jesus Christ for the remission of sins; and you shall receive the gift of the Holy Spirit" [Acts 2:38].

It was in the face of DEATH,
I came to see the TRUTH
It taught me not to take for granted,
My sweet and precious youth.

Amidst the darkness, fear, and pain,
God gave to me his hand
That I could learn and overcome
And yielding understand.

Many disregard their life,
As such a precious gift
I am, but one among the souls
He will "try" and "sift."

For sifting lifts the chaff away
That He with grace removes
ALL that on the Judgment Day
He in Righteousness reproves.

C. Luthey

"All scripture is given by inspiration of God, and is profitable for doctrine, for reproof, for correction, for instruction in righteousness, that the man of God may be complete, thoroughly equipped for every good work" [2 Tim. 3:16-17].

A Prayer

Lord, help me NOT to grieve your heart, but help me change my ways
Grant me grace to know Thy Son, and fill my soul with praise.
Prepare my life for Christ's return, to greet Him as a FRIEND,
And keep me from thy Judgment Lord upon my journey's end. Amen

"In Him we have redemption through His blood, the forgiveness of sins, according to the riches of His grace" [Eph. 1:7].

Four
LIFE IS BUT A VAPOR

"Come now, you who say, "Today or tomorrow we will go to such and such a city, spend a year there, buy and sell, and make a profit"; whereas you do not know what will happen tomorrow. For what is your life? It is even a vapor that appears for a little time and then vanishes away" [James 4:13-14]

I've learned my life is truly but a vapor
Here but then it quickly fades away,
The only thing that I can take to heaven
Is but the FAITH and LOVE I have this day.

This moment from me now is growing dimmer
And there is nothing I can do to stall
The hands of time continue on their ticking
I have no purpose here, but heed God's call.

The call is simply this: Through faith to FOLLOW
To walk with Christ by only grace alone
Amidst life's mountains and its valleys
Until to me His blessed heart is shown.

I've laid my life and will upon God's alter
Yielding EVERYTHING I am within
For truth has shown that all on earth have fallen
Deserving death and hell for every sin.

So we must die to "self" before it leads us
To places where the heart should never be
Surrendering to Christ as LORD to save us
Knowing not, when sleep shall fall on me.

Christene Luthey

Christene Bolte-Luthey

THE BREVITY OF LIFE

Violently and unexpectedly life can change forever! At any moment you can experience adversity, hardships or tragedy. Difficulties that may seize our strength tax our faith and test our character. When unwanted trials vex our lives, we suffer a multitude of emotions. Crisis of any sort may bombard us with feelings of depression, despair, discouragement, and—denial.

Too often very few of us are equipped mentally, physically or emotionally for disaster. I for instance, know what it was like to feel safe and secure one second, and the next being tormented with fear. Disaster upsets everything around us. Within the blink of an eye you're aware of the terrible fact, that without Christ, your world is unsafe and unsure. All you long for are answers to the questions flooding your mind. You long for strength to see you through whatever remains of your life.

When tragedy strikes, you feel that a part of you has been taken. Leaving you with emptiness and grief to bear. Loss is no doubt a deep and devastating valley. Grief is no respecter of persons. Loosing everything I owned brought overwhelming feelings of vulnerability and disbelief. I knew that my life and our world as we knew it—would never be the same. I couldn't help at the time of the tornado wondering WHY and HOW this could happen? It also made me think that we encounter deep despair, because we assume that adversity will knock "someone else's" door.

Some respond in anger when crisis strikes, accusing and blaming in order to cope. When tragedy hit I didn't feel anger, but did succumb to guilt. My heart was broken by the fact that we had to "start over." But I couldn't share my grief. People had DIED—And I was alive. That recurring thought passed through my mind for months. Finally, I came to understand that I was suffering from "survivors guilt," which is just as it says—enduring feelings of guilt and remorse for being a "survivor." But labeling my feelings brought little if no comfort to my heart. WHY was I alive? I couldn't stop asking myself that question. All the while no mind could have possibly imagined just how grateful I was.

Today may I ask WHAT are YOU suffering from? Is there a battle raging in your heart that you can't fight alone? Are you hurting? Are you sad? Are you feeling overwhelmed by the your weight of your worries? Are you afraid? Are you tired? If you have answered yes to any one of these questions I encourage you to let God enfold you in His love...Begin by allowing Him to hold your tomorrows...

LET GOD HOLD YOUR TOMORROWS!

Unlock the bolted door inside,
To make another start
Contentment comes from setting free
The things that bind your heart.

C. Luthey

I PLACE MY TRUST IN THEE

When I fail to do my best and worry taunts at me
Let me first surrender Lord, and place my trust in Thee.
When I fall beside the way, with not the strength to stand,
Let me first remember Lord, to quickly take Your hand.
When my tears are falling fast from being troubled so
Let me trust your grace for me wherever my feet shall go.
When I cannot understand injustice in this world,
Let me not lose faith in you, that I may be unfurled.
When my heart confronts the fear, my situation lost
Let the joy of victory Lord remain above all cost.
When the journey seems too long, and friends abandon me
Let me come to you in prayer, and place my trust in thee.
When I feel so all alone, nearly to the end, let me not forget you Lord
My priceless, precious friend.
And when you come with trumpets sound, there reward shall be
For all who kept you first dear Lord, and placed their trust in thee.

Christene Luthey

TAKE COURAGE

I was successful in rejecting the truth for a while. Yet I needed to talk with someone. If only one person could understand HOW I was feeling, and WHY I was feeling that way, I knew I could carry on. But I couldn't find anyone who had known the terror I'd endured. Let alone understand the thoughts that raced through my mind. Who could I trust? What would they say? How would they respond? These questions I couldn't escape. I didn't know were to go for answers. I felt alone and misunderstood. Before I knew it, I was feeling isolated, trapped and defeated.

Sometimes, you and I may feel discouraged beyond belief. Perhaps even today you are experiencing some of these things? If so, let me say, **take courage**! Believe that although life may have you feeling cast down, you can overcome with Christ as your anchor! Lay hold of the faith God has given you and don't "abandon ship." God is able to see you through the deepest darkest seas. Remain calm and know:

> The One who has said to the wind "Be still!"
> Is stationed there at your side.
> Do not desert Him He cares so for you
> Simply have faith and abide.
> Tell Him your troubles; tell Him your cares,
> He will know just what to do,
> Though torrent, and fear assault you today
> His grace shall see you through.

> **"And a great windstorm arose, and the waves beat into the boat,**
> **so that it was already filling.**
> **But He was in the stern, asleep on a pillow.**
> **And they awoke Him and said to Him,**
> **Teacher, do you not care that we are perishing?**
> **Then He arose and rebuked the wind,**
> **And said to the sea,**
> **Peace be still!**
> **And the wind ceased**
> **and there was a great calm."** [Mark 4:37-39]

It has been upsetting—remembering the day of the tornado. The vivid images of that terrible day have been carved in my mind and will linger in my heart forever. Yet today I do not feel alone, for I have Christ Jesus as my friend. I am comforted in knowing that the Lord will never leave nor forsake me. Today, join me in laying hold of the peace that passes all understanding! Believe that amidst every storm, **THERE IS HOPE**, because **GOD IS IN CONTROL**.

FACE TO FACE WITH OUR VALUES

If it is that you feel no one understands and this frustrates your mind, consider the choices you can make. All of us at one time or another must come face to face with our values, beliefs, relationships, and our mortality. When tragedy is the instrument God allows to make us face them, it can either prompt us to drift away from our family and God, or draw us even closer them. We can lose the faith we have or trust God for a deeper one.

It astonishes that all moments and memories throughout our lives from birth to death influence and affect us. We are all unique. Not two of us are alike. Our existence and the way we view life is determined mainly by the circumstances and relationships we have known. Each experience and every interaction with another human being ultimately molds and shapes us. We are ever changing in the stages of our mental and spiritual growth. By the grace of God if we stay in His will, our portrait when revealed will be found balanced and beautiful in the eyes of our heavenly Father.

I MAY NOT HAVE TOMORROW

At no other point in time would I realize the intensity of the scripture verse, **"Life is surely but a vapor"** than in 1985 tornado. Many of us have not given much thought to it, have we? Many of us never would. Yet in the aftermath of my ordeal, I have contemplated those few words in great depth and believe they are <u>absolutely true.</u>

How do those words make YOU feel? I hope they prompt you to cherish each and every second. I also hope they inspire you daily to thank God for blessings He has bestowed upon your life. <u>Take not one moment for granted</u>. Begin to see and care for life as the passing gift it is. May I ask you to try a little experiment that will prove HOW PRECIOUS our time here is? <u>Go to the nearest mirror or window and breathe on it</u>. What happens? **"It appears for a moment and then vanishes away!"** Just as our lives! **[James 4:14].** It's difficult to argue with what we see. Are we capable of adding to the length of the time the vapor exists? NO, it is not possible. By the time we have taken another breath, it is fading.

This example helps to prove, that we are deceiving ourselves if we believe <u>we</u> are in control. We do not possess power to control the minutes of our lives. Just as a vapor that quickly fades and is gone, we also would cease to exist if not for the grace of God. Therefore, we would be wise to pay attention to these words, **"All things that are exposed are made manifest by the light, for whatever makes manifest is light. Therefore He says, awake, you who sleep arise from the dead and Christ will give you light. See then that you walk circumspectly, not as fools but as wise, redeeming the time, because the days are evil. Therefore do not be unwise, but understand what the will of the Lord is" [Eph. 5:13].**

It's time to redeem that, which has been spent, apart from Christ. God's grace, we cannot mock! Are you and I prepared to meet our Creator? What if today was our LAST? We need to be prepared for this. God at any moment may call for our life. When that instant arrives, all excuses for living apart from Christ will be worthless. The doors to either heaven or hell are going to be shut, and we will find ourselves standing behind one of the two? We then, will spend eternity with either Jesus Christ or Satan. **"As I live says the Lord, every knee shall bow to Me and every tongue shall confess to God. So then each one of us shall give an account of himself to God" [Romans 14:11-12].** MAY 31,ST 1985 God nearly called me TO GIVE AN ACCOUNT of my life. Until that moment, I had never thought about dying. I see now that facing questions like these really don't need to bring us distress. On the contrary, they can bring us CLOSER TO GOD!

ONE TRUE FRIEND

Just one true friend is all I need to tell my troubles to
To open up and bear my thoughts when I am feeling blue.
Just one true friend is all I need when joy has filled my heart
To sing with me in happy times not jealously depart.
Just one true friend to dry my tears that fall in pain and strife
Any hour of the day throughout my course of life.
Just one true friend who knows me well, that's all I really need
One with good intentions to see that I succeed.
Just one true friend who'd DIE for me, that's all I need it's true,
I prayed to God for such a friend, and JESUS, I met YOU!

Christene Luthey

You are my friends if you do whatever I command you. No longer do I call you servants, for a servant does not know what his master is doing;

**but I have called you friends, for all things that I heard from my Father
I have made known to you"
[John 15:14-15].**

WHO SHALL KNOW THE DEPTH OF GOD

If in you dwelt all knowledge
It would be a grain of sand
For none shall ever fathom child, the power in my hand.

When you have held a ray of sun
Or stopped the morning dew
Or captured breezes when they blow, you've shared a secret true.

For THESE would be a drop of rain
Amidst the oceans deep
For who can know my thoughts and ways, they are but mine to keep.

When YOU can cause the earth to move
And grant the moon its light
When you can give a bird its song, or make its wing take flight,

When you have caught a falling star
Or paint an evening sky
When you have gathered every tear, that's fallen from each eye,

When you possess the power to breathe
LIFE into a soul,
When you can take a shattered world, heal and make it whole,

When you can die upon a cross
To set a sinner free,
This shall only be the start, to know the DEPTH of ME.

So do not search for proof to grant
Peace within your mind
The proof you seek of me dear one, you shall never find,

> Accept and trust in what I've said
> Receive in faith today
> I am who I proclaim to be; please throw your doubts away.
>
> No one shall ever match or beat
> The ways of God, it's known
> All knowledge of the depth of him
> RESTS IN CHRIST ALONE.
>
> *Christene Luthey*

"Oh, the depth of the riches both of the wisdom and knowledge of God! How unsearchable are His judgments and His ways past finding out! For who has known the mind of the Lord? Or who has become His counselor? [Romans 11:33-34].

If any <u>fear</u> should grip our soul, it should be that of our life coming to an end *before* we've received Christ as Savior. If any <u>grief</u> should touch our heart, it should be for those who are still prisoners of sin. My motivation in writing this book has **never been to frighten you into receiving Jesus Christ**. I am simply heeding the warnings given in **[Ezekiel 33:3:11]** to those who know the TRUTH of God's punishment for sin, and do not share it with others. **"When he sees the sword coming upon the land, if he blows the trumpet and warns the people, then whoever hears the sound of the trumpet and does not take warning; his blood shall be upon himself. But he who takes warning will save his life. But if the watchman sees the sword coming and does not blow the trumpet, and the people are not warned and the sword comes and takes away any person from among them, he is taken away in his iniquity; but his blood I will require at the watchman's hand."**

Question, shouldn't we all be considering God's gift of grace and His judgment for sin? **[John 12:48] "He who rejects me, and does not receive my words, has that which judges him, the word that I have spoken will judge him in the last day."** God, I sincerely believe will allow many things in the days ahead to gain our attention and trust. This makes me wonder how many tornadoes, floods, earthquakes, and fires the world must endure before we come to our senses? Sometimes even horrible disasters don't humble us?

What demonstrations does man need to prove that GOD is in control? Another question we might ask ourselves is what exactly will it take for God to get us focused on Him, and not this world? Why do you suppose so many lives are suffering tribulation? Could it be that God is allowing us to know adversity in the hope that it might draw us closer to Him? This we can be sure of, God rescues those who place their trust in Him and call upon His name. **"For this is good and acceptable in the sight of God our Savior, who desires ALL men to be saved and to come to the knowledge of the truth." [1 Tim. 2:3-4].**

In triumph Jesus said, **"I have overcome the world" [John 16:33].** No one but Christ Jesus can say this! Therefore, let us not give in to the things of this world that can never redeem your soul or mine on the day God demands it. God's word says there is none that have placed Him first in life. None that have avoided sin, and all are guilty of taking His name in vain. We have not attended God's Holy Communion regularly. Nor have we listened, believed, or lived according to God's ways. We have not shown reverence to Him. Nor have we loved our neighbor as He commanded. We have not gone though our lives without hurting someone. Nor have we helped the sick and needy to the best of our ability. We have not turned from ungodly companions. Nor have we avoided breaking the heart of God. Therefore, let's consider how we shall stand before Him and give an account?

From the beginning of time God has given man free will to make choices and decisions. This still holds true today. Each of us throughout our lives is faced with choices. Many of which affect our lives forever. The questions concerning these alternatives are how many of us take God's counsel into consideration BEFORE making a decision? **[Proverbs 3:5-7] "Trust in the Lord with all you heart; and lean not on your own understanding. In all your ways acknowledge Him and He shall direct your paths. Be not wise in your own eyes; fear the Lord and depart from evil."**

Christene Bolte-Luthey

Nowhere To Hide From God

When you have come to the end of yourself
You find there is no where to hide
There in the light of truth it is seen
In CHRIST you must abide.
Then you shall find that a choice must be made,
In fact, it's required, I know!
And freedom from chains that have bound you to sin
Are broken by just, "letting go."

C. Luthey

Five

THE JUST SHALL LIVE BY FAITH

"The just shall live by faith" [Gal. 3:11]. "For a little while, He who is coming will come and will not tarry. Now the just shall live by faith; but if anyone draws back, my soul has no pleasure in him" [Heb. 10:37-38].

> It seems our hearts are torn in two, by things that we must bear
> Doubt and disappointment, sorrow and despair.
> Often we are bound by things, we cannot understand
> More than not, little here turns out the way we planned.
>
> But gain we will a victory, if we are chosen true
> More than called, we've answered YES to all Christ said to do.
> It is written that the "just shall live, by faith" and so we must
> Forever walk by faith, not sight, and solely place our trust,
>
> In Christ alone, who beckons us, to be the chosen few
> And share with Him eternally
> Life, forever new!
>
> *Christene Luthey*

IS CHRIST THE LORD OF YOUR LIFE

Letting go is never easy. Yet the greatest act obedience toward God is letting go of our self-centered wills. When we do He will guide our lives and be the anchor of our soul. Trusting Him when trials come crashing around us we then can say, **"Truly my soul silently waits for God; from Him comes my salvation" [Ps. 62:5].** He is faithful in every situation. Longing only for us to grow in Christ like character and be strengthened spiritually. It is absolute trust He desires. Trust and total reliance upon that which we cannot see. We cannot see the wind, but we know it is there. So is HE!

When we TRULY "let go" we allow God to make the decisions. Believing that His love is genuine and will hold far more substance in our lives, than we could ever dream. Do we trust God? Or, do we trust in ourselves for our future? I know that it can be very difficult to step onto a "bridge" you've never crossed, but God's word states if we, **"humble yourself, under the mighty hand of God, that he will exalt you in due time, casting all your care upon him, for he cares for you" [1 Peter 5:6-7].**

The most important thing any of us can do is get right with Almighty God. It is a wise soul that humbly receives Christ, for only those who do, shall enter into God's kingdom. **[Heb. 4:6-7] "Since therefore it remains that some must enter it and those whom it was first preached did not enter because of disobedience. Again he designates a certain day, saying in David, TODAY, after such a long time, as it has been said: TODAY if you will hear his voice, do not harden your hearts."** If it is that you haven't entered into God's "rest because of disobedience," you need to know Christ loves you! If you have been wandering, backsliding, sinning, and feel alone know that His word is true, **"if you will hear His voice, He will welcome you into His kingdom."**

[Gal. 2:16] states that, **"a man is not justified by the words of the law but by faith in Jesus Christ."** Can you and I say these words spoken by the apostle Paul? **"I have been crucified with Christ; it is no longer I who live, but Christ lives in me; and the life which I now live in the flesh I live by faith in the Son of God, who loved me and gave Himself for me" [Gal. 2:20]**. Have you turned away from Christ, **"who gave himself for our sins, that he might deliver us from this present age, according to the will of our God and Father" [Gal. 1:4]**. Will we set aside the grace of God? **"For if righteousness comes through the law, then Christ died in vain" [Gal. 2:21].**

> What a sweet gift Christ has given to all
> Who turn from the world and answer his call.
>
> He shines with true glory, like sun on my face
> Revealing with splendor, God's awesome Grace.
>
> Warming my heart with His tender care
> He's always near, to ponder each prayer.
>
> Beloved Redeemer, master and friend
> Because of thy love, my life shall not end.

Christene Luthey

THE DAY HAS COME TO SEARCH OURSELVES

The day has come to search our hearts. Let us genuinely examine our lives. What is it that we might be taking for granted? What beliefs do we consider absolute? What values are established as certain? These questions should be given much thought. You and I live in a corrupt and compromising world. **[Romans 2:9] "Tribulation and anguish shall fall upon every soul that does evil"** we are warned. That is why it is vital that we **"search and try our ways, and turn again to the Lord" [Lamentations 3:40]**. **"The time has come that Judgment must begin at the house of God: and if it first begins with us, what shall be the end of them that do not obey the gospel of God" [1 Peter 4:11]**.

IS CHRIST THE LORD OF YOUR LIFE

Do you fall down and worship humbly and pray
Do you thank God sincerely for blessings each day?
Do you love and adore him, have you made him your own
Is CHRIST the LORD of YOUR LIFE and your Home?

Have you given him all, you hold in your heart?
Have you asked that forever, you shall not part
Do you look up to him, for thoughts of his will?
Does he have control, his purpose to fill?

OR, are you wearing a "Christian" disguise?

Search now yourself while time stands to do
All of the things you know you should do
Take not for granted, that you hold the key
You are under a curse, until Christ sets you free.

So, Please bow before him, humbly and pray:

I make you my Lord with each passing day.
I truly accept your blood for my sin
Come, precious Jesus, my Savior come in!
Enter my heart; make me your own,
Be now my Lord, here's my heart and my home.
I'll be true to your will; I'll turn from control
Be now the keeper of my very soul.
I've not lived my life, as you planned for me
Thank you for Grace and the courage to see
I must be forgiven, to dwell there above
I praise you for saving my soul with your LOVE.

C. Luthey

The Bible tells us, **"Do not be deceived, God is not mocked; for whatsoever a man sows, that will he also reap" [Gal. 6:7].** Lets consider the penalty of living life without Christ as Lord. The word of God tells us, **"The heavens and the earth which now exist are kept in store by the same word, reserved for fire until the Day of Judgment and perdition of ungodly men" [2 Peter 3:7].** Let us check to see, have we, **"Trampled the Son of God underfoot, counted the blood of the covenant by which He was sanctified a common thing and insulted the spirit of Grace." It is God who said, Vengeance is mine, I will repay, and again, the Lord will judge His people. It is a fearful thing to fall into the hands of the living God" [Hebrews 10:29-31].**

Another scripture we need to consider, **"Assuredly, I say to you, unless you are converted and become as little children, you will by no means enter the kingdom of heaven" [Matthew 18:3].** Have we humbled ourselves a "child" and sought God for forgiveness? If we choose not to, we forfeit our Salvation and eternal life in heaven.

A Sinner's PRAYER...

Dear Father, I confess that I am a poor miserable sinner. Your Holy Spirit has revealed this to my soul. Forgive me of my sin.... I sorrowfully accept my unrighteousness before Your Holiness and I sincerely repent of all I have done in thought, word or deed to displease or grieve Your tender heart. I humbly come before Your throne of Grace, and ask You as a trusting "child" to receive Jesus Christ, Your Beloved Son, as my blessed Savior and Redeemer. I believe that Jesus' sinless death on the cross was meant for me as payment in full for my offensive sin debt. I ask you to wash me whiter than snow, that I may one day live with you in your glorious Kingdom. Therefore, please fill me with the Holy Spirit, that my name might be written in your BOOK OF LIFE. From this moment on, I surrender my will unconditionally to You that you may, sit on the throne of my heart, and become Lord of life. Amen

I hope you prayed the sinner's prayer so that TOGETHER in heaven we may rejoice sitting at **JESUS'** feet, and worship Him in Glory! For only horrid **"weeping and gnashing of teeth"** await the "wicked in hell." Surely no words can begin to describe the torments therein the bottomless pit, **[Revelation 9:11 and 17:8],** for those **"whose names are not written in the book of life."** Oh, dear friend, is your name written in God's Book Of Life? Please consider bowing this moment, if you are not and ask Christ to spare your soul from ever knowing eternity apart from God. **"Let us be diligent to enter that rest"** as we are urged in **[Heb. 4:11] "For the word of God is sharper than a two-edged sword, piercing even to the division of soul and spirit, and the joints and marrow, and is a discerner of the thoughts and intents of the heart. And there is no creature hidden from his sight, but all things are naked and open to the eyes of him whom we must give and account" [Heb. 4:11-13].**

> Come, all yea, who are laden with care
> Allow Christ to carry all thy despair.
> Rest in the arms of mercy and grace
> Come, enter into they Lord's resting place.
>
> *C. Luthey*

AGE OF REBELLION

"All have sinned" and the **"wages of sin is death" [Rom. 6:23].** It is clear to see that we cannot walk in wickedness. The Lord cannot allow us to work iniquity in our life. If we do, we will experience the fruit of our rebellion. When will we fear SIN and its judgment? **[Matthew 23:37]** says, **"you shall love the Lord your God with all your heart, and all your soul**

and with all your mind. This is the first and greatest commandment." How many of us, even attending church regularly, disregard what the Bible has to say? Did you know that the Spirit of the "Anti-Christ" leads those who rebel against Christ and His teachings? That they are destined for despair, and will drink the wine of God's wrath? **[Rev. 14:10] "He himself shall also drink of the wine of the wrath of God, which is poured out full strength into the cup of His indignation. He shall be tormented with fire and brimstone in the presence of the holy angels and in the presence of the Lamb."**

Think about your life considering that: this may be God's last call to repentance. What if this was the last opportunity you were given to turn from sin and be saved? Would you act on it? Will today be the day God hears your voice calling out to Him? He says to us, **"In an acceptable time I have heard you, and in the day of Salvation I have helped you. Behold, now is the accepted time. Now is the day of Salvation" [2 Cor. 6:2].**

Age Of Rebellion

How long will God tarry? How long must he give?
How much should a Father forget and forgive?
To see here again, "Sodom" on earth,
We're Mocking God's grace and the depth of its worth.

Ignoring His word, Holy and true
While we never regret, one thing that we do.
Remembering not, His will or his ways,
While taking for granted
Our briefness of days.

C. Luthey

HARDEN NOT YOUR HEART

"Enter into His rest," so it may be that we are as the scripture says, **"Hidden in the day of the Lord's anger" [Zeph. 2:3].** And receive the Grace needed to **"Flee all kinds of evil and pursue righteousness, Godliness, faith, love, patience, and gentleness" [1 Tim. 6:11].** Will we **"fight the good fight of faith, and lay hold of eternal life, to which we were called" [1 Tim. 6:12].** Then we must humble ourselves in the sight of

God **"who gives life to all things, and before Christ Jesus who witnessed the good confession before Pontius Pilate" [1 Tim 6:13].**

Have we humbled ourselves to the will of God? If we haven't is it because we view humility as a sign of weakness? If so, let us take a look at *JESUS*, who humbled Himself becoming obedient to the point of death on a cross. <u>This He did for you and I.</u> **[Phil. Chapter 2]. "He who blessed and only Potentate, the KING OF KINGS and LORD OF LORDS. Who alone has immorality, dwelling in unapproachable light who no man has seen or can see, to whom be honor and everlasting power" [1 Tim. 6:15-16].** What do you think about when you ponder **humility?** I think about the <u>tormenting pain Jesus endured to become the BRIDGE that spans between the Glory of heaven and the torture of hell, for OUR Salvation.</u> No mind could begin to fathom the magnitude of His quest for mankind. Can we possibly imagine for one second walking in His shoes? Knowing that by the <u>Law</u> of God, Christ alone could die for our sin. If not for Christ's' love and obedience, the gift of eternal life would not be offered. Had Christ not paid our sin debt, the gulf between God and man would not have been bridged. **"The sting of death is sin and the strength of sin is the law. But thanks be to God, who gives us the victory through our Lord Jesus Christ" [1 Cor. 16:56-57].**

So, was it in weakness that Jesus died? Absolutely not! The strongest, most courageous soul that ever breathed could not have endured the slightest mental assessment of being CRUCIFIED; let alone suffering physically the racking pain attributed to such a fate. WHO among US could understand Christ's agony as He surrendered Himself to God's perfect will? For us Jesus was crucified. Suffering the CRUELEST punishment known, that you and I might be "saved" because—He loved us so.

COULD WE BEAR HIS CROSS

I stand in awe when I ponder JESUS'S suffering, and willingness to die for sinners such as you and I. Some of us may consider humility to lack strength, yet how many of us would be willing to take His place on the cross? (We know it's impossible, because we're not "sinless") But, <u>what would we do, **IF** God said, that "sinners" must pay their OWN sin debt</u>, should we <u>reject Christ's efforts?</u> Would we appreciate Jesus more?

One day, while I was meditating on <u>this question</u> the following poem filled my mind. I pray that it speaks to your heart as much as it did mine?

Woven throughout the lines I sense strongly our heavenly Father rebuking us, for our lack of thankfulness. May the words cause us to value more Christ's precious gift of love? And see in a different perspective the true depth of God's compassion.

Let us search our own hearts and ask: Have we, **"trampled the Son of God underfoot?"** Have we, **"Insulted the Spirit of Grace?"** Have we, **"Treated the blood of the covenant as a common thing?"** Then, let us consider with reverent fear if it is any wonder why the judgment of God shall one day fall upon this world? How many of us have counted Christ's suffering as NOTHING? I think sincerely we know this scripture is true: **"it will be a fearful thing to fall into the hands of the living God."** Why? Because God offered His son as a <u>sinless living sacrifice,</u> <u>Holy and acceptable for the sins of the world</u>, but found that, **"we esteemed Him not." "He is despised and rejected by men, a man of sorrows and acquainted with grief. And we hid, as it were, our faces from Him; and we did not esteem Him. Surely He has borne our griefs and carried our sorrows; yet we esteemed Him stricken, smitten, by God, and afflicted. But he was wounded for our transgressions, he was bruised for our iniquities; The chastisement for our peace was upon Him"** [Isaiah 53:3-5]

I HAVE A CROSS FOR YOU

Imagine PERFECT INNOCENCE hanging on a tree
Blood pouring out of him that you could be set free.
Yet, Guilty all are you who take, for granted so my grace,
Would it not be counted fair, for YOU to take YOUR place?
And know YOURSELF the laughter, the scoffing and the pain,
The crown of thorns upon your head, for someone else's gain.
Because you do not care to think about the price He paid
It's true you have forgotten, yes you have also strayed.
Consider please THIS thought I say, and think with reverent fear
YOU could be upon the cross, and then it would be clear.
The agony that wretches in your body as you die
Suffocating slowly, you cannot even cry.
Feel the tearing in your chest, each muscle grips and shakes
Knowing even stronger yet your heart as it too breaks.
Each vessel and each bone you feel pounding in your brain
Feeling weak and fainting as water starts to drain.

> For blood and every ounce of life is trickling to the ground
> But adding to your misery, a FRIEND cannot be found,
> To lend a word of thanks or say, "I love you ever true"
> Yet, knowing that this dying one has paid a DEBT for <u>YOU</u>!
> Instead, you take for granted GRACE, going your own way
> Perhaps you could be more sincere, if I said this today?
> YOU come now and pay the debt written in YOUR name
> I no longer shall accept the LAMB who had NO blame.
>
> Each one must pay the debt HIMSELF; I have a cross for YOU
> Maybe then, my Precious Son would mean much it's true.
>
> *C. Luthey*

HAVE WE INSULTED THE SPIRIT OF GRACE?

If we look at Jesus' crucifixion with perpetual hearts, we would create in our mind the horrid and most bewildering execution known to man. Then, if we haven't already, we might cease taking Christ's efforts for granted in suffering the most horrible death a human can endure. Perhaps then we could truly love and adore Him as the supreme treasure He is?

In all honesty, we could never imagine the upright stake in the shape of a T, and how Jesus must have felt being treated like a horrible criminal (although He was completely SINLESS)? Scorned and forced to carry the crossbeam, to the place where He knew He would DIE a horrifying death. Ponder if possible His arms being tied to the stake because His palms could not bear the entire weight of his body. I am sincerely convinced as they drove the large crude nails though His hands, His body burst into devastating pain that would rupture the mightiest heart. Meditate on the peg He stood on for support as they bound and hammered nails through His feet. He must have shivered in brutal agony as He hung on that cross, barely able to breathe because His body was starving of oxygen.

I have to ask, <u>WHO but Jesus could endure the weight of this cup</u>? Who but our beloved sinless Savior could undergo the convulsing spasms that contracted throughout each bone, vessel and muscle in His body? Again, only Christ Jesus! Then, physically weak and dying, incapable of moving, at the moment of death, Jesus spoke to God and said; **"Father, into thy hands I commit my Spirit" [Luke 23:46].** All the while throughout this unimaginable tribulation, He remained unto His last breath, silent throughout the taunts and physical abuse from those passing by. Jesus' undertaking on earth <u>was fulfilled</u>. He had surrendered humbly His will and life in pure obedience—to the will of His Father. Out of selfless LOVE for you and I, Jesus gave up **"His Spirit to God"** and dying, said: **"It is finished" [John 19:30].**

PERFECT LOVE

It was such a gift to give to man; PERFECT LOVE was in God's plan
Unto Us He gave Himself, Perfect love and untold wealth.
Before us He laid down His soul, yielding all that we be whole.
Could we ever comprehend, <u>that God would DIE to be OUR friend</u>?
No human mind could grasp how deep, the heart of God nor love to keep.
He is infinitely wise. Pure and Holy, no disguise.
Where He lives I cannot tell, inside the heart of sinners (now well!)
He has not forsaken me; in everything He's made me free.
NOW I KNOW I AM "SAVED" WITHIN, for Perfect love, blots out sin.

C. Luthey

LOVE SO PURE AND TRUE

What meaning has this act of love placed your heart today? Have we in any way turned our back on the One who died in OUR place? If we have, we are living our lives in vain. Apart from Christ, life has no meaning. Jesus could have denied us the glory, and magnificence of eternal life, by simply refusing to fulfill His Father's will. But Jesus' heart is so full of love and compassion for mankind that He never would have considered walking away from the His commission. His love is too pure, perfect and true. If His Father had asked Him to die for just ONE soul, He would still not have refused. Even for one, He would have totally surrendered without regret <u>because He loves us that much!</u>

Maybe today will be the day we hear (if we have not already) the Holy Spirit affectionately beckoning us to trust Christ Jesus? Possibly you may be someone who has been hurt or has simply lost your way? Are you wandering like a lamb away from your loving Shepherd? If so, Jesus is waiting for you to call on him. He's waiting for you to simply "let go" of your sin and pride, so that he may live in you. You CAN trust Him! Jesus is and forever will be a name that will never let us down. He is worthy of our trust. Therefore, let us allow Him to prove Himself today.

CHRIST ALONE IS WEALTH

In Him we are so rich within, free from bondage of our sin
Paid, He wiped our debts away. Something we could never pay
So instead of earthly things, I receive what true love brings.
A Savior, Lord, grace and peace
And easily, my cares then cease.
And thankfulness soon fills my heart
With joy to last and never part.

C. Luthey

Christene Bolte-Luthey

Six

BEHOLD THE PLUMB LINE
Law/Wickedness/Death

"Amos, what do you see? A PLUMB LINE, I answered. Then He said, I am using it to show that my people are like a wall that is out of line. I will not change my mind again about punishing them. The places where Isaac's descendants worship will be destroyed. The Holy places of Israel will be left in ruins. I will bring the dynasty of King Jeroboam to an end" [Amos 7:7-9]. (This plumb line foretells God's divine decision to execute judgment

I stand with my plumb line ready to test each heart upon the earth
To see when the storm is raging in force, what is your faith really worth?
Will it stand and be thankful trusting in ME or die like a grape on the vine?
Do you not see as Gold is too tested, it will prove who really are mine?

The line has been given, it is time to DECIDE, which side you're standing on
I will not allow both sides of the line, for soon you will see it is gone.
There is only one side that surely will spare you; the other holds no sympathy,
There is no compromise when I look in your eyes, do you follow Satan—
or—Me?

I'm through with your living with such indecision,
For the flood of hard times soon will come,
All who shall suffer will be those too willful
And chose not to follow my Son.
I sent Him to save you from sin's destination
Then I gave you the freedom to choose
Yet time and the line are quickly now fading,
And all who are "LUKEWARM" will loose.

Loose all your belongings, all your false hopes,
All of your senses and schemes
And too late realize, when I look in your eyes,
What a plumb line truly means.

IT IS TIME TO DECIDE

The line has been given and is to divide
Those who love Me—or—those who love sin,
This the last chance, you may have, "enter in."

Beware of the mockers who spitefully mock
You are laughing so loud you cannot hear Me "knock"
And **those who are Mine, but are *living* as not?**
You are mocking My grace and the price you were bought.

I shall not stand for these—be aware,
It is time to DECIDE
Choose My REST or Despair…

Christene Luthey

This should definitely be a wake up call. So far you have had many things to consider; sin, judgment, and death. In *this chapter* I want to talk about the danger of you and I living **"double-minded," "LUKE-WARM LIVES."** Chapter six I hope will assist you in contemplating God's Kingdom, what you believe and possibly making a life long decision to follow and serve Jesus Christ.

IN THE BEGINNING

From the beginning of time God has given man the free will and opportunity to make choices and decisions. When He created Adam and Eve, He gave and freely blessed them. Yet along with those blessings He commanded them, **"Not to eat of the tree of knowledge" [Gen. 2:15-16].** In spite of the Lord's warning that **"in the day that you eat of it you shall surely die."** Although fully aware of God's command, Adam and Eve took the fruit and ate it. In fact, when Eve was asked by the serpent, **"Has God indeed said you shall not eat of every tree in the garden?"** Eve went on to *quote* God's command. Knowingly she and Adam disregarded and ignored God's counsel—and ate.

It was evident that Adam and Eve gave little thought to God's words, **"you shall surely die."** Today, it is still evident that we have not learned very much from *their* disobedience. We have also throughout the ages remained in rebellion to God. Often we like Adam and Eve take no notice of God's word that we might LIVE and not "die" in our sin. Why do we ignore such things? Have we no reverent fear of God? Is it that we believe we can hide from our Creator? God's word tells us that without delay after they had **"eaten,"** that, **"then the eyes of both of them were opened and they knew that they were naked; and they sewed fig leaves together and made themselves coverings"[Gen.3:7].**

I think if we look at our lives and the mistakes we have made along life's way, it would be undeniable that the consequences of sin is always everlasting. That is unless we have allowed Christ to erase our debt? The act Adam and Eve committed by challenging God's warnings caused God to send them out of the garden. Their arrogance deluded them, and they pursued their own wishes. The Devil has not changed his deceptive tactics over the years. He still uses the same lies that have proven successful in deceiving and separating people from God.

Satan with his plots to destroy is always standing by eager to plant his evil seeds of distrust and rebellion. For Satan in his vanity said in his heart, **"I will ascend into heaven, I will exalt my throne above the stars of God" [Isaiah 14:13].** And, **"I will be like the most high" [Isaiah 14:14].** Now let us stop and see if you or I have an attitude that bears a resemblance to his? Let's think, WHO honestly decides what you or I will do with our lives? Is it US or is it God?

Remember these words? **"Trust in the Lord with all your heart, and lean not on your own understanding. In all your ways acknowledge Him and He shall direct your paths. Be not wise in your own eyes; fear the Lord and depart from evil." [Proverbs 3:5-7].** If we are following the desires of our own heart and using our own understanding to make decisions, we *like Satan* are acting in disobedience to God.

WHAT IS OUR MOTIVATION

If you or I don't think there is anything wrong with pleasing ourselves, because we're simply "looking out for number one," we'd better *think again*. If you or I believe this way, we are as vain and prideful as Satan was. When we have this sort of overconfident attitude we are failing to acknowledge our unrighteousness before God. In Satan's case, it was his self-pleasing, egotistical mind-set that made him **"fall from heaven" [Is. 14:12]**.

We are unqualified without the Holy Spirit's assistance to distinguish the enemy (Satan) and the devises he uses to tempt people away from the truth. Sin in our lives makes us trust our own stubborn wills and unbelief, and we end up choosing to live opposite to the Gospel of Christ. It should be known that when we disobey God we are granting authority in our lives to our **"ADVESARY the DEVIL, who walks about like a roaring lion, seeking whom he may devour" [1 Peter 5:8]**.

WHAT IS OUR MOTIVATION

What is our motivation?
Is it Joy?—Prosperity?
Happiness, or health perhaps
Life eternally?

Be careful how we answer please
Be honest and sincere,
Knowing God Almighty too
In Holiness shall hear.

It's true God wishes wondrous things
For each and every heart,
Though often in prosperity
He sees a soul depart.

If we have not looked up to see
All treasures dwell above
Blessings as His <u>mercy</u> and <u>grace</u>
And most of all—His <u>love</u>.

> For these should motivate our lives
> To serve Him endlessly,
> The question still remains dear friend
> What motivateth thee?
>
> Perhaps today you're struggling
> Wanting God to do—
> Could this be a test to see?
> What's motivating you?
>
> If we serve **self**, forgetting God
> Embracing "earthly" treasure
> It's true one day our soul shall grieve
> Beyond one's mind can measure.
>
> It's quite a challenge, is it not?
> To ponder WHO we serve
> OURSELVES? Or God Almighty?
> We'll reap what we deserve.
>
> *Christene Luthey*

It would be wise for us to take a look at the prosperity thinking in our world today. Some people believe that Christianity is linked mainly to wealth and "prosperity," but I sincerely tend to disagree. God's word encourages us NOT to live lives or lifestyles of self-indulgence, but rather of <u>SELF-DENIAL</u>. This more accurately mirrors more the teachings of Jesus Christ.

I have found that Satan must only entice the desire for "self-satisfaction" to effectively achieve what he has set out to do: **"Exalt himself above the Most High."** In this he may attempt to keep man divided from God if at all possible. That is why we are told in **[Col. 2:8-9] "Beware lest anyone cheat you though philosophy and empty deceit, according to the tradition of men, according to the basic principles of the world, and not according to Christ. For in Him dwells all the fullness of the Godhead bodily."**

It is through the lust of the flesh that Satan tries to destroy us. Looking for ways to get a foothold in our lives. His ultimate objective is to rob us of the victory that is ours (if we receive it) through Jesus Christ. When we permit the devil to temp our lives through the flesh, we are in danger of sinning against God. Remember, we are gone astray if we are apart from

Christ, which leads to eternal death and condemnation. The enemy knows that after we sin, we must bear the guilt that accompanies disobedience to God's divine will. Therefore, let us strive to be led by the Holy Spirit!

LEAD ME ONWARD

Obey you Lord I long to do, take my hand I ask of you
Lead me onward, further still, where I'm lacking Father fill.
Fill me with your grace divine, precious Savior Lord of mine,
Guide me onward, help me do, that of what best pleases you.
Grant me wisdom, truth and light, faith within the darkest night
Let me not, fall short of Thee, Blessed Lord who set me free.
Through today and still tomorrow, lead me onward I shall follow.

C. Luthey

A few thoughts to consider:

As mere mortal men, we are destined to die	[Romans 3:23]
Unless though faith we believe;	[Acts 16:31]
And are humbled as children, returning to Christ	[Matt. 18:3-4]
Our souls He cannot receive.	[John 3:3]
For sin separates us from God up above	[Romans 6:23]
Until we receive by grace	[Romans 3:24]
Forgiveness to pardon, thus sets us free	[Col. 1:14]
Only then may we look on His face.	[1 Peter 3:12]
Or He will then say, **"depart now and go, You workers of iniquity,"**	[Eph. 5:6]
I do not know you where are you from? No, you are no friend to me…	[Luke 13:22-28]

C.Luthey

Christene Bolte-Luthey

FIXING OUR FAITH IN THE BLOOD OF THE LAMB

God's word shall be accurate, right to the end
Those who are His, must solely depend
On mercy and grace from Christ who is Love
He shall be ALL "believers" dream of.

Not money or power, nor standing they'll see
They shall be loyal for He set them free
These are the ones who will carry His cross
Risking it all whatever the cost.

They will not be frightened, nor be deceived
These are the hearts that WHOLLY received
CHRIST the anointed, the Savior and Lord
Not loving self, but Him they adored.

Thus washing their sins in the blood of the Lamb
Fixing their faith in the Sovereign "I AM."

Christene Luthey

Throughout history (and today) God's word reveals in many ways WHY we have not always received His promises or rested in His peace. One account is the book of Numbers found in the Old Testament of the Bible. People had made their way toward the land of Canaan, which God had promised would be plentiful in every kind of fruit, honey, wine, water and cattle. God promised all they would ever need or want to live productive lives. Yet they as we sometimes still do today, became very restless, impatient, and resentful of having to wait almost a year at Mount Sinai. Being they were detained they began complaining of the hardships and trials they had undergone on their journey. The Bible tells that **"Scouts which had been sent to investigate this land of Canaan, found it to be filled with promise, just as God had said, but returned with negative reports that prompted (tempted) people to doubt and fall into unbelief."**

How many of us have allowed Satan to get vice-like grips on our lives like this? All of us probably have, at one time or another? But even when things are not going as we expected, we don't have to sin as Satan tempts us. One example of that shows us two who God was <u>not displeased with</u> among this group, **[Numbers Chapter 14]**, Caleb and Joshua. **"They faithfully trusted Him and believed his words saying that he would bring them into the land He promised."** It was due to the lack of faith on this people's part that God decided and gave the decree that they would NOT enter into the land of promise. Instead, because of their complaining they would wander forty years. It would be their children's generation that God would actually bless and bring into Canaan.

I share that story because I sincerely believe that WE sometimes place far too much emphasis on the time and place we are stationed in life also. Oddly enough, the sin of being bad tempered that tempted them into unbelief, began them complaining. Ironically this brought God's punishment and cost them dearly. By this, we see that when we focus mainly on ourselves we are more at risk of suffering disappointment, despair and devastation.

All of us are on a journey like those written about in the Bible. Every hour of the day, we are crossing "rivers", "valleys" and "bridges." Many of which might cause us to become restless, angry, disappointed and discouraged. Yet we must be aware that hardships met along the way if not kept in check, can be used by Satan to encourage us to sin. Remember always the Bible says that he, **"walks about like a roaring lion, seeking whom he may devour" [1 Peter 5:8].**

Each of us is in a "wilderness" of sorts in this world. We are all searching for something to fill the spiritual vacuum in our lives. We may not know it, or admit it, but until Jesus Christ dwells within us, there will always be an immeasurable void that simply cannot be filled. What we must know about this void, is that turning to anything other than the Gospel of Jesus Christ will be futile. That is why we are told to, **"seek first the kingdom of God and His righteousness, and all these things shall be added to you" [Matt. 6:33].** Also, **"Ask and it will be given to you, seek and you will find; knock and it will be opened to you" [Matt. 7:7].** Therefore, anything offered to us—other than the Gospel of Christ is an imitation that Satan has devised to deceive. Again, forget not that he is working to cheat us out of God's perfect will. **"I beseech you therefore, brethren, by the mercies of God, that you present your bodies a living sacrifice, holy acceptable to God, which is your reasonable service. And do not be conformed to this world, but be transformed by the renewing of your mind, that you may prove what is good and acceptable and perfect will of God" [Romans 12:1-2].** This applies to all of us. **"Do not love the world or the things in the world. If anyone loves the world, the love of the Gather is not in him. For all that is in the world is passing away,** and the lust of it; but he who does the will of God abides forever" [1 John 2:15-17].

The Devil does not want us walking in the will of God. Therefore he will use various forms of temptation to lead us astray. Satan has not changed. Consider how many lives he is trying to destroy right now through abuse, drinking, pornography, drugs, theft, etc. the list is endless. We know the Devil is a liar and the Bible says he is an "accuser!" In fact he right now may be trying to deceive you by saying that your sins are justified as long as you're not hurting anyone? Some other lies are that compromise is acceptable, or, that you don't need a Savior. Then there is the LIE that you don't need to be concerned with the eternal fate of your soul. Again, dear friend, all of these are LIES! Do not be deceived!

Today, Satan must only get us to rub shoulders with the world to direct us to sin's death and keep us away from God's best. **[Luke 16:13] "No servant can serve two masters; for either he will hate the one and love the other, or else he will be loyal to the one and despise the other. You cannot serve God and money."** This is why it is imperative that we put a halt to the things we compromise in our lives. Why is this so significant? Because little by little sin will overshadow us and make it very difficult to determine whom TRULY is "Saved." Today we have nearly compromised ourselves to the brink of eternal disaster. Paying little attention to Satan who is watching and accusing every "lost" soul as it is being spiritually drowned in the waters of "Luke-warm" living.

Jesus talked about the will of His Father in **[John 6:39-40], "This is the will of the Father who sent me, that of all He has given me I should lose nothing, but should raise it up at the last day. And this is the will of Him who sent me, that everyone who sees the son and believes in Him may have everlasting life; and I will raise Him up at the last day."** What we must realize is that God's perfect will can only be accomplished in our lives as we humbly place our faith and trust in Christ. Believing in Him and receiving God's free gift of Salvation. **"For by grace we are saved through faith, and that not of yourselves; it is the gift of God, not of works lest anyone should boast" [Eph. 2:8]. "Consequently, just as the result of one trespass was condemnation for all men, so also the result of one act of righteousness was justification that brings life for all men. For just as through the disobedience of the one man the many were made sinners, so also through the obedience of the one man the many will be made righteous. The law was added so that the trespass might increase. But where sin increased, grace increased all the more, so that** just as sin reigned in depth, so also grace might reign through righteousness to bring eternal life through Jesus Christ our Lord" [Romans 5:18-21].

>Though unaware of sin and death,
>You reached out for my hand,
>I struggled at first because dear Lord
>I did not understand.
>
>It took a glimpse of life and death
>To help me change my ways
>Before I yielded to YOUR will
>And gave you thanks and praise.
>
>Today I stand in awe of you
>And lift your Holy name
>Because you helped me die to "self"
>I'll never be the same.
>
>*C. Luthey*

Precious friend, Satan has caused many a careless heart to love the world and the things in it. He does this because the world does not seek God's kingdom or His Righteousness. The world does not seek the approval of God. On the contrary, it cares only about the approval of man. Yet God's word says, **"You are those who justify yourselves before men, but God knows your hearts. For what is highly esteemed among men is an abomination in the sight of God"** [Luke 16:15]. The world serves and satisfies the lusts of the flesh, and will not surrender to the Holy Spirit. Which is why we no longer can risk justifying sin in our lives. We are not to be, **"men pleasers,"** but, **"servants of Christ, doing the will of God for the heart with good will doing service as to the Lord and not, to men"** [Eph. 6:6-7]. Friend, are you presently caught up in the things of this world? Ponder please whether you are a man or God pleaser? Knowing **"what is highly esteemed among men is an abomination to God,"** isn't this a priceless question? Is the devil "pulling the wool over your eyes" by things you're taking for granted?

Christene Bolte-Luthey

SATAN IS LAUGHING AT YOU

If you're taking for granted, tomorrow will come?
As most of us truthfully do,
Open your eyes, my friend realize
Satan is laughing at you.
If you're taking for granted, you need not be "saved?"
And so, put it off till tomorrow,
You'll soon realize to your demises
Satan will laugh at your sorrow.
If you're taking for granted the lives of your loved ones
Not giving them time through the years
Who can you blame, never the same?
As Satan laughs at your tears.
If you're taking for granted that money has power
To make all your dreams come true
You will find one day, it's been stolen away
As Satan is laughing, "poor you."
If you're taking for granted the time you've been given
To make a difference my friend
Refusing your place to share in God's grace
Satan will laugh in the end.
For see all the ways you've helped in his favor
His tactics were easily planted
Destroying your life, and adding with strife
<u>All YOU did was take HIM for granted!</u>

C. Luthey

I'll be the first to admit that I've taken many things for granted in life. Just to name a few: my life, my health, my salvation, and my family, just about everything you can think of. But not so much since the tornado in 1985, because that is when the line of compromise became so clear to me. Since that happened I've taken a tough look at what is right and wrong in my life according to the word of God.

I'm hoping that today might be the day you step off the "starting line" and run in the "race" God has set before us? You and I need to stop wandering around the same sin filled compromising mountains in our lives. They will not lead us to victory. If I can encourage you today to look with me beyond our troubles, and seek God's face, I know that one day you will reach the true summit of contentment. This "summit" is not like the one I mentioned previously when speaking of the gladness I *thought* Scott and I had achieved, but the glorious "summit" where you and I can forever dwell in the midst of God's awesome love and grace. There we may look forward to sharing in His glory forever. Let us give thought to that wonderful goal! Guarding our heart and mind with the knowledge that Satan will try to keep us from basking in the radiance of God's eternal light. This place is where day and night those who have trusted Christ never stop saying, **"Holy, Holy, Holy, is the Lord God Almighty, who was, and is, and is to come"** [Rev. 4:8], **"As they fall down before Him who sits on the throne saying: You are worthy, our Lord and God, to receive glory and honor and power, for You created all things, and by Your will they were all created and have their being"** [Rev. 4:10-11].

In the land of promise, the Bible says that, **"The Glory of God will illuminate the city and there shall be no night there, because the Lamb (Jesus Christ) will be its light"** [Rev. 21:23-35]. In this amazing place, those who have surrendered their lives to the will of God, **"receive the crown of life which the Lord has promised to those who love Him"** [James 1:12 & Rev. 2:10]. Can you imagine the jubilation in this extraordinary place as God Himself the Bible says, **"will wipe away every tear from their eyes,"** and **"there shall be no more death, nor sorrow, nor crying, and no more pain, because all of these things will have passed away."** [Rev. 21:4].

THE WICKEDNESS OF MAN

Scripture tells us that **"The day of the Lord will come as a thief in the night, in which the heavens will pass away with a great noise and the elements will melt with fervent heat; both the earth and the works that are in it will be burned up"** [2 Peter 3:10]. I know what it's like to have my life "flash before me," and experience the horrible feeling of knowing my spirit was sinking. That is why it is extremely important that you not only consider what I am sharing, but also take God's words into your heart.

We don't know WHEN our lives will end. We don't know when, the **"Lord will come again."** Therefore, you and I must believe that: <u>there will not be any time to make peace with God if we haven't already done so when either of these two things occurs</u>. I sincerely believe that if it had not been for the tender mercy of God, I would have reached the "point of no return" on May 31st, 1985. In that instant, I would have been forced to live forever in darkness. Again, I sincerely believe that <u>had I died that day without Christ as my Lord and Savior, I would have been bound to spend eternity with the devil suffering the judgment of my sins. This would have held for me throughout infinity, regret, misery and torture.</u> May I ask you friend to consider this end, and search your own soul? You may or may not know me, but I hope what I've just shared will get your full attention! May it perhaps cause you to consider your eternal fate?

Let me ask, do you think that I "deserved" to go to hell? Well, that would depend on WHICH SET OF STANDARDS you were judging me by. If by the **world's** standards, probably not? BUT the BOTTOM LINE is: <u>GOD SAYS I AM A "SINNER!" AND REGARDLESS OF HOW "GOOD WE ARE OR TRY TO BE" YOU AND I BECAUSE OF SIN ARE SEPARATED FROM GOD AND HIS HOLINESS. THEREFORE unless we KNOW JESUS CHRIST as our SINLESS SAVIOR, we bear God's Judgment of Sin.</u>

I'm sharing that truth because there are a lot of people in the world today that are under the dangerous impression that as long as you do your best to "live by the Golden Rule" you will be "saved" and "go to heaven" when you die. NO! My friend, there is but one and <u>ONE WAY ONLY to receive Salvation that leads to eternal life. That is only through faith in JESUS CHRIST!</u>

[2 Cor. 11:31-32] advises that, **"If we would judge ourselves, we would not be judged, but when we are judged we are chastened by the Lord, that we may not be condemned with the world."** God has set LIFE and DEATH before us; let us not take either of them for granted! Instead, let us ask God to begin inspecting and proving our hearts so that we may experience the true life-changing salvation that leads to a life of fruitfulness. May you and I seek the courage to look within ourselves and see what God sees when He searches our hearts? That way, we may **"walk in integrity, trusting in the Lord without wavering" [Ps. 26:1]. "But know this, that in the last days perilous times will come: For men will be lovers of themselves, lovers of money, boasters, proud, blasphemers, disobedient to parents, unthankful, unholy, unloving, unforgiving, slanderers, without self-control, brutal, despisers of good, traitors, headstrong, haughty, lovers of pleasure rather than lovers of God" [2 Tim. 3:1-4]**.

TRUTH:	Quite often can be painful. Especially when it reveals that which dwells within our own heart.
HONESTY:	Is the key that unlocks the door to what we are afraid to see in our self.
COURAGE:	Is what we require to admit what we find therein.
HOPE:	Believes that we CAN change, becoming a better person.
GRACE:	Is the wondrous means by which we may become truly WHOLE.
LOVE:	Is the way to press on toward the heavenly goal!

C. Luthey

"Till we all come to the unity of the faith and the knowledge of the Son of God, to a perfect man, to the measure of the stature of the fullness of Christ that we should no longer be children tossed to and fro and carried about with every wind of doctrine, by the trickery of men, in the cunning craftiness by which they lie in wait to deceive, but speaking the truth in love, may grow up in all things into Him who is the Head Christ, from whom the who body is joined and knit together by what every joint supplies, according to the effective working by which every part does its share, causes growth of the body for the edifying of itself in love" [Eph. 4:13:16].

THE JUDGMENT OF THE UNGODLY

Just as it was in the days of Noah, there are going to be scoffers who mock people who strive to trust in Jesus Christ, and follow Him in obedience to God's will. The Bible tells us the earth was **"corrupt"** and **"filled with violence"** in Noah's day, and so it is in ours. As God looked upon the earth, He saw that it was corrupt, as all flesh had corrupted his way. God spoke to Noah and said, **"The end of all flesh has come before me; for the earth is filled with violence through them, behold I will destroy them with** the earth" **[Gen. 6:11-13]**. Punishment had come to the evildoers, as God always keeps his promises!

Yet, God in His mercy kept Noah and his family from the judgment that came upon the land saying, **"make yourself an ark" [Gen. 6:14]**, and **"I will establish a covenant with you; and you shall go into the ark, you your sons, your wife and your son's wives with you" [Gen. 6:8]**. Why? Because we are told in **[Gen. 6:22]** that Noah DID according to all that God commanded him and the **"Lord shut him in the ark." [Gen. 6:8]**.

Perhaps you are wondering why I am sharing these Old Testament scriptures with you? Maybe you don't feel they apply to us? Oh, dear friend they do! You see God's anger was kindled by mankind's wickedness yet in the midst of death and destruction, God spared Noah and his family because they had DECIDED to follow God's commands. We are told that, **"Noah was a righteous man, blameless in his generation" [Gen. 6:9]**. Noah and his family were SPARED FROM THE JUDGMENT of "wickedness," on the earth, because of his faith, obedience and trust in God.

I sincerely believe that the heart of God must be DEEPLY GRIEVED when He looks upon mankind TODAY and sees how far from Him we have strayed. Corruption, violence, and murder are on the increase and yet we resist to humbly reach out for Christ's hand to see us through life's difficulties. It's easy to see that where there is lack of BIBLICAL righteousness, there are no fixed standards. Each of us then sinfully resign ourselves to do whatever we feel or believe is right. I ask you; if we go on taking what is Biblically righteous and replacing it with evil, HOW LONG will it be until God's anger AGAIN is kindled? What will happen when it is? Will it be that you and I that experience what the Bible describes as the LAST JUDGMENT? **"For the time has come for judgment to begin at the house of God; and if it begins with us first what will be the end of those who do not obey the Gospel of God? Now, if the righteous one is scarcely saved, where will the ungodly and the sinner appear?" [1 Peter 4:17-18]**.

Common sense and our own consciences should tell us that judgment is destined to come. Friend, the infallible word of God, warns us of the final reckoning. This will be the time when the fate of every soul will receive this promise, **"Then the sign of the Son of man will appear I heaven, and then all the tribes of the earth will mourn, and they will see the Son of Man coming on the clouds of heaven with power and great glory" [Matt. 24:30]**. At that time, **"He will send out His angels with a great sound of a trumpet, and they will gather together His elect from the

four winds from one end of heaven to the other" [Matt. 24:31]. God will grant in great measure, tribulation to every soul that taunted, teased, and tormented the followers of Christ. These, the Bible says will be cast into the **"lake of fire"** for rejecting the GOOD NEWS because they wouldn't receive the LOVE OF GOD in their hearts.

Like it or not, the meaning within these pages are obvious. God requests each and every one of us to take these things into our hearts: accountability, responsibility, loyalty, respect, reconciliation, restoration, disobedience, rebellion, trust, obedience, judgment, righteousness, repentance, faithfulness, salvation, God's grace, mercy, peace, hope, forgiveness and love… I KNOW these things are weighty and thought provoking subjects. <u>PLEASE DO NOT FAIL TO REMEMBER that wrote this book over a period of SIXTEEN YEARS</u>. DO NOT BE OVERWHELMED by the scripture verses, questions or my thoughts, PLEASE. I simply ask if you would thoughtfully consider these things and take them into your own heart? Because I know a decision to trust Christ will forever change and bless YOUR life!

Borrowed—are the hours
God has given to REPENT
Soon all eyes shall look and say
Too late, my time is spent…C.L.

IN HIS ARMS I LONG TO BE

If you listen you can hear it though its subtle it is there,
His sweet voice is softly calling all to come to Him in prayer
There He'll answer those who trust Him with their heart and trust His love
Through their faith he will carry, all believers home above.
It's so simple yet so many fail to hear His loving call,
Unaware that without Him, they will tumble down and fall.
Not much longer will He grant us time to choose our destiny
This decision will determine where we spend eternity.
He is calling! Have you answered? Saying "yes" dear Lord take me,
When you come with trumpets sounding, in your arms I long to be.
For Jesus said, to us in scripture "except a man be born again,"
"He cannot see God's kingdom" have you ears, take heed my friend.

Christene Bolte-Luthey

"Verily, verily, I say unto you,
He that hears my word and believes on Him that sent me
has everlasting life,
and shall not come into condemnation,
but is passed from death unto life" [John 5:24]

JUDGMENT IS COMING

A storm is surely coming, greater than we know
In likeness to a whirlwind, the Lord has shown me so.
He has true revealed to me, the distant muffled roar
Described, I have the dangers, that I may then implore,
Not long we have, for it is true, we see it in the world,
Will you enter "in His rest?" Or will we be unfurled?

God takes no pleasure in the cries, of the innocent and dying
Yet while we take for granted GRACE, the world has started sighing.
We cannot carry on and on, doing OUR OWN will
Will we not care and realize, the <u>greatest fear</u> until—

The trumpets sound and break apart, the clouds up in the sky
But then within an instant, the world will start to cry.
For all shall then break forth in fear, knowing this was true,
<u>God gave us many warnings, and told you what to do.</u>

So please dear one do not neglect, the passages I gave,
To disregard God's warnings, would be then NOT to save.
May your heart consider, the TRUTH you see within
And offer up yourself to Christ, and please "repent of sin."

C. Luthey

Morality shall be the supreme value by which our nation is judged. I cannot stress this enough. We shall be held responsible for the moral and social transgression, regardless of how insignificant they may seem. The nations shall be weighed on God's divine scales and found extremely wanting, **unless <u>HUMBLY we return to the Lord.</u>** I sincerely trust that

God will punish any nation when it is found guilty. God's word states, **"My people are destroyed for lack of knowledge: because you have rejected knowledge, I will also reject you, from being a priest to me. And since you have forgotten the law of Your God, I also will forget your children"** [Hosea 4:6].

THE COST OF SIN

All too often all too late
Many find God's closed the gate
As the winds soon cover the land
Regrettably, we'll understand,
Those with hardened hearts to Thee
Darkness they shall only see.

Yet those who found a place to pray
Shall be found in light's array
Gleaming like a candle's glow
Into GLORY these shall go.
Passing through the gates to be
At God's side eternally.

C.Luthey

As I write, I am trying to paint with words a picture of what I sincerely believe will one day occur when Christ comes to gather His own unto Himself. I am in NO WAY predicting when or where that might occur. **God only knows such things**. I cannot even say whether or not it will be in my lifetime or yours? I am simply saying, I truly believe that what I experienced on May 31st, 1985 in the tornado will in no way measure up to what is *yet to come*, that is described in God's Holy word in the book of ***Revelation.***

REVELATION'S THUNDER will come with God's final judgment. I do not think that enough of us are aware of that, **"Since it is a righteous thing with God to repay with tribulation those who trouble you, and to give you who are troubled rest with us when the Lord Jesus is revealed from heaven with His mighty angels, in flaming fire taking vengeance on those who do not know God, and on those who do not obey the Gospel of our Lord Jesus Christ. These shall be punished with** everlasting destruction from the presence of the Lord and from the glory of His power, when He comes, in that day, to be glorified in His saints and to be admired along with all those who believe, because of the testimony among you was believed" [2 Thes. 1:6-10]. If ever the Spirit of God was calling us to know Jesus Christ, and beckoning us to put on the **"breastplate of righteousness,"** it is NOW! The Bible is being fulfilled before our eyes and, we have not yet taken to heart the realities of the judgment those souls shall endure who, **"trample the son of God underfoot,"** and **"insult the Spirit of Grace"** [Heb. 10:29]. I pray that if this book has reached your hands you will seek humbly God with your whole heart (if you have not already)? Find shelter in the arms of grace and mercy while you are able.

Let us take heed to the warning signs that surround us, quickly repenting of sin. **"Little children, let no one deceive you. He who practices righteousness is righteous, just as He is righteous. He who sins is of the Devil, for the Devil has sinned from the beginning. For this purpose the Son of God was manifested, that He might destroy the works of he Devil. Whoever has been born of God does not sin, for His seed remains in him; and he cannot sin, because he has been born of God"** [1 John 3:7-9].

CONSIDER THE LATTER END

We must cast off the WORLD'S philosophy; it will not make healthy the hearts that are broken. Man's philosophy will not bring permanent comfort, joy and peace to a soul. Perhaps some may disagree? But I sincerely believe that ONLY GOD can provide the healing truth and light we have need of today. **"This is the message which we have heard from Him and declare to you, that God is the light and in Him is no darkness at all. If we say we have fellowship with Him, and walk in darkness, we lie and do not practice the truth. But if we walk in the light as He is in the light, we have fellowship with one another, and the blood of Jesus Christ His Son cleanses us from all sin. If we say that we have no sin, we deceive ourselves, and the truth is not within us. If we confess our sins, He is faithful and just to forgive our sins and to cleanse us from all unrighteousness. If we say that we have not sinned, we make Him a liar, and His word is not in us"** [1 John 1:5-11].

Any method used to cure the afflictions of the heart and soul OTHER than having a PERSONAL RELATIONSHIP with JESUS CHRIST is certain to be unsuccessful! This is why those who trust in the world for their emotional healing and answers to life's problems are continuously experiencing anger, fear, disappointment, depression and despair, etc. True and lasting victory over these feelings are obtained only through the GRACE of God. Why? GRACE is not of this world. Therefore, it cannot be acquired by any other means than through the Lord Jesus Christ.

FALSE WORSHIP AND TEACHERS

Beware of any person, in any position who DOES NOT PREACH the GOSPEL of Truth. In the days to come, people will be led astray IF we have not learned to abide in Christ and seek God's word for counsel. Today, there are some who consider them selves to be "ministers" of the Gospel of Jesus Christ, but sadly they are *not preaching* what Christ taught. They talk ABOUT the messenger (Jesus), and His personality, but they do little to actually educate people about that which Jesus preached. **"Let no one defraud you of your reward, taking delight in false humility and worship of angels, intruding into those things which he has not seen, vainly puffed up in is fleshly mind, and not holding fast to the head from whom all the body, nourished and knit together by joints and ligaments grows with the increase which is from God" [Col 2:18-19]. "These things indeed have an appearance of wisdom in self-imposed religion, false humility, and neglect of the body, but are of no value against indulgence of the flesh" [Col. 2:23].**

The only way to not be misinformed will be if we are faithfully abiding in Jesus. We also must KNOW for ourselves what the Bible actually says is TRUTH. Neither you nor I can truly know Christ through what *other people* tell us of Him, or what He preached. We have to know Him personally as our Savior. What I share with you of my faith and what Christ has meant to me I hope will be uplifting and possibly encourage you? But YOU can in no way be completely whole UNTIL you know him YOURSELF. At that moment your heart will confirm that JESUS CHRIST IS REAL! You WON'T have to take anyone's word for it. In fact, not anything anyone could say will measure up to to the joy YOU will feel when HIS LOVE lives inside of YOU.

Perhaps you have searched for answers but haven't found them yet in a "church?" Dear friend, I offer my love and sympathy. Is it possible that you have been hurt? I sympathize in that I too have found that some of God's "shepherds" today are interested in "climbing the ladder of success," and "making a name for themselves" more so than seeing to and meeting the needs of "their people?" Some, (NOT ALL), preach out of selfish ambition and are not SINCERE about teaching the Gospel of Christ. But there is something you can do. Find a Holy Bible in a translation you understand, and begin READING. If you want to learn more about Jesus, begin there and you will find beautiful accounts of Him and His ministry. In the meantime, seek God and ask Him to show you a church that is filled with God's Holy Spirit. In doing these things you will find answers and direction for your life.

Jesus spoke on many occasions about those whom He considered to be **"hypocrites"** as we see in this scripture verse. **"When you see it is evening you say, it will be fair weather, for the sky is red and threatening. Hypocrites! You know how to discern the face of the sky, but you cannot discern the signs of the times. A wicked and adulterous generation seeks a sign and no sign will be given to it except the sign of the prophet Jonah" [Matt. 16:2-4] [Jonah 1:17 & 3:5].** I must say that I am grieved by the care-less positions of *some* (again, NOT ALL) ministers. Every heart especially those in ministry should be alert to the **"signs of the times."** Striving to do all they can to send serious warnings to this wicked generation. Let us stay alert for **"watchmen who are blind, without knowledge, dreaming, lying down and loving to slumber" [Isaiah 56:10-12].**

The Bible states that: God's word is, **"living and active, sharper than any two edged sword, piercing to the division of soul and spirit, of joints and marrow and discerning the thoughts and intentions of the heart" [Heb. 4:12].** Yet, some ministers have dulled this **"sword"** into a smooth butter knife, which does nothing to direct "sinners" to repentance. Do not be deceived, if you ARE attending a church, perish etc, that is NOT sharing with you the scriptures like you are reading throughout these pages, you need to know that they are NOT doing you a favor. Even though we may cringe at what we are being told in the word of God regarding sin in our lives, every soul is in terrible danger if it is not hearing the TRUTH. Therefore if in hearing God's word we are NOT convicted of sin or the areas we need to give attention in our lives, then the God's will is not being accomplished. Please be careful of any "minister" that pampers you, or builds sermons on or around what <u>you or the rest of his congregation will or won't hear</u>. If you are a person that makes life rough on someone who is determined <u>to tell you the TRUTH</u>, God help you! Unless you are being presented with the word of God, which may sometimes feel like a "sword," then he is <u>not doing the work he was called to do</u>.

If you and I are not being told these truths then we aren't being cared for spiritually. Anyone who does not share God's word because he is worried that *less money may be put in the collection plate*—will answer to God. This person is definitely NOT concerned about our spiritual life or your eternal destination. In fact, rather than waking us spiritually so that we may repent and LIVE, they instead, are lulling us into a deep spiritual sleep. That can be tragic. Jesus himself said: **"Watch therefore, for you do not know what hour your Lord is coming"** [Matt. 24:42].

No one enjoys being told they are wrong. Nor do we enjoy being shown where there is truth proving it, but if we think about it, we have a lot to gain by simply humbling ourselves and admitting our faults and failures. When we receive the word of God "full strength" as necessity, it would (or should) cause us to wake up and take notice of any sin in our lives. That is why we cannot be "sleeping spiritually." Jesus himself has told us to **"be watching,"** but instead, we allow ourselves to be led astray by **"peace and safety"** sermons. Don't misunderstand, I believe in peace and safety, but only that which we obtain through life in Jesus Christ.

A *few* ministers today seem to carry on as though they didn't know or care that the day is coming when all will be judged according to their deeds. **"But as to the times and the seasons, brethren, you have no need to have anything written to you. For you yourselves know well that the day of the Lord will come like a thief in the night. When people say, there is peace and security, then sudden destruction will come upon them as travail comes upon a woman with child and there will be no escape"** [1 Thes. 5:1-3 & [2 Thes. 1:8-9].

Any one who is a <u>false teacher</u> who practice unhelpful, unscriptural doctrines; need reminding that trouble awaits them, **[2 Peter 2:1-2] "But there were also false prophets among the people, even as there will be false teachers among you, who will secretly bring in destructive heresies, even denying the Lord who bought them, and bring upon themselves swift destruction. And many will follow their destructive ways, because of whom the way of truth was blasphemed. By covetousness they will exploit you with deceptive words; for a long** time their judgment has not been idle, and their destruction does not slumber."

Let's think about that scripture verse one minute? Something that speaks loud to my heart are the words, **"by <u>covetousness</u> they will <u>exploit</u> you with <u>deceptive</u> words."** See how wonderful God's word is? This is a warning! By reading this verse you and I know now that there will be **"false teachers"** who will use **"deceptive words"** to **"exploit"** us by **"covetousness."** Therefore, in other words you and I know that: *<u>**FALSE TEACHERS**</u> WILL USE <u>**GREED**</u> OR <u>**MATERIALISM**</u> TO <u>**TAKE ADVANTAGE**</u> OF US THROUGH <u>**MISLEADING WORDS**</u> THAT ARE <u>**NOT TO BE TRUSTED**</u>!* How much wiser you and I are to "false teachers" now, because we have taken God's word into our heart. See my friend? God doesn't want you and I to be misled! He doesn't want us following teachers who will lead us astray. That's why he's provided us with the Holy Bible! It is God's letter to us so that we may know and avoid such things!

These are ministers and leaders who are NOT turning to God or his word for wisdom and direction. They rely on their own understanding to counsel and comfort those seeking spiritual guidance. Today if you're in need of counseling, please don't turn away from anyone who directs you to JESUS or the HOLY BIBLE. Any person whom trusts himself and not the word of God is without a doubt a "blind" and "false" leader. So please do as the Bible says and test your spiritual leaders by what is written in the word of God!

REMEMBER YOUR WAYS

Today we need to be aware as a society that we have become so laidback that the devil is comfortable in our midst. By this I mean that we have compromised our beliefs and our morals so much that many of God's very own chosen people are losing their "flavor" and "light." We should feel embarrassed and ashamed if we have fallen into a lifestyle of "Luke-warm" living! All the while Satan, I'm sure is "accusing" and applauding our lack of conviction. Let us not forget, Satan knows in our "Luke-warm" position that God's word clearly states, **"I know your works, that you are neither cold nor hot. I could wish that you were cold or hot. So then, because you are lukewarm, and neither cold nor hot, I will vomit you out of My mouth"** [Revelation 3:15].

In many ways we need to be aware of Satan's "accusing" in our lives. Think about some of the ways he entwines his wickedness in our lives? Always trying to gratify his addiction, **"to ascend above the clouds, and be like the Most High" [Is. 4:14].** He has waged war against all that Christ has accomplished. Remember, it is CHRIST to whom the song shall be sung, saying; **"You are worthy to take the scroll, and to open its seals; for you were slain, and have redeemed us to God by your blood out of every tribe and tongue and people and nation, and have made us kings and priest to our God; and we shall reign on the earth" [Rev. 5:9-10].**

Satan is in conflict with everything Jesus is and stands for. He knows **"the wages of sin is death, but the gift of God is eternal life through Jesus Christ our Lord" [Romans 6:23]. "Oh death, where is thy sting? Oh grave, where is thy victory?" [1 Cor. 15:55]. "But thanks be to God, which gives us the victory though our Lord Jesus Christ" [1 Cor. 15:57].** Does the word VICTORY mean anything to you? It means a lot to Satan! He knows very well that, **"Jesus who was made a little lower than the angels for the suffering of death, crowned with glory and honor, that He, by the grace of God should taste death for every man" [Heb. 2:9].** Satan also knows that Jesus Christ has made this promise, **<u>"Verily, verily, I say to you, if a man keep my saying, he shall never see death," and again he said, "if a man keep my saying, he shall never taste death"</u> [John 8:51-52].**

For this purpose Jesus Christ, the only Begotten Sinless Son of God, reigns in glory today and evermore!!! <u>If you hear, trust and believe on His name you can be sure that the Son of God is able to deliver you from the **"sting of death"** and will one day take you to be with Him in Glory!!!</u> That is my friend; Heaven! Where the Bible says a **"mansion"** waits, which has been prepared for those of us who believe on His precious name! Oh yes, Jesus will most assuredly deliver all whose names are **"written in the book of life,"** and make alive those that once were dead. To all who have trusted Him, he will give eternal life! To Jesus Christ only is this power and authority given, not to any other on earth, in heaven or in hell. Jesus Christ alone is worthy. He was the sinless lamb that was slain for those who trust in Him. All glory is given to Him in heaven where He reigns. No other holds this promise. No other possesses this power. Jesus Christ is the key that unlocks the door to Salvation. By no means shall any person enter the gates of heaven than by Jesus Christ alone. **"He who believes in Him is not condemned; but he who does not believe is condemned already, because he has not believed in the name of the Only Begotten Son of**

God. And this is the condemnation, that the light has come into the world, and men loved darkness rather than light, because their deeds were evil. [John 3: 18-19].

PLUNGED INTO DARKNESS

Speaking of <u>false teachers</u>, I thought I might say here that even though the Holy Bible clearly states Jesus Christ has broken the chains of "death," some still refuse to place their trust in Him. Rather there are those who have chosen to follow <u>New Age Teaching</u> (for instance). These souls have placed their faith, and trust in beliefs of <u>"reincarnation."</u> But in talking to a few of these people I've learned that they have been <u>*DECEIVED by the "false teaching" that the Holy Bible supports New Age beliefs? BUT IN REALITY, THESE HAVE FALSLY TWISTED JESUS' WORDS TO SUIT THEIR IDEAS.*</u>

Friend, incase you are a believer in New Age, I thought I would share with you EXACTLY what Jesus did and did not say, Jesus said, **"Except a man be BORN AGAIN, he cannot see the kingdom of God" [Matt. 3:3].** In saying this, Jesus was explaining the question that was asked Him by a man who inquired, **"How to enter his mother's womb the second time."** Jesus replied, **"Except a man be born of Water and of the Spirit, he cannot enter the kingdom of God." [John 3:5].** Jesus spoke to us about being **"born again,"** does NOT refer to *"reincarnation."* Jesus' words specifically state that one must not only experience a physical birth **"of water,"** but a rebirth of **"the Spirit."**

The **"rebirth"** Jesus is speaking of is <u>NOT</u> what *New Age believers consider of the passing through many lifetimes, (reincarnation), physical or other, to access the attributes of God. Or to acquire peace or the perfection, which New Age believers think are possible.* Being **"BORN AGAIN of the water,"** <u>is the birth we experience when we enter this world through our mother's womb. Being **"born of the Spirit,"** is that which Jesus tells us about in</u> **[John 14:15-16], "If you love me keep my commandments. And I will pray the Father and He will give you another comforter, that He may abide with you forever." [John 14:26], "But the comforter, which is the Holy Spirit, whom the Father will send in my name, He shall teach you all things, and bring all things to your remembrance, whatsoever I have said unto you."**

In the book of Matthew, there are scripture verses that *New Age Beliefs have falsely <u>misconstrued,</u> by <u>implying</u> that Jesus said, that Elijah was "reincarnated" in*

John the Baptist's body. **ABSOLUTELY NOT! [Matthew Chapter 11&17]. Jesus has said NO SUCH THING! Nor has JESUS given any reason for you or I to believe in any New Age beliefs or "reincarnation."** Just for the reason that John the Baptist's ministry brought Elijah's to mind, <u>DOES NOT mean that John WAS Elijah "reincarnated."</u> Dear friend, do not be deceived, the Bible will verify this if you read it. When John the Baptist was asked, **"Are you Elijah?"** <u>He answered, **"I AM NOT!"**</u> **[John 1: 21]. "Now this is the testimony of John, when the Jews sent priests and Levites from Jerusalem to ask him, "Who are you?" He confessed, and did not deny, but confessed, 'I am not the Christ." And they asked him, "What then? Are you Elijah? He said, "I am not." "Are you the Prophet?" And he answered, "No." [John 1:19-21].** Therefore *it is only through John's similarity to Elijah that New Age beliefs have used this scripture to DECEIVE YOU and further promote Satan's wicked agenda to deceive the world.* Again, I <u>beseech you to read the Bible YOURSELF</u>. Seek Christ Jesus and don't be deceived.

Remember, **"By this you know the Spirit of God; every Spirit that confesses that Jesus Christ has come in the flesh is of God, and every spirit that does not confess that Christ has come in the flesh is not of God. And this is the ANTICHRIST, which you have heard was coming, and is now already in the world" [1 John 4:2-3].** If it is that you or someone you know has chosen to place trust in New Age, please hear what the <u>Holy Spirit is testifying to your soul</u>. <u>A lying spirit is deceiving you that will lure and lock you in a never-ending place darkness and terror</u>...

<u>If you believe in New Age teaching, please consider this</u>: WHAT IF? "Reincarnation," is nothing more than a cunningly invented plan to deceive? What if? Your soul in trusting "reincarnation" is actually plunged into hell? What if? In hell, your soul is required to suffer forever a living death where it is tormented with everlasting fear and pain? What if? "Reincarnation" is a vicious circle of never ending weeping, darkness and fire? What if? Your soul throughout infinity is persistently tortured by the REGRET of your own conscience? What if? "Reincarnation" is a lie, but you rejected the TRUTH of the Gospel of Jesus Christ? WHAT IF?

What if, the enemy of Christ—bating your ambitious soul to venture out in search for MORE "self" recognition—has only fabricated reincarnation? What if, reincarnation is a false and empty delusion? What friend will you do if JESUS CHRIST IS THE ONLY ONE WHO CAN TRULY GRANT YOUR SOUL LASTING PEACE? Will you choose to follow a belief that challenges your soul to live a limitless number of lifetimes in order to achieve perfection?

Friend, if you are aiming for perfection, hear the Holy Spirit speaking to your heart! **[Heb. 9:27] "And as it is appointed for men to die once, but after this the judgment."** Then, **"For our citizenship is in heaven, from which we also eagerly wait for the Savior, the Lord Jesus Christ, <u>who will transform our lowly body that it may be conformed to His glorious body,</u> according to the working by which He is able even to subdue all things to Himself." [Phil. 3:20-21]**. Those who trust Christ will be IMMEDIATELY transformed and given a GLORIOUS BODY! They will NOT suffer lifetimes of trial, hardship, pain and toil. On the contrary, **"God will wipe away every tear from their eyes; there shall be no more death, nor sorrow, nor crying. There shall be no more pain, for the former things have passed away" [Rev. 21:4].** Would you rather follow JESUS CHRIST, who offers you ETERNAL LIFE and IMMEDIATE EVERLASTING PEACE, or would you rather follow reincarnation and be a "wandering soul" aimlessly lost forever? Again, if you are a New Age Believer, please consider the following thoughts on "Reincarnation," which I have placed in poem form.

WANDERING SOULS

A glimpse of reincarnation

Wandering souls, lost in their lust
Sadly they'll fall into the dust,
And breathing in powder their lungs will cry out
"Lord, bring us help, what is this all about?"
For they've seen no wrong in the wrong they've done
So see their pain has just begun.
These are they with <u>pride</u> and <u>spite</u>
Who sought to test God's power and might.
Though unaware they have no clue
All that they shall suffer through,
Regret, hardships, toil and more
Shall come to those who chose to ignore,
The warnings God gave them not long ago
They tossed to the wind as if not to know
That refusing to make a change in their heart
Shall cost them the sorrow of being apart

From the one who had given so much in their life,
For that, they shall know true suffering and strife.
Then no one shall help them although they cry
And left all alone they'll ask, "Lord why?"
AND Christ shall then answer, remember your ways?
You now may regret them all of your days.
Now begging forgiveness after your fill
But I'll turn away for you're not in my will,
Then just as Satan in the pit I shall throw
All who aren't mine in the flame they will go.
And up from the fire their screams shall not be
For the gulf between heaven and hell shall see
That evil cannot and will not prevail
As all shall then see as I lift the veil.
Then accusing and gnashing, Satan they'll see
And wish, how they'll wish they had not turned from me.

C. Luthey

"And just as it is appointed for men to die ONCE, and after that Comes the Judgment." [Hebrews 9:27]

Friend, one last question regarding reincarnation. What will you do when you learn too late that the *"grand precise moment"* you have so anxiously waited for <u>never arrive, but instead you receive only torment and judgment</u>? Just as those who sinned by turning to other gods. Today just as it was in the days of Moses, Satan's greatest joy was none other than acting on ANY opportunity that brought about Sin and accusing as he watched the people REBEL against God and His commandments.

Imagine the joy Satan received when he saw God's own people gathered together corrupting themselves, creating a **"golden calf"** to serve as a god? Today, just as so very long ago, people whom God has granted life are still turning away from His statutes and love to participate in corrupt and sinful things. Scripture tells us that **"God's wrath burned hot against the people"** who allowed themselves to be corrupted and become **idol worshipers**. Let us keep in mind that <u>anything we place before God</u> in life is considered <u>Idol worship</u>. God has NOT changed considering these things.

Today we run an even greater risk of angering our Creator, being that He sent Jesus to "save" us from our sin.

TRUE REGRET

Let us not forget: <u>Until the return of Jesus, there will be a spiritual battle going on between GOOD and EVIL</u>. Throughout the time you have been reading you may have found yourself fighting the TRUTH in God's word? <u>To believe these words would mean that you and I must continually examine ourselves and admit that we are in desperate need of CHANGE!</u> In God's word we are continually reminded that we have ALL **"fallen short"** of living the life God intends for us. In this we then must humble ourselves, putting an end to our sinful rebellion.

I think most of us would agree that OBEDIENCE is something we expect of our children, but WE battle as adults. Especially when it comes to obeying Almighty God. It seems difficult for many of us to do, being that we live in a world that encourages SELF-satisfaction and man's approval. The WORLD'S standards are LENIENT and totally disregard sin, which we know leads to severe defiance and separates us from God. The battle that rages today is a Spiritual one. That is why we can NEVER FORGET that Satan wants to ROB, STEAL and DECEIVE you and I. The Bible says that he is called, **"The serpent of old who deceives the whole world" [Rev. 12:9]**.

Think about it, as long as people are "too busy" to read the word of God, Satan can deceive souls one by one with little or no effort at all. If you are "too busy" to spend time with Christ in the word of God, or in prayer, you really have NO IDEA what the TRUTH of God's word is. That means that anyone could tell you *anything* and you would not know whether or not it was the truth or a LIE. As I've said before, please READ and TEST EVERYTHING to see if it is in agreement with God's word before you act. **"Test all things; hold fast what is good" [1 Thes. 5:21]. Beloved, do not believe every spirit, but test the spirits, whether they are of God; because many false prophets have gone out into the world. By this you know the Spirit of God: Every spirit that confesses that Jesus Christ has come in the flesh is of God, and every spirit that does not confess that Jesus Christ has come in the flesh is not of God. And this is the spirit of the Antichrist, which you have heard was coming, an is now already in the world." [1 John 4:1-3].**

TRUE REGRET

Truth Received, **U**nclaimed **E**ntrance
Refusing **E**very (opportunity) **G**od **R**endered **E**ternal **T**ime (with Him)
You ask me about REGRET? This my child do not forget
It is a pain you cannot take, it causes all your bones to ache.
It haunts you from each morn to night, and makes the strongest lose their might.
It never ceases, not one hour. And as it grows it gains more power.
It grieves the heart and cuts the soul. In time consumes and takes its toll.
It controls each thought within, it was meant to sever sin.
Although many know its name, they pass it off as just a game.
A thought that passes though the mind, emotions that seem so unkind.
And disregarded some then say, "It's in the past," and laugh away.

Yet, this dear one they'll never see, until too late to set them free.
TRUE REGRET that fades no more shall come to those who slammed the door.
And would not listen when I cared, and sent my Son whose blood not spared
Could have welcomed them within, to pardon them from death and sin.

Oh, the nagging of their pain, tears they'll weep but all in vain.
For TRUE REGRET shall surely be, the cost for sin's vast penalty
Then the wicked complaining voices shall swell,
as sin's weight pulls their souls to hell.

The TRUTH: a conscious misery
That; **<u>JESUS COULD HAVE SET YOU FREE</u>**!!!
But you believed an evil plot, and now must bear this burning lot.
Too bad, too late, hell's tortured pet that you must live with SIN'S regret!

Christene Luthey

Jesus said, **"If your hand causes you to sin, cut it off. It is better for you to enter into life maimed, rather than having two hands, to go to hell, into the fire that shall never be quenched—where their worm does not die, and the fire is not quenched.' And if your foot causes you to** sin, cut it off. It is better for you to enter life lame, rather than having two feet, to be cast into hell, into the fire that shall never be quenched—where their worm does not die and the fire is not quenched.' And if your eye causes you to sin, pluck it out. It is better for you to enter into the kingdom of God with one eye, rather than having two eyes to be cast into hell fire—where their worm does not die and the ire is not quenched.' [Mark 9:43-44]. "For everyone will be seasoned with fire, and every sacrifice will be seasoned with salt. "Salt is good, but if the salt loses its flavor, how will you season it? Have salt in yourselves, and have peace with one another." [Mark 9:49-50].

FIND A BIBLE BELIEVING CHURCH

We must be definite that any counsel we take is coming from one who truly believes in God's word and depends upon it for direction. Take heed that any self-indulgent tactics do not mislead you. All leaders are to be obedient to the word of God. They are not to preach or teach only for money or to seek the admiration of people. Financial gain should never be the motivation ruling a person's heart. The commission that was given to by Christ was to preach the Good News of the Gospel.

Remember, strength is found when you spend time alone with God in prayer and meditate on His word. Therefore don't limit the time you spend with the Lord and perhaps you will find the answers to your questions in life. There is freedom when we seek shelter in the arms of the Almighty. As we move on to consider the OTHER SIDE of the "plumb line," I want you to believe that sin's chains can be broken when we trust God to set us free! May you find peace today in God's resting place!

HIS RESTING PLACE

Let us ponder not the view, only what's inside of you.
Yield: it's in God's perfect will, that He may fashion you and fill,
All the spaces that you need, to help others to succeed.
Stop running, searching though all weather,
Finding not the answers ever.
Due to lack of faith you see, though in chains you could be
Given freedom, and granted peace

For through Gods' grace all pain does cease.
For everyone who seeks His face, Shall behold His resting place.
Christene Luthey

CHOOSE LIFE NOT DEATH

Dear friends, take the wisdom of the following Scripture verses into your mind and please allow God's Holy Spirit to speak to your heart concerning God's word. Keep in mind as you read that the **BOLD PRINT is God's word** speaking to your heart and mine.

The time is soon coming that all shall call Jesus Christ Lord, whether or not they believe: **"That at the name of Jesus every knee shall bow in heaven and on earth and under the earth, and every tongue confess that Jesus Christ is Lord, to the Glory of God the Father" [Phil. 2:10-11].**

There will be tears flowing for the depth of true regret in having had God's Son, by those who chose Him not in the time they had to receive Him. **"And the devil, who deceived them, was cast into the lake of fire and brimstone where the beast and the false profit are. And they will be tormented day and night forever and ever. And I saw the dead, small and great, standing before God, and the books were opened. And another book was opened, which is the BOOK OF LIFE. And the dead were judged according to their works, by the things that were in it, and death and Hades delivered up the dead who were in them. And they were judged each one according to his works. Then Death and Hades were cast into the lake of fire. This is the second death. And anyone not found written in the BOOK OF LIFE was cast into the lake of fire" [Rev. 20:12]. "For the Father has life in Himself, so He has granted the Son also to have life in Himself, and has given Him authority to execute judgment, because He is the Son of Man" [John 5:26-27].**

The stone, which the builders rejected **[Matt. 21:42, Mark 12:10, Luke 20:17],** is true right and perfect in the sight of God. He shall judge and his judgment is just. **"According to the grace of God which was given to me a wise master builder I have laid the foundation, and another builds on it. But let each one take heed how he builds on it. For no other foundation can anyone lay than that which is laid, which is Jesus Christ. Now if anyone builds on this foundation with gold, silver,** precious stones, wood, hay, straw, each one's work will become manifest; for the day will declare it, because it will be revealed by fire; and the fire will test each one's work, of what sort it is. If anyone's work is burned, he will suffer loss; but he himself will be saved as though by fire" [1 Cor. 3:10-15].

<u>Unbelievers shall not receive eternal life, or rewards on that day</u>: "No man is justified by works of the law but through faith in Jesus Christ, even we have believed in Christ Jesus in order to be justified by faith in Christ, and not by works of the law, because by works of the law no one will be justified" [Gal. 2:16].

<u>Does not the Lord's heart ache with frustration at the hardness of our hearts? I am sure in the sight of wickedness, his anger runs deep</u>: "My people are destroyed for lack of knowledge. Because you have rejected knowledge, I will reject you from being priest for me; because you have forgotten the law of your God, I will also forget your children. Because the people have broken my covenant and rebelled against my law, and regarded them as something alien" [Hosea 4:6,8,12].

<u>To each of us, God offers LIFE</u>: "And this is eternal life that they know Thee, the only true God, and Jesus Christ whom thou hast sent" [John 17:3]. Jesus said, "I am the resurrection and the life. He who believes on Me, though he may die, he shall live" [John 11:25]. Jesus also said, "Most assuredly I say to you, you see me not because you saw the sign, but because you ate of the loaves and were filled. So not labor for the food which perishes, but for the food which endures to everlasting Life, which the Son of Man will give you, because God the Father has set his seal on Him" "What shall we do, that we may work the works of God? "This is the work of God, that you believe in Him whom He sent" [John 6:26-29]. Jesus said, "No one comes to the Father except through Me" [John 14:5]. "And this is the testimony, that God gave us eternal life, and this life is in His Son. He who has the Son has life, he who has not the Son of God has not life" [1 John 5:11-12].

<u>Still, in spite of the LIFE that is in the Truth, many choose death</u>. "The wages of sin is death" [Romans 6:23]. <u>Many carelessly follow Satan</u>, "To which the end of those things is death" [Rom. 6:21]. <u>Oh, the tears I am sure God has wept for those who will not bow, for He has loved us so; so much more than we will ever know</u>. "He who does not love does not know God, for God is love" [1 John 4:8]. "We love Him because He first loved us" [1 John 4:19]. "For God so loved the world that He gave His only begotten Son that who eve believes in Him should not perish,

but have everlasting life" [John 3:16]. "God demonstrates His own love toward us, in that while we were still sinners, Christ died for us" [Rom. 5:8].

<u>Yet in spite of God's love many still choose to follow Hate:</u> "For everyone practicing evil hates the light and does not come to the light, lest his deeds should be exposed" [John 3:20]. Jesus said, "He who hates Me hates My Father also" [John 14:23]. Therefore, "He who hates his brother is in darkness and walks in darkness, and does not know where he is going, because the darkness has blinded his eyes" [1 John 2:11].

<u>Time is fading in which God will tolerate this wicked rebellion against Him:</u> "Therefore, as the Holy Spirit says; Today if you will hear His voice, do not harden your hearts as in the rebellion, in the day of trial in the wilderness" [Heb. 3:7-8]. "Therefore put to death your members which are on the earth: fornication, uncleanness, passion, evil desire, and covetousness, which is idolatry. Because of these things the wrath of God is coming upon the sons of disobedience" [Col. 3:5-6]. "For many walk, of whom I have told you often, and now tell you even weeping, that they are the enemies of the cross of Christ: whose end is destruction, whose god is their belly, and whose glory is in their shame, who set their mind on earthly things" [Phil. 3:18-19].

<u>If only we would turn from the evil which delights us, and seek Christ's face. We would know His love and boundless mercy:</u> "If My people who are called by My name will humble themselves, and pray and seek My face, ad turn from their wicked ways, then I will forgive their sin and heal their land" [2 Chron. 7:14]. As Paul was recounting his conversion Jesus sent him out, "To open their eyes and to turn them from darkness to light, and from the power of Satan to God, that they may receive forgiveness of sins and an inheritance among those who are sanctified by faith in Me" [Acts 26:18]. "Let him turn away from evil and do good; let him seek peace and pursue it. For the eyes of the Lord are on the righteousness, and his ears are open to their prayers; but the face of the Lord is against those who do evil" [1 Peter 3:11-12]. "Who is the man who desires life, and loves many days, that he may see good? Keep your tongue from evil, and your lips from speaking guile. Depart from evil, and do good. Seek peace and pursue it. The eyes of the Lord are on the righteous, and His ears are open to their cry. The face of the Lord is against those who do evil, to cut off the remembrance of them from the earth" [Psalm 34:12-16].

To turn from evil, we must all become obedient to God and submit to His will: "Therefore, I urge you to reaffirm your love to Him. For to this end I also wrote, that I might put you to the test, whether you are obedient in all things. Now whom you forgive anything, I also forgive. For if indeed I have forgiven anything, I have forgiven that one for your sakes in the presence of Christ, lest Satan should take advantage of us; for we are not ignorant of his devices" [2 Cor. 2:8-11].

GRACE, TIME and MERCY shall not be an opportunity much longer, for the day will come God will not tolerate wickedness and sin on the earth. "And do this, knowing the time, that NOW it is high time to awake out of sleep; for now our salvation is nearer than when we first believed. The night is far spent the day is at hand. Therefore, let us cast off he works of darkness, and let us put on the armor of light. Let us walk properly, as in the day, not in revelry and drunkenness, not in licentiousness and lewdness, not in strife and envy. But put on the Lord Jesus Christ, and make no provision for the flesh, to fulfill its lusts" [Rom. 13:11-14]. "In an acceptable time I have heard you, and in the day of salvation I have helped you. Behold, now is the acceptable time; behold now is the day of salvation" [2 Cor. 6:2]. "That in the dispensation of the fullness of the times He might gather together in one all things in Christ, both which are in heaven and which are on earth, in Him" [Eph. 5:10]. "Redeeming the time, because the days are evil" [Eph. 5:16]. "Walk in wisdom toward those who are outside, redeeming the time" [Col. 4:5]. "But concerning the times and the seasons brethren, you have no need that I should write you. For you yourselves know perfectly that the day of the Lord so comes like a thief in the night" For when they say, peace and safety, then sudden destruction comes upon them as labor pains upon a pregnant woman. And they shall not escape. But you brethren, are not in darkness, so that this day should overtake you as a thief" [1 Thes. 5:1-4]. "He indeed was foreordained before the foundation of the world, but was manifest in the last times for you" [1 Peter 1:20].

All shall surely see, as each knee bows to Christ, that it will be too late, to enter through God's gate, as blood begins to flow and every heart shall know, that HE ALONE IS GOD. "Then I looked, and behold, a white cloud sat One like the Son of Man, having on His head a golden crown, and in His hand a sharp sickle. And another angel came out of the temple, crying with a loud voice to Him who sat on the cloud, thrust in your sickle and reap, for the time has come for you to reap,

When Shadows Fall: A Journey of Faith

for the harvest of the earth is ripe. So He who sat on the cloud thrust in his sickle on the earth, and the earth was reaped. Then another angel came out of the temple which is in heaven, he also having a sharp sickle, saying thrust in your sickle and gather the clusters of the vine of the earth, for her grapes are fully ripe. So the angel thrust his sickle into the earth, and gathered the vine of he earth, and threw it into the great wine press of the wrath of God. And the wine press was trampled outside the city, and blood came out of the wine press, up to the horses bridles, for one thousand six hundred furlongs" [Rev. 19:15-16] (Blood: in a flood 180-200 miles long, and about five feet deep)

<u>Do we see and understand that we are taking God's mercy and grace for granted? Utterly mocking His tolerance and love?</u> "When they had twisted a crown of thorns, they put it on His head, and a reed in His right hand. And they bowed the knee before Him and mocked Him, saying, Hail, King of the Jews! Then they spat on Him, and took the reed and struck Him on the head. Then when they had mocked Him, they took the robe off Him, put His own clothes on Him, and led Him away to be crucified" [Matt. 27:29-31]. "Likewise the chief priests, also mocking with the scribes and elders, said, He saved others; Himself, He cannot save. If He is the King of Israel, let Him now come down from the cross, and we will believe Him" [Matt. 27:41-42]. "Behold, we are going up to Jerusalem, and the Son of Man will be delivered to the chief priests and to the scribes, and they will condemn Him to death and deliver Him to the Gentiles; and they will mock Him and scourge Him, and spit on Him, and kill Him. And the third day He will rise again" [Mark 10:33-34]. "Do not be deceived, God is not mocked for whatever a man sows, that he will also reap" [Gal. 6:7]. "If you are wise, you are wise for yourself, and if you scoff, you alone will bear it" [Prov. 9:12].

<u>We who proclaim to be (followers of Christ) "Christians," are not to be sinning! Hypocrites are causing many hearts to turn away from God.</u> "Therefore, my beloved brethren, let every man be swift to hear, slow to speak, slow to wrath; for the wrath of man does not produce the righteousness of God. Therefore lay aside all filthiness and overflow of wickedness, and receive with meekness the implanted word which is able to save souls" [James 1:19-21]. "So speak and so do as those who will be judged by the law of liberty. For judgment is without mercy to the one who has shown no mercy. Mercy triumphs over judgment. But whoever has this world's goods, and sees his brother in need, and

shuts up his heart from him, how does the love of God abide in Him? And by this we know that we are of the truth, and shall assure our hearts before Him" [1 John 3:17-19].

Will Non-believers have motivation to REPENT when they watch God's very own people mocking His statutes and laws? "Will it be well when He searches you out? Or can you mock Him as one mocks a man? He will surely reprove you if you secretly show partiality. Will not His excellence make you afraid, and the dread of Him fall upon you" [Job 13:9-11]? "Awake to righteousness, and do not sin; for some do not have the knowledge of God. I speak this to your shame" [1 Cor. 15:34]. "For if we sin willfully after we have received the knowledge of the truth, there no longer remains a sacrifice for sins, but a certain fearful expectation of judgment, and fiery indignation which will devour the adversaries. Anyone who has rejected Moses' law dies without mercy on the testimony of two or three witnesses. Of how much worse punishment do you suppose will he be thought worthy who has trampled the Son of God underfoot, counted the blood of the covenant by which He was sanctified a common thing, and insulted the Spirit of Grace? For we know Him who said, vengeance is mine; I will repay, says the Lord." And The Lord will judge His people. It is a fearful thing to fall into the hands of the living God" [Heb. 10:26-31].

Are we beginning to see why God's wrath shall fall upon evil? "For the wrath of God is revealed from heaven against all ungodliness and unrighteousness of men, who suppress the truth in unrighteousness, because what may be known of God is manifest in them, for God has shown it to them. For since the creation of the world His invisible attributes are clearly seen, being made, even his eternal power and Godhead, so that they are without excuse, because, although they knew God, they did not glorify Him as God, nor were thankful, but became futile in their thoughts, and their foolish hearts were darkened. Professing to be wise, but became fools, and changed the glory of the incorruptible God into an image made like corruptible man, and birds and four footed beasts and creeping things. Therefore God also gave them up to uncleanness, in the lusts of their hearts, to dishonor their bodies among themselves. Who exchanged the truth of God for the lie, and worshiped and served the creature rather than the Creator, who is blessed forever. Amen. For this reason God gave them up to vile passions. For even their women exchanged the natural use for what is against nature. Likewise also the men, leaving the natural use of the woman, burned in their lust for one another, men committing what is shameful, and receiving in themselves the penalty of their error which was due. And even as they did not like to retain God in their knowledge, God gave them over to a debased mind, to do those things which are not fitting; being filled with all unrighteousness, sexual immorality, wickedness, covetousness, maliciousness; full of envy, murder, strife, deceit, evil-mindedness, they are whisperers, backbiters, haters of God, violent, proud, boasters, inventors of evil things, disobedient to parents, undiscerning, untrustworthy, unloving, unforgiving, unmerciful; who knowing the righteous judgment of God, that those who practice such things are worthy of death, not only do the same but also approve of those who practice them" [Romans 1:18-32].

<u>Many of God's beloved children cry out to him each and every hour of the day for an end to their pain and hunger:</u> "How precious is your loving kindness, oh God! Therefore the children of men put their trust under the shadow of your wings" [Ps. 36:7]. "I waited patiently for the Lord; and He inclined to me, and heard my cry" [Ps. 40:1]. "Out of the depths I have cried to you, Oh Lord" [Ps. 130:1]. "He will fulfill the desire of those who fear Him; He also will hear their cry and save them" [Ps. 145:19].

<u>God has not yet sent His wrath upon us, for the sake of many, yet when he delivers those who trust in Him, it will be for always. Then all upon the earth will know that He is God, and has come to set His captives free!</u> "They shall neither hunger anymore nor thirst anymore; the sun shall not strike them, nor any heat; for the Lamb who is in the midst of the throne will shepherd them and lead them to living fountains of waters. And God will wipe away every tear from their eyes" [Rev. 7:16-17]. "And I saw a new heaven and a new earth, for the first heaven and the first earth had passed away. Also there was no more sea. Then, I John, saw the Holy city, New Jerusalem, coming down out of heaven from God, prepared as a bride adorned for her husband. And I heard a loud voice from heaven saying, behold, the tabernacle of God is with men, and He will dwell with them, and they shall be His people, and God Himself will be with them and be their God. And God will wipe away every tear from their eyes; there shall be no more death, nor sorrow, nor crying; and there shall be no more pain, for the former things will have passed away" [Rev. 21:1-4].

I trust that God's precious heart must grow weary in hearing the cries of his people. It must break His loving heart to watch them suffering and in pain. When will we understand that God has allowed suffering for the sake of many souls? The Bible says that He is wanting, "All men to be saved and to come to the knowledge of the truth" [1 Tim. 2:4]. "Do I have any pleasure at all the wicked should die? Says the Lord God. And not that he should turn from his ways and live? For I have no pleasure in the death of one who dies, says the Lord God. Therefore, turn and live! [Ezek. 18:23,32]. "For the grace of God that brings salvation has appeared to all men" [Titus 2:11]. Read also please when you can: [2 Tim. 2:25/Rom. 5:1-4/Rom. 8:18/Heb 2:10/Phil. 3:8-11/1 Pet. 4:12-13].

Will we refuse God's loving call to repentance? For many generations He has granted for the sake of our souls—GRACE to seek Him that we might LIVE. Is it not TIME for YOU to CHOOSE? "I call heaven and earth as a witness against you, that I have set before you LIFE and DEATH, BLESSING AND CURSING; therefore choose LIFE, that both you and your descendants may live" [Deut. 30:19]. "Therefore, be careful to observe them; for this is your wisdom and your understanding in the sight of the peoples who will hear all these statutes and say, surely this great nation is a wise and understanding people" [Deut. 4:6]. "And if it seems evil to you to serve the Lord, choose for yourselves this day whom you will serve whether the gods which your fathers served that were on the other side of the river, or the gods of the Amorites, in whose land you dwell. But as for me and my house we will serve the Lord" [Joshua 24:15]. Also [Prov. 1:29/ Is. 66:4].

Recall Hell's torment: "and being in torments in Hades, he lifted up his eyes and saw Abraham, afar off and Lazarus in his bosom. Then he cried and said, Father Abraham, have mercy upon me, and send Lazarus that he may dip the tip of his finger in water and cool my tongue; for I am tormented in this flame. But Abraham said, Son, remember that in your lifetime you received your good things, and likewise Lazarus evil things; but now he is comforted and you are tormented. And besides all this, between us and you there is a great gulf fixed so that those who want to pass from here to you cannot, nor can those from there pass to us. Then he said I beg you therefore father, that you would send him to my father's house, for I have five brothers that he may testify to them, lest they also come to this place of torment" [Luke 16:23-28]. "Those who have not the seal of God on their foreheads" [Rev. 9:4-5], "shall also drink of the wine of the wrath of God, which is poured out full strength into the cup of His indignation. And he shall be tormented with fire and brimstone in the presence of the Holy angels and in the presence of the Lamb. And the smoke of their torment ascends forever and ever; and they have no rest day or night, who worship the beast and his image, and who ever receives the mark of his name" [Rev. 14:10-11].

Consider <u>HEAVEN'S GLORY</u>: "For all the gods of the nations are idols, but the Lord made the heavens" [1 Chr. 16:26]. "Of old You laid the foundation of the earth, and the heavens are the work of Your hands" [Ps. 102:25]. "The heavens declare the glory of God; and the firmament shows His handiwork" [Ps. 19:1]. "At that time Michael shall stand up, the great prince who stands watch over the sons of your people; and there shall be a time of trouble, such as never was since a nation, even to that time. And at that time your people shall be delivered, every one who is found written in the book. And man of those who sleep in the dust of the earth shall awake, some to everlasting life, and some to shame and everlasting contempt. Those who are wise shall shine like the brightness of the firmament, and those who turn many to righteousness like the stars forever and ever" [Daniel 12:1-4].

In regard to <u>EVERLASTING LIFE:</u> READ, [Matt. 19:29 & 25:46/ John 3:16, 3:36, 4:14, 5:24, 6:27, 6:40-47, Acts 13:46/ Rom. 6:22]. In regard to <u>PARADISE</u>: Read,

[Luke 23:43/ 2 Cor. 12:3/ Rev. 2:7].

Dear Friends, the promise remains, will you enter into God's place of peace and rest? Much work must be done in all of our lives—<u>Christ Jesus IS coming again</u>. Understand that when Jesus returns this time he will not a babe in a manger, but a HOLY AND RIGHTEOUS JUDGE! "God is a just judge, and God is angry with the wicked every day" [Ps. 7:11]. "God shall judge the righteous and the wicked, for there shall be a time there for every purpose and for every work" [Ecc. 3:17 and also see Luke 19:15-27].

***<u>Those who have repented and live believing the words spoken by Jesus shall be saved:</u> "The time is fulfilled, and the kingdom of God is at hand. Repent, and believe in the Gospel" [Mark 1:15]. For "If you confess with your mouth the Lord Jesus and believe in your heart that God has raised Him from the dead, you will be saved" [Rom. 10:9].

***<u>Those who have trusted in Christ, have no need to fear:</u> "In Him we have redemption through His blood, the forgiveness of sins, according to the riches of His grace which He made to abound toward us in all wisdom and prudence, having made known to us the mystery of His will, according to His good pleasure which He purposed in Himself, that in the dispensation of the fullness of the times He might gather together in one all things in Christ, both which are in heaven and which are on earth, in Him, in whom also we have obtained an inheritance, being predestined according to the purpose of Him who works all things according to the counsel of His will, that we who first trusted in Christ should be to the praise of His glory. In Him you also trusted, after you heard the word of truth, the gospel of your salvation; in whom also, having believed you were sealed with the Holy Spirit of promise who is the guarantee of your inheritance until the redemption of the purchased possession, to the praise of His glory" [Eph. 1:7-14]. "But now in Christ Jesus you who once were far off have been made near by the blood of Christ. For He Himself is our peace, who has made both one, and has broken down the middle wall of division between us, having abolished in His flesh the enmity, that is, the law of commandments contained in ordinances, so as to create in Himself one new man from the two, thus making peace, and that He might reconcile them both to God in on body through the cross, thereby putting to death the enmity" [Eph. 2:14-16].

Christ put to death **"The enmity"** (that means, the hostility, the feelings of hatred, the bitterness, that once existed between God and man, Jew and Gentile). For the sake of our souls, Jesus Christ Himself suffered. Suffered horrible agony that we may through Him be RECONCILED TO THE FATHER. This will not be an act of obedience and love that God will take lightly (if it is refused). **"The wicked man will see and be vexed, he will gnash his teeth and melt away; the longings of the wicked will come to nothing"** [Ps. 112:10]. "The wicked plots against the just, and gnashes at him with his teeth. The Lord laughs at him, for he sees that his day is coming. The wicked have drawn the sword and have bent their bow, to cast down the poor and needy, to slay those who are of upright conduct, their sword shall enter their own heart, and their bows shall be broken" [Ps. 37:12-15]. "When a wicked man dies, his expectation will perish, and the hope of the unjust perishes" [Prov. 11:7].

Here's a thought! What if God <u>reveals every opportunity we have been given to receive the Eternal Life He offered?</u> **"I call heaven and earth as witnesses today against you, that I have set before you life and death, blessing and cursing"** [Deut. 30:19]. How many times have you and I heard the Good News spoken about the Gospel of Peace? Have you received it with a humble heart, or have you turned your back on it? <u>And those whose names are not written in the Book Of Life are taken and bound forever with Satan in perdition where God will hear them no more.</u> **"But if the Lord creates a new thing, and the earth opens its mouth and swallows them up with all that belongs to them, and they go down alive into the pit, then you will understand that these men have rejected the Lord. So they and all those with them went down alive into the pit; the earth closed over them, and they perished from among the congregation: [Numbers 16:30,33]. "Let death seize them; let them go down alive into hell, for wickedness is in their dwellings and among them" [Ps. 55:15]. "Behold! The Lord is coming out of His place; He will come down and tread on the high places of the earth. The mountains will melt under Him, and the valleys will split like wax before the fire, like waters poured down a steep place" [Micah 1:3-4]. "The Lord is known by the judgment He executes; the wicked is snared in the work of his own hands" [Ps. 9:16].**

***<u>Those who trust God shall be delivered to PARADISE:</u> **"He who has an ear let him hear what the spirit says to the churches. To him who overcomes I will give to eat from the tree of life, which is in the midst of the paradise of God" [Rev. 2:7]. "Jesus answered him, I tell you the truth, today you will be with me in paradise" [Luke 23:43]. "And I know such a man, whether in the body or out of the body I do not know, God knows, how he was caught up into paradise and heard inexpressible words, which it is not lawful for a man to utter" [2 Cor. 12:3-4].**

***<u>Only the voices of the angels shall be herd, singing songs of praise and honor for the precious Blood of the Lamb.</u> **"The living, the living man, he shall praise you, as I do this day; The Father shall make known your truth to the children about your faithfulness. The Lord will save me, and we will sing with stringed instruments all the days of our lives in the temple of the Lord" [Is. 38:19-20]. "I will not die but LIVE, and will proclaim what the Lord has done" [Ps. 118:17].**

<u>May every heart know the length, breadth, and depth of God's compassion for all?</u> **"Can you search out the deep things of God? Can you find out the limits of the Almighty? They are higher than heaven. What can you do? Deeper than Sheol, what can you know? Their measure is longer than the earth and broader than the sea" [Job 11:7-9]. "That Christ may dwell in your hearts through faith; that you, being**

rooted and grounded in love, may be able to comprehend with all the saints what is the width, length and depth and height, to know the love of Christ which passes knowledge; that you may be filled with all the fullness of God" [Eph. 3:17-19].

Friend, please <u>do not think for one moment</u> that I am trying to bring fear upon you by sharing these scriptures. I have shared these thoughts and scriptures so that you may hear the TRUTH (if it is that you haven't heard it before?) Know that above all, GOD LOVES US! The question we need to ask ourselves is how much do we love Him?

GOD LOVES YOU

The question is: Do YOU love HIM?

By this I know you love Me, do you seek MY will?
On what things do you rely to satisfy and fill?
By this I know you love ME, do you seek MY face?
Be ready always-dearest child, to show forth My grace.
By this I know you love ME, Bear My name and do,
All that I have said, I served, and so should you.
By this I know you love Me, Clothe and feed MY sheep,
Comfort and do not condemn, those who grieve and weep.
By this I know you love ME, give as I have taught,
Love, compassion, mercy, time, of which cannot be bought.
By this I know you love Me, Be always near, abide,
And you will understand and know, MY way, for I'll confide.
By this I know you love ME, Simply be my friend,
No greater will you ever find, on which you can depend.

Christene Luthey

Jesus said, "Greater love has no one that this, than to lay down one's life for his friends. You are my friends if you do whatever I command you" [John 15:13-14].

BEHOLD THE PLUMBLINE
Grace / Righteousness / Life

Jesus said, "The time is fulfilled, and the kingdom of God is at hand. Repent, and believe in the Gospel" [Mark 1:15]. "The ungodly are like chaff which the wind drives away. Therefore the ungodly shall not stand in the judgment, nor sinners in the congregation of the righteous. For the Lord knows the way of the righteous, but the way of he ungodly shall perish" [Ps. 1:4-6].

The battle raging in each life, is one of peace and woe
One submits to God above, one will not let go.
It is a war of Spirit and Flesh, both wanting so to win.
Wrestling ever endlessly—back and forth within.

The Flesh: Just wants to have its way, always for its own,
Causing us to tread on ground, our feet should not have known.

The Spirit: seeks to please always, the one who set it free
Yielding to the cup and cross, whatever it may be.

Who shall win? Please ask yourself, knowing one must fail
The Spirit yes with grace is sure, to certainly prevail!

The flesh must die; for it destroys each time we let it win
So we must learn how to deny, each and every sin.
The flesh must lose, although the fight, shall never cease until
The beating of my earthly heart, God decides to still.

What a battle, what a war, tis one you cannot see
Raging each and every hour, deep inside of me.

Oh but grace, sweet precious grace, shall see me through I know
Through peace and strife I'll carry on, Faith has told me so.
I must only strive to TRUST, the One who died for me
His power, strength and priceless blood, has promised VICTORY!

Christene Luthey

THE DEPTH OF GOD

[Proverbs 1:7] says, "The fear of the Lord is the beginning of knowledge, but fools despise wisdom and instruction." I pray that neither you nor I despise the instruction or wisdom God has given us to receive Christ. He is calling us to come to Him. His words are being made known to our heart. He is stretching out His hand to keep us from falling into sin's condemnation. If we refuse His love let us look at **[Prov.1:26-31]**, where God warns those who have HARDENED their hearts against His teaching. **"I will laugh at your calamity; I will mock when your terror comes. When your terror comes like a STORM, and your destruction comes LIKE A WHIRLWIND, when distress and anguish come upon you. Then you will call upon Me, but I will not answer; you will seek me diligently, but you will not find Me because you hated knowledge, and did not choose the fear of the Lord, nor would you have my counsel, and despised all My Reproof. Therefore you shall eat the fruit of YOUR OWN WAY and be filled with your own fancies."**

We have been informed of the CONSEQUENCES of turning away from God's counsel. We can also be CERTAIN that if we have hardened our hearts against Him, we had better be PREPARED FOR THE WORST! God tells us about an UNPARDONABLE SIN that will NOT be forgiven... That sin is the **"Blasphemy against the Holy Spirit"** [Matthew 12:31]. **"Anyone who speaks against the Holy Spirit will not be forgiven either in this age or in the age to come"** [Matt. 12:32], God in His mercy and grace said, **"In an acceptable time I have heard you, and in the day of salvation I have helped you. Behold, NOW is the acceptable time; Behold now is the day of salvation"** [2 Cor. 6:2]

GOD WILL NOT BE MOCKED

"Do not be deceived; God is not mocked, for whatsoever a man sows, that he shall also reap. For he who sows to the flesh shall reap corruption, but he who sows to the spirit will of the spirit reap everlasting life" [Gal. 6:7-8]. That is something to think about. Let us "Arise you who sleep, arise from the dead, and Christ will give you light. See then that you walk circumspectly, not as fools, but as wise.

Redeeming the time, because the days are evil. Therefore do not be unwise, but understand what the will of the Lord is" [Eph. 5:13-17].

Let us do as the Lord would have us do, so that we may be considered blameless before Him. [Is. 1:16-18] says, "wash yourselves make yourselves clean; put away the evil of your doings before My eyes. Cease to do evil, learn to do good; seek justice, reprove the oppressor; defend the fatherless, plead for the widow. Come now and let us reason together says the Lord, though your sins are like scarlet, they shall be white as snow; though they are red like crimson, they shall be white as wool."

<u>A PRAYER:</u> Almighty God, Have mercy upon me. Count not my sins against me,
But rather forgive me of my faults and failures,
So that I may Lord, find favor in your beloved eyes and not vengeance.
Spare me oh merciful Redeemer from your judgment, and keep me safe from harm.
I sorrowfully repent oh God of my half-hearted attempts at being a "Christian."
Forgive me for not upholding your statutes, laws and ways before those around me.
I am ashamed of my lack of boldness to be the example you have commanded me to be. Help me please. Help me heavenly Father to do and know your perfect will.
Grant me unyielding courage to stand against the enemy and fight the good fight of faith. Oh, Lord God, do not abandon me, (although I deserve to be abandoned.)
Throughout all my earthly days, stay with me and have complete control of my will.
Teach me to follow you regardless of the cost. Lead me and guide me in the truth.
Grant me wisdom, peace and grace to live amidst this world and all of its darkness.
Shine your everlasting light of love and life upon my soul and live through me. Amen

Christene Bolte-Luthey

THE SCARLET THREAD

There is a scarlet ribbon, which flows between two friends
Possessing in its Crimson color, love that never ends.
Just as the blood of Christ was shed, to set the sinner free
His love for those who trust in Him shall last eternally.
Hearts which bear the scarlet thread, live forever more
Just as the grace of God our Father, spans from shore to shore.
It's wondrous how Almighty God, turns crimson into white
Leaving only glory friend, to light the darkest night.

S-Is for the **S**on of God, whose blood has dyed with color
Crimson, what could not be done, on earth by any other.
A-is **A**lways lifting us, above the storms of life,
Rescuing with mercy true, freeing us from strife.
L-is for the **L**ove He's shown, **E**ncircling us with grace
That we in blood stained holiness, may look upon His face.
T-is for the **T**ie that binds, for sin then, God won't see,
But purely that great Crimson stain, He used to set us free!

Christene Luthey

Friend, have you been washed in the Blood of Christ so that your sins have been made "white as snow?" Paul wrote in **[Rom. 12:1-2], "I beseech you therefore brethren, by the mercies of God that you present your bodies as a living sacrifice, holy acceptable to God, which is your reasonable service. And do not be conformed to this world, but be transformed by the renewing of your mind, that you may prove what is good and acceptable and perfect will of God."** Why would we want to follow this counsel? Because it is written, **"As I live says the Lord, every knee shall bow to me and every tongue shall confess to God. So then each of us shall give an account of himself to God' [Rom. 14:11-12].**

Therefore we should strive to make our way perfect, as He is perfect. Then we will not fear the end of our time on earth, for we will have the blessed assurance of peace, hope and glory. **[2 Cor.4:16-18]. "Therefore, we do not lose heart, even though our outward man is perishing, yet the inward man is being renewed day by day."**

When Shadows Fall: A Journey of Faith

FEAR NOT THE WAY TO GLORY

When on my deathbed I do lie, I'll wait without a tear
For then my spirit shall embrace, the love of God so dear.
Though faintly I now hear Him call, I know it won't be long,
Until I enter through His gate, and hear the victory song.
Long awaited there I've been, by my beloved friend,
Who has taken care of me, and still unto the end.
Prepared, I know a mansion waits, were I may rest in love
Lovingly He beckons me, to meet him there above.
I shall not fret or fear the way that opens that great door,
Compassion turned the key for me; no I need fear no more.
Farewell, dread not deaths gloomy porch, Venture through with peace
Once passed the moment quickly spent, all care and woe shall cease.
Onward now without a tear, I bid a fond "good-bye,"
To greet my Lord and Savior
To LIVE, I first must DIE.

Christene Luthey

"For our light affliction, which is but for a moment, is working for us a far more exceeding and eternal weight of glory, while we do not look at the things which are seen. For the things which are seen are temporary, but the things which are not seen are eternal" [2 Cor. 4:17-18].

IF NOT FOR GRACE

The Bible says that, **"The day will come that everyone's work will be put through the fire, and all can see what sort of work it is" [1 Cor. 3:13].** At the age of twenty-five I was forced to look at and ponder all I have shared with you. If I had not, I would not ask YOU to consider them. I only hope that you find these questions as vital to your life? May you then contemplate them and give them the attention they deserve? <u>Again, neither you nor I know what TOMORROW will bring.</u> If it were not for the grace of God, I would not be alive today. I want to share with you these truths for they have not only given me direction and Christian guidance; they have also helped me live a fruitful life. I hope your life and faith will also grow?

Would you take a moment to think about this? Jesus was asked, **"Are you the Christ, the Son of the Blessed?"** He answered, **"I am. And you will see the Son of Man sitting at the right hand of the power and coming with clouds in heaven." [Mark 4:61-62]**. What we believe concerning THIS scripture verse DETERMINES whether or not we will receive **"the promise of the Spirit through faith" [Gal. 3:14]**. God's righteousness comes only through <u>faith in Jesus Christ</u> on those who believe in <u>Him</u>. Do you believe that HE is the CHRIST? I inquire because: <u>ETERNITY IS IN THE BALANCE</u>, while the destiny of your soul and mine is fixed in what we *believe*. Please understand. Up until the day of the tornado I NEVER THOUGHT about WHAT I BELIEVED. Nor did I ever ponder that MY TIME to decide was RUNNING OUT. I also never really faced the actuality that if I didn't make a choice myself, the word of God would make one for me.

I pray that you have by now fixed your heart on the truth that is in Jesus Christ? **"The just shall live by faith" [Rom. 1:17]**. Remember, **"Faith in the Gospel of Christ, for it is the power of God to salvation for everyone who believes" [Rom. 1:16]**. If we trust the word of God **[John 1:12]** saying, **"as many as received Him, to them He gave the right to become children of God, even to those who believe on his name."** We can be sure that, <u>**"Whoever calls upon the name of the Lord shall be saved"**</u> **[Rom. 10:13]**.

But for those among us who will not receive Him, God said, **"And this is the condemnation, that light came into the world and men loved darkness rather than light, because their deeds were evil. For everyone that does evil hates the light, neither comes to the light lest his deeds be reproved" [John 3:19-20]**. Understand my friend, if you or I walk in darkness, it is by choice, because Jesus stated in **[John 8:12], "I am the light of the world; He that follows Me shall not walk in darkness, but shall have the light of life."**

We all know that walking in both darkness and light is impossible. One is darkness the other is light. Just as one choice set before us is DEATH, the other is LIFE. The same then is true; a person CANNOT walk according to the will of God (obeying the Holy Spirit) and at the same time walk in his own will (the flesh). **[James 1:18] explains, "A DOUBLE-MINDED man is unstable in all his ways."** But, **[2 Sam. 22:31], "As for God, His way is** perfect; The way of the Lord is proven; He is a shield to all who trust in Him." So it is that until you and I have yielded our heart, mind, body and soul to the will of God we are still trusting in OURSELVES.

TIME TO CHANGE

Scripture my friend is being fulfilled like never before. **"When you hear of wars and commotions, do not be terrified; for these things must come to pass first, but the end will not come immediately. Nation will rise against nation, and kingdom against kingdom. And there will be great earthquakes in various places, and famines and pestilences; and there will be fearful sights and great signs from heaven"** [Luke 21: 9-11]. This is why we should to look at our lives and decide whether or not there may be any areas that need changed? We are told that the, **"The great day of the Lord is near; it is near and hastens quickly"** [Zeph. 1:14].

LAY HOLD OF THE GIFT OF GRACE

GRACE: Is not to be taken lightly
It is not to be "trampled on,"
It is; by mercy offered
To those who realize sin and wrong.

To lay a strong foundation,
One must humble himself, his life, and his will to me
Only when you see yourself a "SINNER"
May My blessed grace set you free.

Many want my love and blessings
But will not seek, or hear My calling voice
As time is fading just as a vapor
I summon ALL to make a CHOICE!

Choose a strong foundation that won't falter
Amidst the storms of life you battle through
<u>WHAT you decide will surely determine</u>
<u>Whether DEATH or LIFE shall come to you.</u>
Christene Luthey

Let us **"Watch therefore, [Matt. 24:42], "For as in the days of Noah were, so will the coming of the Son of Man be. For as in the days before the flood, they were eating and drinking, marrying and giving in marriage, Until the day that Noah entered the ark, and did not know until the flood came and took them all away, so also will the coming of the Son of Man be" [Matt. 24:37-39].** Jesus said, **"But of that day and the hour no one knows, no, not even the angels of heaven, but My Father only" [Matt. 24:36].**

There have been several weighty thoughts to consider throughout the beginning of this book? <u>Please do not be overwhelmed by them</u>. God places a variety of choices before us. <u>But do not rush into anything. I encourage you to research the Holy Bible for yourself and examine the scriptures well.</u> **[Deut. 30:15-16] "I have set before you today; LIFE and GOOD— DEATH and EVIL. In that I command you today to love the Lord your God, to walk in His ways, and to keep His commandments, His statutes, and His judgments, that you may live and multiply; and the Lord your God will bless you in the land in which you possess."** This advice is for everyone we know and us. **"I call heaven and earth as witnesses today against you, that I have set before you LIFE and DEATH, BLESSING and CURSING, therefore CHOOSE LIFE, that both you and your descendants may live" [Deut. 30:19].**

Within the heart of every man there dwells a certain place
Where emptiness abides unless, it's filled with love and grace.

Perhaps you've noticed something friend lacking in your soul?
A need to feel accepted? And wish you could be whole?

You're not quite sure of *what* it is that you are longing for?
But quietly you wish for it and peace you do implore?

Recognize that you are "lost" and floundering in sin
Repent and Christ will enter, your heart and live within!

He's waiting for your yielding, unto His perfect will,
To come abide within your soul, Himself, your void to fill.

Christene Luthey

A CHOICE IS REQUIRED OF YOU

Though savage winds around me blow
Deep within my heart I know
The steady hand of God is near
To shield me till the sky is clear.

I have known the fear of sin
When storm clouds come you search within.
Yet much too late, you ponder there,
All you've done without a care.

In this, regret is all you feel
For death—you realize is real.
From truth you find you cannot hide,
No place of refuge to abide.

Only that which you recall
Christ has paid sin's debt for all.
Then search you must your very soul
To find within—you're half, not whole.

If Christ dwells NOT therein your heart
Like chaff from wheat the two must part.
As light and darkness can't embrace
It's death through sin, or life by grace.

These things I tell you friend are true
A CHOICE IS BEING REQUIRED OF YOU.

Christene Luthey

John the Baptist said speaking of JESUS: **"I indeed baptize you with water unto repentance, but He who is coming after me is mightier than I, whose sandals I am not worthy to carry. He will baptize you with the Holy Spirit and fire. His winnowing fan is in His hand, and he will thoroughly clean out His threshing floor, and gather His wheat into**

the barn; but He will burn up the chaff with unquenchable fire" [Matt. 3:11-12].

IN THE LIGHT OF TRUTH
NO DARKNESS REMAINS
THUS GRANTING SWEET FREEDOM
FOREVER, FROM CHAINS!

C. L.

Seven
ETERNITY IN THE BALANCE

"According to the grace of God which was given to me, as a wise master builder I have laid the foundation, and another builds on it. But let each one take heed how he builds on it. For no other foundation can anyone lay than that which is laid, which is Jesus Christ. Now if anyone builds on this foundation with gold, silver, precious stones, wood, hay, straw, each one's work will become clear; for the day will declare it, because it will be revealed by fire; and the fire will test each one's work, of what sort it is" [1 Cor. 3:10-13].

WHEN BEFORE THE LORD I STAND

When before the Lord I stand, I wonder will He take my hand
And with a smile say to me, "**Well done my faithful servant** see"
"The treasures you laid up are here, where moth nor rust could not come near."
Behold, your efforts were not in vain, for see here written in your name.
Are precious gems, of silver and gold. For you served Me as you were told
Loving first the scared and lost, you fed My sheep and count the cost.
Submitting to My will and ways, come now blessed, receive thy praise.
Hear with joy the pardoned sing, glory to your God and King.
These once lost and dead in sin, heard the truth and entered in.
How beautiful are YOU that GAVE, humbly serving Me as slave.
Or yet in Satan's chains they'd be, never knowing Jubilee.
Their voices praise My name today, because you took the time to pray.
Beloved, enter, as My friend, into Life, which has no end.

OR.... When before the Lord I stand, will he with SADNESS take my hand?
And say to me in deep despair, "**Depart from Me**, you did not care"
You gave Me NOT One thing to save, neither food nor clothes to Me you gave.
No mercy did you show your Lord, now go, and receive your just reward.
The least of these My brethren claim, to these and Me, you've done the same.

Then both the "cursed" and "righteous" say, "When did brethren come our way?"
Judging then, I'll say to thee, "As such you've done you've done to Me."
"Now go, receive thy just reward, each to which you've shown your Lord."
[Matthew 25:21-46]

Christene Luthey

Please do not be DISCOURAGED with anything you read on these pages. I know that God's "PRUNING" and "TRIMMING" is not always easy. In fact, it's down right difficult and makes us miserable at times? Yet if we trust God who created us, we will yield good "fruit" from His loving hand on our life. When we love Him we want to live our lives for Him, that will bring glory to His name. I hope you feel the same way? If you do, then don't ever be offended by what you read in God's word for it will ultimately mold and shape your Christian character.

Getting back to where I left off, God has placed extremely heavy on my heart—that it is time for all people to decide where their loyalty is. We can't risk being fickle with our beliefs any longer because: **"God's promise is not slack concerning His coming." "He is long suffering toward us, not willing that any should perish, but that all should come to repentance" [2 Peter 3:9].** We can't claim to be a "Christian" while rejecting Christ or the doctrine of Christ's Deity. We shouldn't be engaged in wicked practices, speaking the language of Christendom, but indecisively <u>living it</u>. Simply acknowledging God is not enough to be right with God. Understand that God's word states that it is a sin to be taking part in adultery, perverted sex and sorcery. If our statement of repentance and gratitude before Christ is not apparent by our behavior, then we deceive ourselves and contradict our confession of faith. Many people today claim to be Christians, while at the same time take part in wicked practices such as: seeking spirit guides, channeling, worshiping angels. We have to observe our confession. God knows our thoughts, our works and our ways. If we involve ourselves in these things, God's word states that these **"shall have their part in the lake which burned with fire and brimstone; which is the second death" [Rev. 21:18].** Sin never leads to salvation. **"For whatever is born of God overcomes the world. And this is the victory that has overcome the world, our faith" [1 John 5:4].** Ponder if you will, **"But in accordance with your hardness and your impenitent heart you are treasuring up for yourself wrath in the day of wrath and revelation of the righteous** judgment of God, who will render to each one according to his deeds. Eternal life to those who by patient continuance in doing good seek for glory, honor, and immortality; but to those who are self-seeking and do not obey the truth, but obey unrighteousness, indignation and wrath, tribulation and anguish, on every soul of man who does evil, of the Jew first and also of the Greek; but glory, honor and peace to everyone who works what is good, to the Jew first and also the Greek" [Romans 2:5-9]. "But I want to remind you, though you once knew this, that the Lord, having saved the people out of the land of Egypt, afterward destroyed those who did not believe" [Jude 5].

Friend, indecision, compromise, hypocrisy and double standards are NOT a part of living the Christian life. Neither you nor I can allow the door of our way of life to swing both ways. The Bible says that **there will be NO "LUKE-WARM" souls** dwelling in the kingdom of God! Therefore, shouldn't we consider where we might be compromising God's word? Until we do, how can we put an end to hypocrisy in our lives?

I sincerely believe the "whirlwind" I saw would not compare to the terror a soul will encounter that has not trusted in Christ on the day of God's Final Judgment. That is why I feel strongly that God is calling everyone to righteousness through faith. Though we know not when (no one knows when), God will send forth the decree to gather the wheat from the ends of the earth. Shouldn't you and I seriously consider our faith, beliefs, and absolutes, by God's standards?

CHRIST THE CORNERSTONE

Recall the scripture in of Amos where it is written, **"Behold the Lord stood on a wall made with plumb line, with a plumb line in His hand" [Amos 7:7]**. God is standing in front of this wall, for it is the pattern by which He shall use to judge our lives. It will grant God a *true picture* of our labor. In his hand is a plumb line by which He shall judge the nations. With justice He shall judge according to what is written in His unchangeable word. What is written is fixed, settled and unalterable.

I sincerely believe JESUS and His teachings will be the STANDARDS by which God will judge us. Jesus taught us by His perfect and sinless example to love, honor and obey God and submit to His will at all cost! That is why Christ is the example we must follow (not the world). Do not misunderstand or be discouraged. Am I implying that God expects us to be perfect as Jesus was perfect? No! I am only saying that God knows our heart and to what degree we desire to mirror the character of Christ's devotion and affection to Him.

Pondering these things myself, I to some extent imagined a set of scales. I began to wonder how God might possibly judge ME? In considering that, I envisioned some weights He might place on the scale, and what they could have written on them. Below are a few of the labels I thought God might possibly assess my obedience? It didn't take long after meditating on these that I developed an even GREATER appreciation for God's grace and what Christ did on the cross. Perhaps you might like to ponder a few for yourself?

FAITH, HONOR, COURAGE, GENTLENESS, SUBMISSION, OBEDIENCE, LOVE, FAITHFULNESS, HUMILITY, RIGHTEOUSNESS, REPENTANCE, WORKS, UNDERSTANDING, LOYALTY, PERFECTION, TRUTH, HUMILITY, CHARACTER, GIVING ALMS, INTEGRITY, PRAYER, FASTING, FORGIVENESS, PATIENCE, LONG SUFFERING, MEEKNESS, KINDNESS, MORALITY, FORNICATION, PRIDE, BLASPHEMY, SIN, COVETOUSNESS, WRATH, GREED, ANGER, DISOBEDIENCE, WICKEDNESS, BITTERNESS, MURDER, JEALOUSY, EVIL DESIRE, IDOLATERY, MALICE...The list could go on and on...

Would the righteous weights outweigh the wicked in our lives? God's scales won't lie. A productive fruitful life can only be obtained though our faithful obedience to God's word. Putting in to practice what we have seen demonstrated in the life of Christ. For life apart from Christ, HAS NO MEANING at all.

WEIGHED AND FOUND LACKING

God stood before me with scales in his hand
What is this Lord, I don't understand?
Come nearer He said let judgment begin.
Now hand He the weight
Inscribed there with "SIN."
Trembling I reached for it just as He said
But the stone was so large that I just hung my head,
I can't lift it dear Father, it's too much for me,
I KNOW THAT, He answered, recall CALVARY?

Now what would I do as He stepped toward the scale?
What is it dear child, you look slightly pale?
Then placing some other stones in the bowl
He said, now let's measure the worth of thy soul.

There was no denying the TRUTH that I saw
Each weight on the scale was God's Holy law.
In having forsaken CHRIST and His ways
God's word would determine my eternal days.

"Depart then," I heard, and I knew I was lost
I had taken for granted, my SIN and its cost…

**So, friend, ponder God's Judgment,
Consider *this* end,
<u>Let Christ be your Savior, Your Lord and your friend</u>.**
Christene Luthey

    Christ Jesus has set a standard. Being that He will judge us, shouldn't we know how He walked and what He taught while on earth? Have you or I studied examples of how JESUS loved, forgave, submitted and surrendered to God's will? God gave us the Ten Commandments to give our lives a structure, but Christ added to them by the example of His life. That is what is meant by **"be yea perfect" [Matt. 5:48].** Christ was the **"stone the builders rejected."** Laying down his life, He emptied Himself of His own desires and permitted God's will to be done through Him. In reverence and respect, Jesus submitted totally and unconditionally to God's will. So must we if we want to be like Him?

    Can we say these things of ourselves? If we searched our motives and the desires of our heart, would we be shocked at what we might see? If righteousness is the standard by which we will be judged, shouldn't we pray daily for a pure heart? Jesus said that, **"Unless you change and become like little children, you will never see the kingdom of heaven" [Matt. 18:3].** In order for you or I to become like the **"little children"** Jesus spoke of, we must learn to trust him without reservation or doubt. In doing this we consent to Him to changing us within. This can be accomplished by believing God's word, taking up Christ's cross, and following Him. Whatever the cost or sacrifice might be? Humbling ourselves and admitting that we are "sinners" is NOT an easy thing to do. Yet if we are able to come to the point of understanding that we need to place ourselves in the hands of God, we <u>will</u> experience indescribable peace and immeasurable joy.

CHRIST IS THE STANDARD

The cornerstone God has chosen and laid
Has also become a great colonnade
A blessed memorial of love that is pure
A heart that is perfect, faithful and sure.

Though builders rejected Him, when choosing their stone
He's a rock that is tested, proven and known
Would one day determine whether a house fall or stand,
Explaining the plumb line God holds in His hand.

He shall weigh in the balance
FAITH, TRUTH and LOVE;
With Christ as the standard
Of God's judgment above.

It is by Him and through Him
We will be measured
It is also by Him all bonds shall be severed.

Look close at the Gospels and surely you'll see
The standards He'll measure, our—eternity.

Perhaps some may argue and say it's not true?
Ignore what is said, or just follow through?

The standards He's set are written and sure
To weigh true repentance
In the hearts of the world.

Christene Luthey

CHRIST OUR FOUNDATION

Most of us would have to admit that we are terribly deficient in righteousness, repentance and things of this nature. But if we begin to distinguish our faults and failures, God can form the foundation that our faith can build on. Woe unto us if we trust in anything other than Christ. God commanded us to build on the ROCK of thy Salvation that is Jesus. He is the base upon which all homes (lives) shall stand. This is God's solemn promise. Every house that is NOT built upon this cornerstone (Jesus) shall break and know great sorrow. All other forms shall wash away leaving only regret, misery and shame. I sincerely believe that time is fading in which we may choose this precious stone. One day we shall be called to meet our Maker. Therefore we cannot risk taking this stone for granted nor the time we have to build upon it. I say this because we simply do not know the hour in which God shall require our soul.

Have we also taken into consideration that one day God will also appraise the **"Spiritual gifts"** He has given us? Did we put them to use for His purpose and glory? Did we also know that the Bible says everything we have done for ourselves will **"burn like chaff"** in the wind? If we don't use our gifts for God's glory, we will feel very ashamed when we stand before Him. God's word also tells only what we have labored for God's glory will remain amidst the consuming fires of the final judgment. Knowing these things, shouldn't we be diligently serving Him?

<u>I truly believe that God is stretching out His rod across the land and is beginning to evaluate who is with Him and who is rebelliously following sin.</u> I think God's sifting has begun and will shake many foundations. This process will separate the repentant hearts from the rebellious. This may seem harsh and unbelievable, but I cannot help but feel that our faith is daily going to be uncovered. God will determine also in this sifting the source from which we receive faith. Do we look to the world for our substance and strength? Or do we long for Christ Jesus, **"the living water"** that quenches our spiritual thirst? Is Christ **"the bread of life"** that feeds our soul when it hungers for wisdom and truth? Or do we turn to the world? These are questions we need to ponder honestly. WHO and WHAT rule your heart and mine?

Christene Bolte-Luthey

HIS LOVE BOUGHT VICTORY

Though I taught and I preached the Gospel of TRUTH
Only a few hearts would hear.
The message within that rescues from sin
That in **FAITH alone** I come near.
By the words that I spoke I was tested and tried
Found guilty although I was not.
But only through BLOOD could I wash clean
The souls that Satan had sought.
So I offered myself, all I could give
My body, heart and soul
Unto the pain of sin and death
That YOU may become whole!
Apart from Me you can't be whole
No, just an empty shell
Destined by sin's awful curse
To suffer judgment's hell.
But, **I bled and died upon the cross**
Where Satan too could see
No longer could he bind in chains
Those who trusted Me.
His wicked schemes to torment then
Men's souls upon the earth
Were undone for **LOVE**, not hate
Had granted "second birth."
In darkness I confronted sin,
Alone but not with fear
For this I knew, was NOT the end
REDEMPTION soon was near!
Iniquity pronounced with joy
"That it had won," (but NOT)
The battle was not over yet,
Sin's victory, (but a thought).
I listened while it mocked my love
And twisted what I said,
"So you'll have victory over the grave?"
"Not true, for you are dead."

> On and on sin's wicked words cut me to the bone
> UNTIL I heard LOVE'S sweet command,
> **To ROLL AWAY THE STONE!**
> Then evil heard like thunder loud
> **HE'S RISEN FROM THE GRAVE!**
> **HE ROSE AGAIN JUST AS HE SAID**
> **ALL SOULS FROM HELL TO SAVE!**
> *Christene Luthey*

I hope that poem blessed your heart? I pray that in reading it we ponder the physical and mental HELL Jesus endured so that you and I could be free from sin's curse? Today, in reading that poem I hope <u>if you have not made the decision yet to trust Christ as your personal Savior, you soon will</u>? <u>He loves you so much that He died in horrid agony to prove it</u>. Who else has ever done such a thing? No one ever possibly will because it's impossible! Today because of God's immeasurable love we are being called to repentance.

Jesus said, **"abide in me, and I in you. As the branch cannot bear fruit of itself, unless it abides in the vine, neither can you unless you abide in me" [John 15:4].** We are created human beings with a divine Creator. <u>WE ourselves ARE NOT DIVINE</u>, nor do we have the right to claim or consider ourselves divine. Those who refuse to distinguish between the Creator and created human beings are in danger of God's Supreme judgment. **"For thus says the Lord, who created the heavens, Who is God, Who formed the earth and made it, Who has established it, Who did not create it in vain, Who formed it to be inhabited; I am the Lord, and there is no other" [Is. 45:18]** Also read, **[Ezek. 28:1-10]**.

We are human beings subject to death, physical and spiritual. We are not mentally, physically, or spiritually able to possess the knowledge, power, wisdom or attributes of God. **[1 Tim. 6:15-16]** states that <u>CHRIST ALONE</u> is **"blessed and only Potentate, the King of Kings and Lord of Lords. Who alone has immorality, dwelling in unapproachable light, whom no man has seen or can see, to whom be honor and everlasting power."**

The only "transformation" we need today is that which comes by an act of God's Holy Spirit. **"I beseech you therefore brethren, by the mercies of God, that you present your bodies a living sacrifice, holy, acceptable to God, which is your reasonable service. And do not be conformed to this world, but be transformed by the renewing of your mind, that you** may prove what is that good and acceptable and perfect will of God" [Rom. 12:1-2].

The question is: Are you and I in the will of God or are we trying to BE God? It would be wise to ponder this question before we stand before our Creator. There is only one life to live. Realize that DEATH closes the door of opportunity. When we leave this world, you and I WILL IMMEDIATELY stand before God whether or not we're prepared. [Heb. 9:27]. There are no second chances when flesh and soul depart. True Christ saved Christians may look forward to glory, but only darkness and terror await the unsaved.

Because of God's wondrous love He is *even now* permitting us time to prepare for the day we will meet Him. Again, let us remember God's words, **"I know thy works that you are neither cold or hot. So then because you are Luke warm, and neither cold nor hot, I will spew you out of my mouth," "As many as I love, I rebuke and chasten: be zealous therefore, and repent."** [Rev. 3:15,16,19]. I sincerely believe the "pangs" spoken of in the Gospel of Matthew have already begun. Those of us who have not loved God or attempted to serve Him WILL NOT dwell with Him in His heavenly kingdom.

Are we partakers of His glory? Will we be the **"chosen" few,** the **"elect"** who have forsaken the things of this world and taken up our cross to follow Christ? Ask yourself, am I serving God as Christ served? Am I enduring life's trials as Christ endured? Do I love, forgive and walk as Christ Jesus did? Am I allowing God's will to be done in as Christ did?

We should strive daily to do these things. Abiding in Him and permitting Him to be our source of peace, hope, strength and love. For in these things the grace of God is revealed. In them we also receive confidence and trust. By following Jesus Christ we not only by faith receive the blessings of God, but are also granted the faith to receive our heavenly crown. Unless we ABIDE IN CHRIST and allow God's Holy Spirit to guide us, our Christian walk will be weak and unstable. Remember—it is a perilous thing to be separated from God. Let us not forget, Satan is the accuser who seeks our destruction, and will until Christ returns. Remember that it was the enemy who led Eve into sin **[Gen. 3:1-5],** Sought to destroy Job **[Job 2],** and even attempted to tempt Jesus. **[Matthew 4:1-11].**

SATAN: THE ADVESARY OF OUR SOUL

We have a wicked enemy, who seeks to rob and kill
A murderer who looks to harm, his own desires to fill.
His goal, to tempt your very soul, with compromise and pleasure
To take eternal life from you, God's greatest gift and treasure.

He wants so to destroy your faith,
He'll tempt and try you well
And should he win, be sure my friend
He'll live with you in hell.

There is but only ONE WAY known
To resist him and stand,
Proclaim the word of God in truth
And take faith's "sword" in hand.

Say, "It is written, I have won
I'm forever free!
Rising from the dead, Christ sealed
Every victory!"

Christene Luthey

The word of God tells us to, **"Be sober, be vigilant; because your adversary the Devil walks about like a roaring lion seeking whom he may devour. Resist him, steadfast in the faith, knowing that the same sufferings are experienced by your brotherhood in the world" [1 Peter 5:8-9].** One of the first things we can do to help protect ourselves from the enemy is to SINCERELY repent of sin. Doing that, we free our consciences of that which Satan can use "accusing" us.

A CALL TO REPENTANCE

In light of your ways your statutes and grace
"Create in me Lord, a clean heart."   **[Psalm 51:10]**
Lead me and guide me, keep me oh God
That I may not error, nor depart.

For who precious Father is able to please you
Except those who bow to your will,
And **"Renew a right Spirit within me to follow"**   [Psalm 51:10]
That my life before you is real.

Please **"Cast me not, away from thy presence"**   [Psalm 51:11]
But help me obey thy commands
And **"take not Thy Holy Spirit then from me"**   [Psalm 51:11]
And daily make use of my hands.

"Restore unto me, the Joy of Salvation"   [Psalm 51:12]
That others may see YOU in me
Oh what a blessing to know dearest Father
The love that has set sinners free!

"Then I will teach transgressors Thy ways"   [Psalm 51:13]
With a heart destined only to serve
It is the least I can do for my brothers
Knowing Lord all You deserve.

Create in me God, a heart with true hunger
To **"seek first your kingdom"** and Grace   [Matt. 6:33]
"Blessed are those whose hearts are pure"
For **"they shall see your face"**   [Matt. 5:8]

Help me to be all that you desire
Loving, faithful and true
Help me proclaim your precious name   [Acts 4:12]
In all that I say and do.

Use me always, for YOUR glory   [John 15:8]
That flows forever on;
Be my sweet, sweet inspiration
Be my heart's true song!
Christene Luthey

I hope that you prayed that prayer and meant it from your heart? When we do if we've meant it, we will be less apt to fall into the sin of PRIDE.

[Proverbs 3:1-11] Tells us wisdom brings blessings. **[Verses 1-11]**, "Do not forget my teaching, but keep my commands in your heart. For they will prolong your life many years and bring you prosperity. Let love and faithfulness never leave you; bind them around your neck, write them on the tablet of your heart. Then you will win favor and a good name in the sight of God and man. Trust in the Lord with all your heart and lean not on your own understanding. And in all ways acknowledge him. And he will make your paths straight. Do not be wise in your own eyes; fear the Lord and shun evil. This will bring health to you body, and nourishment to your bones. Honor the Lord with your wealth, with the first fruits of all your crops. Then your barns will be filled to overflowing and your vats will brim over with new wine. Do not despise the Lord's discipline and do not resent His rebuke, because the Lord disciplines those He loves, as a Father the son delights in. Preserve sound judgment and discernment, do not let them out of your sight; they will be life for you, an ornament to grace your neck. Then you will go on your way in safety, and your foot will not stumble when you lie down, you will not be afraid, when you lie down your sleep will be sweet. Have no fear of sudden disaster, or of the ruin that overtakes the wicked, for the Lord will be your confidence and will keep your foot from being snared."**

When we take a good look at wisdom, we may see why some may not be receiving the blessings of God. Are we seeking His wisdom? Have we in disobedience strayed from His teaching? Are we keeping His commands? Have we allowed love, wisdom, and faithfulness to leave our lives? Are we leaning on our own understanding? Are we honoring him with our wealth, and the first fruits of our earnings? Do we greatly despise any discipline that comes from the Lord? Are our judgments distorted?

Despite the blessings we just read about, have we turned away from God's sovereign wisdom? Have we become envious, violent people who choose all and any other ways BUT the Lord's? If we answer yes to any of these we need to realize that, **"the Lord's curse is on the house of the wicked" [Prov. 3:33],** and that **"He mocks proud mockers" [Prov. 3:34].** Blessings are ours only when we seek and follow God's wisdom and counsel. **"Blessed is the man who finds wisdom, the man who gains understanding, for she is more profitable than silver and yields better returns than gold. She is more precious than rubies, nothing you desire can compare to her. Long life is in her right hand; in her left are riches and honor. Her ways are pleasant ways, and all her paths are peace.**

She is the tree of life to those who embrace her; those who lay hold of her will be blessed" [Prov. 3:13-18].

God's word tells us: **"The Lord detests a perverse man, his curse is on the house of the wicked, he mocks proud mockers and fools he holds up to shame"** [Prov. 3:32-35]. Why in our nation are we choosing these curses rather than God's blessings? Don't you agree that it's time we sought God's good judgment and entrusted ourselves in obedience to follow it? If we would—we then could rest assured in these promises. **"The Lord takes the upright man into his confidence, He blesses the home of the righteous, and gives grace to the humble"** [Prov. 3:32-34].

I believe that it is a wise person who reverently fears God. But many throughout the world do not fear God or His judgment. **[Ps. 33:8]** states **"Let all the earth fear the Lord; let all the inhabitants of the world stand in awe of him"** [Prov. 8:13] says, **"The fear of the Lord is to hate evil."**

Let's ask ourselves, what on earth do we fear more than God? What do we trust or love more than Him? As a nation do you think we put just about everything before God? Does it seem to you that we want to pursue His statutes? Or do you think that we mainly follow our OWN? We have neglected greed? Have we observed it as an instrument the enemy can use to bind and destroy our lives? Have we thoughtfully considered that GREED is a one-way road that can end in the depletion of our meaning? Is it our motivation?

ALL IS VANITY

Friend, we can't forge ahead into the future and please God with this world's present attitude of perpetual indulgence. Always getting if not taking what we want, endlessly. Doesn't it seem that our appetites are growing more and more every day? Isn't it obvious that we are teaching the generations that follow us that materialism is typical and acceptable? In doing this we are unwisely ignoring the warnings God gave all who are greedy for gain. If you happen to be one who pursues gain, or is pacifying the desires of your children, consider this passage of scripture that addresses the sin of greed. **"So are the ways of everyone who is greedy for gain; it takes away the life of its owner"** [Proverbs 1:19].

FORTUNE AND FAME

Fame and fortune quickly fade, amidst the jewels of God
Compare them, one is golden, the other, merely sod.

Riches, honor, pleasures all, become a passing thing
Finding with a twist or turn, the woe events can bring.

Only FAITH can follow us, beyond our "earthly" life
Not belongings we have gained hard through toil and strife.

Therefore we must guard our heart, and thoughts that lead astray
Our lives, by seeking only things, that surely fades away.

Let us rather ponder deep, Faith and all its wealth
But first to do this we must try, to DISCIPLINE OUR SELF!

C. Luthey

"Therefore, put to death your members which are on the earth: fornication, uncleanness, passion, evil desire, and covetousness, which is idolatry. Because of these things the wrath of God is coming upon the sons of disobedience" [Col. 3:5-6]. "For this we know, that no fornicator, unclean person, nor covetous man, who is an idolater, has any inheritance in the kingdom of Christ and God" [Eph. 5:5].

Why are so many of us throughout the world trying to gain more and more? Isn't it evident to us by now that greed for gain, **"takes away the life of the owner?"** We have established that our lives are **"but a vapor,"** and yet being greedy for gain, we end up supporting the enemy. Considerably cutting short the number of our days here on earth. Is this because very few of us have learned to be content with what we have? Are our NEEDS in life twisted out of perspective? Are we so diluted by the temptations of this world that we are willing to cut down the days of our lives?

I know it would be difficult, but if we could learn to *WANT* only what we *NEED*, a smaller number of us would be held in the bondage of DEBT! If we could strive to better discipline the lusts of our flesh, we would be blessed with peace and contentment. Why? Because NEEDS will not bind us nor make us greedy for gain. *Needs* are those things which are <u>necessary</u> to provide for ourselves, whereas WANTS are not truly necessary.

Recall that it was Satan who said, **"I shall"** for he wants what he knows could destroy us. Christ Jesus offers us freedom from debt if we heed the knowledge of His counsel. Realize that when we want or obtain much, we must also be ready and willing to part with it for Christ. Take heed to this: **"What do I lack?"** The rich young ruler asked Jesus, and Jesus answered him, **"If you want to be perfect, go, sell what you have to the poor, and you will have treasure in heaven; and come, follow me" "But when the young man heard that saying, he went away sorrowful, for he had great possessions"** [Matt. 19:20-22].

Today, if we were asked to SELL EVERYTHING WE OWN and give it to the poor, what would we do? That's a pretty huge question isn't it? Would we walk away from Jesus like the rich young ruler did? Would we be willing to walk away from everything we own to FOLLOW Christ? If we wouldn't, then we need to consider what Jesus said, **"And he who does not take his cross and follow after me is not worthy of me. He that finds his life will lose it, and he who loses his life for My sake will find it."** [Matt. 10:37-39]. I am not saying these things to anger you. I have thought about them in great depth myself. I'm only putting these questions out to you in hope that if we take heed to God's wisdom, we will be spared much hardship and sorrow.

WHERE IS OUR TREASURE

Let's talk a minute about the **"pruning"** God is doing in our lives. It is known that a tree must be pruned in order to grow well and produce quality fruit. If a tree is left alone and not pruned it will rapidly grow out of control and produce little or nothing of value. Therefore, you and I must allow God to "prune" our lives spiritually. As he "prunes," through instruction and love, we learn to set limitations, becoming Christ centered, disciplined people. Then we'll produce good fruit that will make it more difficult to fall into sin. Today, are we willing to resign ourselves to be possibly spiritually ruined by becoming obsessed with the pleasures of this world? If not, then we must consider today the areas we need to safeguard our hearts from the temptations Satan might be using to draw us away from God and our precious families?

HONESTY

(Is the beginning of healing)

Humbly placing heart and soul
On the throne of Grace
Needing a Savior
Exchanging Sin for Righteousness
Sanctifying our heart
Transforming our lives
Yielding our will to God…

C. Luthey

LET CHRIST BE OUR FRIEND

Hear this plea unto your heart; let Christ be your friend
He is a rock amidst life's storms, in which you can depend.

No other has more love for you, nor longs to hold you near
No other can erase your pain, or wipe away all fear.

He is our Savior in all things so let him carry you
You need never walk alone; As Lord He'll see you though.

Let him prove Himself to you, simply take His hand
Step by step just as a child, He'll help you understand.

One by one He'll turn for you the problems in your soul
And all that makes you half inside will surely become whole.

C. Luthey

Let us all realize the things in life that hold much quality and bearing. Let us strive with all our might to protect and defend them. Let us realize that life is a short and passing season. Let us take no day for granted. We must learn to live each day as God intended, and do our best to lay a strong foundation that will stand the test of time. Through each and every one of life's trials, let us learn the peace and assurance that comes when we follow Christ's example of obedience and unconditional love. May we evaluate our lives and think seriously about how we are living. Remembering that we are only travelers en route for eternity.

WHERE IS YOUR TREASURE

Walk cautiously beloved child do not be deceived
Temptation is much nearer now than when you first believed.
I've brought you far beyond your hopes, and given you your dreams
Be watchful and be wise lest you, fall victim to life's schemes.
Have I said to want so much that I be left behind?
Have I said to search and seize? No, rather "seek" and find.
Find that in My truth you'll see, WHERE your treasures are
Then, beloved child you'll grow and you shall journey far.
The world says it is in My will, to profit you with gain?
But when you read My word you'll know, that riches are in vain.
Unless your greatest dream is this, to first deny yourself?
To bear the burdens of the cross, no good is all your wealth.
Be wary with the time you have, to walk upon this earth,
One day I shall appraise your life, what shall I say it's worth?
What sacrifices will you make to set My people free?
For there shall come your true reward, what YOU have given ME.

C Luthey

"Riches do not profit in the day of wrath, but righteousness delivers from death" [Pr. 1:4]

Perhaps it would help if more parents were able to stay at home with their children? There are so many leaving them behind in order to "buy" things. Things that are being obtained for either them or ourselves which will quickly be outgrown or will fade away? Could it be possible that if we could devote more time with our children, that fewer of them across the nation might be living rebellious lives? I sincerely believe **[Prov. 15:27]** is true, **"He who is greedy for gain, troubles his own house."** Why? Because sadly I have witnessed several examples of couples I know who work from sunup to sundown to make "more money." The more money they make, the more they buy their children. The more they buy their children, the further out of control those children become. The further out of control those children become, the more their parents work. Now, the parents can't cope with the chaos at home. So the parents spend even fewer hours at home, and the children are left to fend for themselves even more. In the end, the vicious circle continues until the children end up relying on their own resources for love and attention, wherever it may be.

I suppose we should all look at our homes and ask if there is any trouble like this? If there is, we need to evaluate why we are seeking so much gain? Whatever it may be we need to take the time to think about it. Are these things that we <u>want</u> or need? Then we could ask our self if we would be able to justify our actions if standing before God? Would God think our reasons for being away from our families were justifiable? Seriously, let's stop one moment and ponder all the reasons we work so many hours? Are our motives truly worthy of our life and time? Are we compromising our responsibility and commitment to our family? Are the things we're working for <u>worthy of the time we are sacrificing with our children</u>?

That is a very solemn question. Consider that we cannot reclaim those years with our children. Once those precious tender years have passed, they are gone forever. Another thing to consider is whether or not I am placing my family in the pathways of any temptations where the end result is heartbreak? Think about it. If you feel that in pondering these things you believe that your family needs you at home, simply pray my friend and ask God for wisdom. He will grant you direction. He will show you how you may bring things about that will bless and protect your family. Just seek His counsel, remembering always that He wants what is best for you. Trust that He has the answers and will sustain you.

After my near death experience I promised the Lord to do my best to see to it that my CHILDREN were the number ONE priority in our life. They always had been, but what was truly important in life became definitely clear after the tornado. I realized that they needed a mother at home more than they needed "THINGS." In making that pledge I sought God in prayer and was lead to stay at home with them until they are finished with high school. That decision for many years meant that Scott and I would have to make a variety of sacrifices, but we agreed that being a main part of their upbringing would definitely be worth it.

Their needs have always been met, and God has faithfully blessed our family throughout nearly twenty years now. Scott has had to work long hard hours, but he has lovingly provided for our family of four. Six years ago through much prayer and consideration I stepped out in faith to educate them privately at home using a Christian curriculum with Biblical perspectives. Today I know that all of our efforts have not been in vain. On the contrary, I have shared with them the most precious and valuable years of their lives. Throughout that time, I have been blessed with the opportunity to instill deep within them, the moral fiber and Godly foundation they will require to build lives of their own.

Yet we by no means according to this <u>world's standard</u> would be considered "rich," but we live extremely happy and contented lives. Our home is quaint, but the love of God fills every room. For generations my family and my husband's family have been tightly woven in the strongest tapestry known to exist, <u>FAMILY</u>. No, our children may not have EVERYTHING "money can buy," but they do have something that will NEVER fade with time. They also have something that can never be taken away from them. They have the sweet assurance, confidence, and love of two dedicated parents who value THEM above EVERYTHING in this world! You see, the most blessed gift we can give them is; TIME.

So, if it should be that God would call Scott or I away tomorrow, I trust that in the years I have invested in them, and the time we have spent together, they have been given much more than "money" could have ever bought them. Much more meaningful and momentous things that will see them through the strongest storms life may bring. Therefore, do not be disheartened if it is that you cannot "buy" your children everything. Simply give they what money cannot buy! Your precious time, support, and love which they will need to survive in this world. Today I encourage you to think about your life and the lives of your children (if God has blessed you with them)? Begin giving your children the greatest gift you have to give, <u>YOURSELF</u> and your priceless time. I promise that you will NEVER regret it.

BORROWED ANGELS

Humbled by your sweet embrace, throughout the time you play
I feel it right my children dear, to tell you this today.
You both are "borrowed" angels, granted only mine,
God sent you from heaven, **to love for just a time.**

I know that I acquired you through God's astounding grace
He lovingly reminds my heart each time I see your face.
So graciously I seek each chance, I have upon this earth
To love and guide you carefully, I know your precious worth.

It makes me feel quite blessed inside, being entrusted to,
Oversee such priceless gifts, as are the two of you.
That's why I'm very cautious, and strive for no mistake
It's quite important to us all, I've found for heaven's sake.
So now you know the reason, I hold you oh so tight
My "borrowed" little angels, you're precious in God's sight.

Christene Luthey

ALL THEY NEED IS YOU

Children <u>NEED</u> their <u>PARENTS</u>, throughout these precious years;
Not toys or things that money buys. Can tokens dry their tears?
We think that what the WORLD gives, will make them "happy"—True?
Not so, for in a CHILD'S heart, none take the place of YOU!
I understand your want to work, believe I know your sorrow
But ponder this my dearest friend, **what if there's no tomorrow**?
I can only speak for me, but this is what I've found
Tomorrow is not promised to us, we may not be around...
So just suppose it was to be, you ONLY HAD TODAY—
What exactly would you do? What then would you say?
What would really matter then?
Ask yourself and see,
When you think of life this way
You learn PRIORITY.
The way I think and feel is this, **if I just have TODAY?**
I want to spend it loving them
For LOVE won't pass away!
The love I give... is all they'll have... To get them through this life
The love I give... They'll stand upon; when they are faced with strife.
The TIME I give ... will make them strong; with it they'll come to know
All the things they need in life... To LIVE, SURVIVE, and GROW!
See, LOVE is ALL I've stood upon... To get me through MY tears
I've drawn from it this wisdom true, to see me through these years...

> So see, there's more to giving love
> More than meets the eye
> That's MY answer when I'm asked
> That's my reason WHY!
> Our children's future is at stake
> Believe me—it is true,
> Though you may work to "Give them <u>MORE?</u>"
> **ALL THEY NEED IS <u>YOU</u>!!!** C Luthey

"Behold, children are a heritage from the Lord, the fruit of the womb is a reward. Like arrows in the hand of a warrior, so are the children of one's youth. Happy is the man who has his quiver full of them; they shall not be ashamed, but shall speak with their enemies in the gate" [Psalm 127:3-5]. "Train up a child in the way he should go, and when he is old he will not depart from it" [Prov. 22:6].

THE FINAL ASSESSMENT

Please do not misunderstand; it is <u>not</u> that I am saying we shouldn't have nice things. I've been blessed with much myself. I am merely stating that it is heartbreaking to see worldly possessions being gained, while the futures and foundations of our children are at risk of potential calamity? If we are too busy "working to buy them things," and are not actively taking part in their lives, where will they receive the SELF ESTEEM, SELF WORTH, and CONFIDENCE they need? These characteristics will sustain them, not the "things" we buy. Many of us know this is true. Due to our hasty lack of TIME and NURTURING, we are carelessly overlooking the most precious years of our children's lives. Taking time for granted, we allow them to grow up without being taught the basics of building strong foundations that will help them endure life's storms and adversities.

If we truly desire our children to triumph over circumstances they will experience as they journey through life, we must <u>make our children a personal priority.</u> We must strive to prioritize our lives and eliminate the unnecessary "wants" that put our beloved angels in "day care centers," etc. Realizing that in centers SOMEONE ELSE is instilling their thoughts, ways and practices in the hearts and minds of our children. We need to consider then, from what resources our children will draw strength, courage, and faith? Will it be from OUR life lessons and beliefs, or from those of a stranger? Questions like this may make us uncomfortable, but if we reflect upon these serious subjects, perhaps we will see that our CHILDREN and their rearing are more significant than "things" we are trying to obtain?

We know that it is a sinful to seek more, the pleasures of this WORLD than God. We cannot afford to store up earthly things. Remember, they are passing away. Therefore let us focus not on that which we "don't have," but instead let us rather, **"fear Him who is able to destroy both soul and body in hell"** [Matt. 10:28].

If we believe we can avoid the FINAL ASSESSMENT that is coming, and take for granted the TIME God has granted us to prepare ourselves, we are sadly mistaken. Not one of us will be able to hide from God, no matter what we do. **"The Lord standing by the alter said, strike the doorposts, that the thresholds may shake, and break them on the heads of them all. I will slay the last of them with the sword. He who flees from them shall not get away, and he who escapes from them shall not be delivered. Though they dig into hell, from there I will take them; through they climb up to heaven, from there I will bring them down; and though they hide themselves on top of Carmel, from there I will search and take them; though they hide from my sight at the bottom of the sea, from there I will command the serpent, and it shall bite them; though they go into captivity before their enemies, from there I will command the sword, and it shall slay them. I will set My eyes on them for harm and not for good"** [Amos 9:1-4]. **"For surely I will command, and will sift the house of Israel among all nations, as grain is sifted in a sieve; yet not the smallest grain shall fall to the ground. All the sinners of my people shall die by the sword, who say the calamity shall not overtake us nor confront us"** [Amos 9:9-10].

It is clear that neither you nor I will be excused from bending our knees before the Lord. **"Whom He has appointed heir of all things, through whom also He made the worlds. Who being the brightness of His glory and the express image of His person, and upholding all things by the word of his power, when He had by Himself purged our sins, sat down at the right hand of the majesty on high, having become much better than the angels, as He as by inheritance obtained a more excellent name than they"** [Heb. 1:2-4].

Christene Bolte-Luthey

CHOOSE LIFE, NOT DEATH

(Be "Born Again")

Love bought victory over the grave
And took its sting away
That we might live eternally
Through faith in Christ today.

He will not force His love on us
We can but receive
Trusting to believe this truth
Decide what we believe?

Separate yourself from sin
It leads to death, not life.
Causing deep regret within
No peace but only strife.

By grace you're saved, through faith alone
This truth—is reality.
**Choose Life not death; be "born again,"
And Christ shall set you free.**

His arms are were open on the cross
And they are open still
Come, abide in Him and let,
His Spirit quench and fill.

Be not an empty shell my friend
Give to Him your soul
Fear not again the sting of death
For Christ shall make you whole.

Christene Luthey

**"Most assuredly, I say to you, unless one is born again,
He shall not see the kingdom of God"
[John 3:3]**

Christ Jesus is a portrait of God's astounding GRACE. He is that which is TRUE, RIGHT AND JUST. In Him we find salvation. In Him we receive sanctification. In Him we experience peace. He offers what this world by no means can ever hope to give. Without God's Holy Spirit dwelling our heart, our lives are empty. God is the discerner of our heart and is aware of those who come to Christ in faith. He knows whether or not we have honestly forsaken the world? He knows who will walk obediently to His word, and those who will take up His cross? He knows which hearts are submissive and who seek after His truth? **"All things were made by Him; and without Him was not anything made that was made" [John 1:3]**. Is there anything in this world that could be more important than knowing Christ who, **"cleanses us from all sin?" [1 John 1:7]** Through suffering and death He has said to those who trust Him, **"Lo, I am with you always, even unto the end of the world" [Matt. 28:20].** Therefore when we abide in Him we will truly know what it is to be rich! **"Thanks be to God, which gives us the victory though our Lord Jesus Christ" [1 Cor. 15:57].**

So now the question is: on what in life do we spend our time and effort? Is it to own a bigger house, or to make more money? Is it to achieve a higher position? Or is it to receive greater recognition? (Again, *DO NOT MISUNDERSTAND ME*), I am not saying there is anything wrong with these things. I am only saying that it would be wise for us to SET limitations. Material things must not and cannot be gained at GOD'S EXPENSE, and at the putting off of our loved ones. I pray that you and I will grow in understanding this subject that we may begin setting HEAVENLY GOALS that never pass away. Keeping in mind that God will one day appraise our goals, actions, intentions and beliefs.

If we question this, reflect on God's word, **"He is ordained of God to be the judge of the living and the dead" [Acts 10:42]. "He will judge the world in righteousness by that man whom He has ordained" [Acts 17:31]. "The word that I have spoken, the same will judge him in the last day" [John 12:48]. "Of that day and that hour knows no man, no not the angels which are in heaven, neither the Son, but the Father." [Mark 13:22]. "The end of all things is at hand" [1 Peter 4:7].** Let us never forget that God will not judge us by the WORLD'S standards. He judges by HIS OWN.

Let's consider for one moment—**time**. What are you and I doing with it? What are we accomplishing for the kingdom of God? Many of us may be gathering things that bring gratification, but are these things bringing glory to God? Are the people around us aware that we are a Christians? That is, IF you have received Christ? When was the last time we reached out to witness to someone about the love or grace of God? Have we given any thought to the eternal destination of our loved ones? What are our priorities? What are our goals in life?

If you've never really given any thought to these subjects, you may be feeling overwhelmed? Again, please don't be. That is not what I want from sharing this with you. These questions are only to help people revaluate their lives so that the time we have on this earth is not taken for granted. One of the greatest lessons I have learned is that, <u>there is but ONE account in which we need place your faith and trust</u>. That account, I hope you realize <u>is JESUS CHRIST</u>! Because friend, the world can't save us… The world doesn't care about you or I at all, but JESUS CHRIST DOES! We're told that He's coming again to judge the world and take with Him those who truly seek His face. **"The day of the Lord comes as a thief in the night, in which the heavens will pass away with a great noise, and the elements will melt with fervent heat; both the earth and the worlds that are in it will be burned up. Therefore, since all these things will be dissolved, what manor of persons ought you to be in holy conduct and godliness"** [2 Peter 3:10-11]?

Remember, if we refuse Christ's love, we'll ultimately stand before God without excuse. Because the Gospel of TRUTH has been heard but may have been rejected? That is why we must remember daily, our mortality. Remember friend that death is a reality. May we consider the latter end knowing that if we chose to live our life without God, we will die without Him also? In having made that decision, we would be banished from Him throughout eternity. <u>Yet, those of us who have chosen to RECEIVE Christ into our hearts will be received with open arms into the kingdom of God to exist for all time.</u>

LIFE OR DEATH

God sets before us LIFE and DEATH
Good and Evil too;
Choose blessing, not the curse I ask, and
Decide what you shall do…

C. Luthey

PLEASE don't think FOR ONE MOMENT that I am trying to be unkind or critical. REMEMBER, I am sharing with you the SOUL SEARCHING questions I have asked myself during the past fifteen years. I am giving out these things for the sincere reason that you might perhaps ponder these matters for yourself and judge <u>your own life and relationship with God</u>? Then, if you have not done so already, you might be inspired to make PEACE with Him through Christ Jesus? **Today**, after personally taking these things to heart, **<u>I don't fear standing before God</u>, because Jesus Christ as my personal Savior has bridged the gulf between God and myself. Today I experience God's <u>unending forgiveness and compassion toward me,</u>** (a poor miserable, wretched, sinner, saved by His awesome grace.) Perhaps in my testimony to you, you may have noticed the wondrous DIFFERENCE my personal relationship with Christ has made in my life? Like night and day, as His light entered my life, the fear of death vanished and my life has been forever changed. How I hope yours will too?

If you are or have been a Christian for some time, I pray you will be motivated to thankfully lift high your praises to God for the GRACE, love and mercy that has spared our soul from sin's condemnation? May these truths, which you may already know launch your heart into a deeper more precious relationship with the One who set your soul free!

ALL IS VANITY

The days of childhood innocence have long forsaken me
For surely I have truly learned, that ALL IS VANITY.

No longer do I stand deceived, of breath beyond tomorrow
Vain and foolish is the one, who knows not, TIME we borrow.

Life with every moment spent, entirely is lost
Empty and unfruitful lest, we esteem the cost

Of Christ who's sweet surrender, encountered death alone
Undertaking every sin, the world has ever known.

In vain are all our earthly days, if Christ is not our friend
Established only deep regret precedes that bitter end.

So flee from all in life that takes, your heart away from love

Envy, malice, lust, and hate, these come not from above.

Instead, show kindness toward all men
Be justified by grace,
Knowing ALL IS VANITY
Lest you've beheld Christ's face.

Christene Luthey

[Ecc. 1:2] "Vanity of vanities; all is vanity."

Vain and vanity are used in the Bible as follows: Entirely empty. Fruitless. Worthless. Absurdity. Futility. Nonsense. Believe dear friend, that the "things" of this world are empty substitutes for GOD! <u>All is vanity.</u> It's a lesson we must learn. The world holds only TEMPORARY things. We obtain—we lose. <u>NOTHING on earth will last forever</u>. One "season" we're children, the next we're adults. One "season" we live, and die in the next. All that is seen here is temporary. Just as the scripture says, **"Therefore we do not lose heart, even though our outward man is perishing, yet the inward man is being renewed day by day. For our light affliction, which is, but for a moment, is working for us a far more exceeding weight of glory. While we do not look at the things which are seen, but at the things which are not seen. For the things which are not seen are eternal" [2 Cor. 4:16-18]**.

Have you ever thought that perhaps we know disappointments in life mainly because we've allowed ourselves to become exceedingly secure in the "temporary things" of this world? We've read that everything here is but a "vapor." Recall the instance of the mirror? There is freedom and contentment in this priceless wisdom if we lay hold of it? Why? Because we cannot <u>lose</u> that which has been "temporary' from the beginning. Although it is difficult, we need to face the reality that everything is given a selected amount of time to exist. For example, people, places, thoughts, feelings, and things. If we would lay hold of this knowledge, perhaps we might spend more time with those we LOVE and less time trying to acquire possessions? We might also be less apt to take our time with loved ones for granted? I thank God for this precious truth. What is unseen is eternal!

Today are YOU and I content? Do we know perfect peace? Do we have unexplainable joy deep within us? Are there any who can answer <u>yes</u> to all of these questions? Indeed, there are! Perhaps that may surprise you? There are many who claim to be very content in all situations. Yet by the "world's standards," most these would not be considered "very wealthy" people. I know a few who declare they know perfect peace <u>because they've placed their trust in Christ.</u> These people understand that every hour is <u>borrowed. Tomorrow is hoped for, but not promised.</u>

These people have learned not to take life for granted. They express gratitude to God for reach and every day. These people have also received the glorious knowledge of Jesus into their heart, and have made Him Lord of their life. These people celebrate in the blessed assurance of the friendship they share with Him. Christ is their "rock" and foundation. **"For no other foundation can anyone lay than that which is laid, which is Jesus Christ" [1 Cor 3:11]. "Now therefore, you are no longer strangers and foreigners, but fellow citizens with the saints and members of the household of God, having built on the foundation of the apostles and prophets, Jesus Christ Himself being the chief cornerstone, in whom the whole building, being joined together, grown into a holy temple in the Lord, in whom you also are being built together for a habitation of God in the Spirit" [Eph. 19:22]. "For this reason I also suffer these things; nevertheless I am not ashamed, for I know whom I have believed and am persuaded that he is able to see what I have committed to Him until that day" [2 Tim. 1:12].**

In ending this chapter let me include that I believe our integrity is on the line. Let us ask ourselves what our character has to say about: our marriages, reputations, finances, morals, etc? Honestly, can we say today that we are walking in integrity before God? I ask because I sincerely believe that Satan is trying to rob us of our faithfulness and is using compromise to bring it about. We are told in God's word to be **"SALT" and "LIGHT."** (If we are followers of Jesus Christ), **"You are the salt of the earth; but if the salt loses its flavor, how shall it be seasoned? It is then good for nothing but to be thrown out and trampled under foot by men. You are the light of the world. A city that is set on a hill cannot be hidden. Nor do they light a lamp and put it under a basket, but on a lamp stand, and it gives light to all who are in the house. Let your light shine before men that they may see your good works and glorify your Father in heaven" [Matthew 5:13-16].**

If we are called to be **"salt"** and have lost our flavor, what good are we to Christ and God's kingdom? This is related again to being **LUKE WARM!** Friend, I don't want to be **"thrown out"** and away from God, do you? Then, what about the Bible saying we are to be "light." Are we in a similar way shining as a lamp for all to see? Or has our "Luke-warm" lifestyle caused us to become so weak in our confession that our Christian witness no longer is credible? Hopefully you and I will begin (if we haven't already) sorting out our lives and cleaning out everything that would make us **"lose our flavor"** as children of God? We must stand against compromise and get rid of anything that might lead to a "sloppy" Christian life. This is why we should know the will of God and be fervent about living it. As we attempt with glad hearts to do this, our "light" will shine before men, and the power of God will flow through our lives. Friend, we know light conquers darkness. Therefore let us not permit any sin in our lives that might obstruct or diminish our light. We have been given the liberty to decide what we'll do with the life God has given us. For that reason, may we with gracious hearts serve the One who has loved us so much?

The Bible says that very few people in the days ahead will follow Christ. I pray that you and I never become souls who go our OWN way? We are told in the Bible that only the **"elect"** will inherit the kingdom's riches by denying them selves to follow Christ. These obedient souls will have chosen to: serve as Christ served; love and Christ loved, and walk as Christ walked in agreement with His Father's will.

Eight
WHEN SHADOWS FALL

"See that you do not refuse Him who speaks. For if they did not escape who refused Him who spoke on earth, much more shall we not escape if we turn away from Him who speaks from heaven. Whose voice then shook the earth; but now He has promised, saying yet once more I shake not only the earth, but also heaven. Now this, yet once more indicates the removal of those things that are being shaken, as of things that are made, that the things which cannot be shaken may remain. Therefore since we are receiving a kingdom which cannot be shaken, let us have grace, by which we may serve God acceptably with reverence and godly fear. For our God is a consuming fire"[Hebrews 10:25-29].

No servant ever lived for God that has escaped the FIRE
Testing solely deep within, the heart and its desire.
This I know before I leave this "temporary" shell,
All intents and every deed will be examined well.

By God my Father who has called, according to His will
My life to be conformed to which, His purpose may fulfill.
Purging and removing all, that clouds His awesome grace
"Blessed are the pure in heart, for they shall see His face" [Matt. 5:8]

It's only though His cleansing fire, the soul is true refined
And blamelessness determined, within the Master's mind.
As innocence and purity, sincerity and love
Revealed for us the heart of God, who from His throne above,

Made obvious though Christ his Son, the <u>CORE of Life's true goal,</u>
<u>To walk within God's will and feel, His presence in your soul.</u>
                                                    -Christene Luthey

Christene Bolte-Luthey

YIELDING TO THE MASTER'S HAND

THEREFORE, I MUST TRUST IN CHRIST
YIELDING TO THE HEAT
THAT GOD MAY SANCTIFY MY HEART
MAKING FAITH COMPLETE….

C.L.

It is amazing to me—that in the quietness of my prayer time/devotion I can sense the love of God enveloping me. Enfolding me amidst the storms of life. One evening as I sat contemplating the "wilderness" I seemed to be in, I sensed the Lord's Holy Spirit softly whispering, **"Do not be discouraged..."** For a moment I remained quiet. Listening for His influence. Then again it came… *"By the things you endure…"* And I suddenly knew a *poem* was about to be written. Taking a pen in hand, I waited until words began to flow… *"I must ALLOW them,—That I may be sure…"* Sure about what? I did not know, until I had finished the poem.

GOD'S LESSON OF ENDURENCE

Do not be discouraged by the things you endure
I must allow them… That I may be sure…

That when you are "GROWN UP," Matured in your heart
You may go forward, fulfilling your part.

It is <u>not</u> what this world or men do to you
It is how you endure the trials you walk through…

It is how you endure the pain in your heart
It is how you endure the race from the start.

**It is how you endure LIFE with its "crosses"
Counting them all for ME, worthy losses…**

Christene Luthey

What did the Lord mean, WORTHY LOSSES…? It seemed that many trials followed my family and I after the tornado. First, came the horrendous storm... Then the uncertainty of our unborn baby's life... Then, we had to SURRENDER everything to the will of God...

This time it was "Dolly." A few years had passed and we by the grace of God had found another home. All seemed to be getting back to normal, until she came to me one afternoon complaining that "her throat hurt." I saw that the glands in her neck were swollen. Without delay we went to the doctor. Upon examining her, he suggested that she be admitted that moment to a hospital. Now this may not have been earth-shattering news, but I was very concerned. Throughout the years before kindergarten "Dolly" had previously suffered five allergic reactions to antibiotics. In fact they were so severe we had to rush her to the emergency room. Currently, the doctor was telling me that whatever was going on in her glands, would have to be taken care of by "intravenous injection."

My first emotion was fear. Knowing not what might happen. As Scott and I entered the hospital it was evident that we needed to pray. The only thing I could request was that God would grant the doctors wisdom. She required something to battle the infection making her ill. Scott and I placed her in God's hands and stayed beside her bed. That night as I sat beside her I took a piece of paper and wrote the following poems.

LITTLE ONE SO ILL

Your body warm with fever high, I feel your pain with every sigh
The morning hours will pass so slow, the fear I feel you could not know.
Your voice is weary when you speak, I watch you, as you lay so weak
For you are ill my child it's true, what can mama do for you?
My darling little one so ill, the hours together we will fill
Close at your side I'll surely stay, throughout the night and into day.
I have much to offer you, count on me to see you through
This, my love and everything, life through time may know and bring.
Praying at your side I'll keep, now close your eyes and go to sleep.
This sickness causing you to ache, God I trust to quickly take.

C. L.

Christene Bolte-Luthey

I MAY NOT HAVE TOMORROW

I may not have TOMORROW, to carry out God's plan
So I must strive to make TODAY, as precious as I can.

For I have come to realize, we live on "borrowed time,"
It is only by the grace of God, each "earthly" hour is mine.

I know not WHAT each passing day, or moment spent might bring
I've learned it's true, not to take for granted, ANYTHING.
Such as time because you see, it can't be bought or sold
Therefore being priceless, with value still untold.

For nothing in this world could mean as much to me as this
A loving smile a warm embrace, a soft or tender kiss.

From those have come the fondest times, I've known within my heart
Throughout my life these smallest things have played the greatest part.

Not the things that money bought, that some on earth may treasure
But those of which cannot be bought, mean more than one could measure.

So that is why I seek each chance to cherish every day
<u>I may not have tomorrow, but God gave me TODAY!</u>

Christene Luthey

    Amazingly, all went well! After receiving antibiotics for five days in the hospital, our precious little girl was well enough to go home. She had been diagnosed with "cat scratch fever." Little did we realize what danger a scratch could cause our "Dolly?" We learned while in the hospital that a little kitten she'd been playing with at a friend's house had scratched her.
    While leaving the hospital, I was handed a sheet of paper with a prescription on it to "have filled." There were five remaining days that she was to continue taking the medicine. However, when we arrived at the pharmacy we found to our dismay that of the FIVE bottles she was to take, only "TWO existed in the county were we lived." The two bottles existing were in the pharmacies of two hospitals in the city. The pharmacist told us,

When Shadows Fall: A Journey of Faith

"that these two bottles could be obtained, but the remaining THREE would have to be specially ordered."

"What are you telling me?" I said, "Why are there only two other bottles known in the county?" "Didn't they tell you?" He questioned, with an odd look on his face. "They quit manufacturing this medicine YEARS ago, because it's known to be dangerous!" I stood in shock. I couldn't believe my ears. "WHY is it so DANGEROUS?" I asked. "Well," he replied, "It was known to deplete white blood cells." **"She might possibly come out of this with Leukemia."**

Horror instantly flooded my mind! All of the sudden things made sense. Throughout the time she had been in the hospital, "Dolly" had received thirteen blood tests. It was clear at this moment why our little angel's wrists resembled pincushions. We had been told that when she'd "finished the prescription, to take her back for a final blood test." Suddenly I was furious! The doctors at the hospital had never given us this information. Standing there for a second Scott and I conversed about the fact that she'd been given this drug for five days. Now we were being told that we had to orally administer five additional bottles.

What would you have done in this situation? Standing there glancing at my little girl, I knew there were only two choices we could make. Either disintegrate under the weight of fear, or stand on the faith that we had PRAYED in the hospital. We had placed everything in God's hands before she'd been given the first dosage. I won't tell you that it was simple, but I decided, to continue giving her prescription. As we returned home with the medicine, it was apparent that we were going to have to SAY A LOT OF PRAYERS.. With each and every dose I prayed as I gave that medicine to our precious little girl. Yet no words could begin to express how long and difficult those five days were—for us all.

The enemy harassed my heart and mind with fear, anxiety, and anger during the course of each day. It seemed that Satan's cruelty never ceased, as he taunted, "WHAT IF?" But in faith, I tried not to pay attention to his wickedness, and determined in my mind to carry on trusting God. Satan continued mocking, "what will you do?" It wasn't easy, but I kept in mind that enemy was hoping I would break under the pressure of the situation. But I focused my trust on the hope that God could make her well. Still, the more Satan tempted me to worry, the HARDER I BEGAN TO PRAY! I prayed like I had never prayed before. I suppose you could say, **"without ceasing"** as the Bible tells us to do. "What if?" I thought. "What will I do?"

I will do the only thing I can do.... TRUST GOD, despite the consequences or the circumstances.

We continued giving the medicine until the five days had ended. It was time now to make the appointment for the final blood test. The only thing different this time, was that we were aware of what they were searching for. Again, I knew our faith was going to be tried. Waiting for the test results is never easy. This time, we had to consider the fear that our little girl might have—Leukemia? The contemplation of that sent chills throughout my entire body. Now is it not true that times like these will <u>determine WHETHER OR NOT we have "BUILT OUR LIVES ON THE ROCK OR ON SAND?"</u> It is as I have shared with you in this book. Laying a strong foundation is what eventually helped us not only ENDURE, but also prevail over life's uncertainties.

<u>At no other time do we realize how VITAL it is to build on Christ, than when TRAGEDY has beaten on our door</u>. Like the scripture says, **"Each one's work will be clear"** as to WHAT our foundation is built on. In the midst of these trials we find out that no amount of gold, money, savings, or stock would be able to grant us peace, or resolve the problem. Believe it or not, there ARE things that money CANNOT buy! One priceless and precious thing is the <u>PEACE OF GOD</u>. All I knew in the midst of this situation was that I urgently needed peace. I required it more than anything—the night BEFORE the final blood test. As I turned to God's word that evening for comfort, I came upon this blessed verse, **"Rejoice in the Lord always, again I will say, Rejoice! Let your gentleness be known to all men. The Lord is at hand. Be anxious for nothing, but in everything by prayer and supplication, with thanksgiving, let your requests be known to God; and the peace of God, which passes all understanding will guard your hearts and minds through Jesus Christ"** [Phil. 4:4-7].

NEEDING THE PEACE OF GOD

In each trial we've known, I wanted and needed more than anything, to experience the PEACE of God to see me through. Especially when the doubts and worries seemed to flood my heart and mind concerning the circumstance. In this instance although it was difficult, I **did** what God's word commanded me to—**rejoice**. Miraculously, I recognized that when I began rejoicing about the hope I had in Christ, I began feeling the peace of

God lifting me higher than my cares. Just as the scripture said, I began **"letting my requests be known."** As I prayed, comfort came to my heart and mind. Yes, throughout my prayers tears steadily flowed in constant streams to the ground, but as cried, I prayed. And as I prayed I humbly surrendered my little angel to the will of God. Surrendering those you love to God's will is not an easy thing to do, but when we are able, we will receive God's peace.

It was with this particular testing that God helped me understand in a wondrous way How Abraham (spoken of in the Bible) must have felt as he humbly obeyed God by faith. He was tested in a similar method to offer up his son. God told Abraham to take Isaac to the land of Moriah and offer him as a burnt offering on a mountain [Read **Gen. 22:1-18**]. It became clear to me how simple it is to <u>SAY</u> you trust God, and that we are living for him. Perhaps even that we are willing to serve Him? But the true proof of our faith becomes unmistakably apparent when we stand face to face with crisis.

Uncertainty was all we knew. What would the blood test reveal? Again, we were forced to decide whether or not our faith and trust in God was <u>**sincere.**</u> Was our surrender to God's will conditional or unconditional? Was it a deep an all-trusting surrender, or was it a surface type of submission? I knew in my heart that this was the question God was challenging me to answer. God sought to know whether we were with Him or not. What was my faith really worth in the middle of this tragedy? The question was— HOW were we going to weather THIS "storm?" Were we going to be battered and beaten by the horrible winds of fear and anxiety? Or were we going to rest in the loving arms of Jesus who speaks to the winds of pain and discouragement, "peace, be still?" Again, I want to say that the faith and trust in God is harder to lay hold of in the center of a storm. If it is that you have NEVER before learned how trust Him in life's small uncertainties.

On bent knees I prayed this prayer, "Dear Lord, I surrender my baby girl to YOU, knowing that she is a precious gift from heaven. I praise and thank you for entrusting her to my care, and I pray that you will have mercy upon us, and allow us to have more time together. Lord God in heaven let not these tests reveal that she has Leukemia, but rather I ask that you use this opportunity to glorify yourself in making her well. Protect her body from harm! I know that I can but seek your tender mercy, knowing all the while that in the end, YOUR WILL MUST BE DONE…"

As the hours passed long into the night, I remained on my knees before God in prayer. Strange is it not? How incredibly humble we can become when we are at God's mercy for something? As I prayed throughout the evening and into early morning hours, I could sense in my heart again, the Spirit of God whispering gently to me, "You have vowed to love me, trust me, serve and follow me, all the days of your life?" "I raise this question to you, will you continue to be true to MY WILL and maintain obedience in all these things—REGARDLESS of what tomorrow brings?"

As those words made their way though my mind I began to weep so loud that I woke Scott, who was sleeping in the bedroom upstairs. **"YES LORD,"** I answered, **"YOU KNOW THAT I WILL!"** Following that vow, I emotionally placed my little girl's life and health on God's spiritual alter (inspired by Abraham's faith), and surrendered her UNCONDITIONALLY to GOD'S WILL. As I did that, I "let go" of my fear believing that "Tomorrow, was in God's capable hands. So were the results and her future. With that finally settled in my heart and mind, I received the peace I needed—to sleep.

As the sun came up "Dolly" and I joined hands together and prayed before her appointment. At seven years of age this little angel had been blessed with faith that was strong. She had been a little trooper (learning trust in God of her own). So we agreed to whatever "God's will would be for her life." This, shared faith, in the end brought glory and praise to God when as our hearts overflowed with joy with the tests returning as "Normal." Pondering those difficult moments now, I can't help but get teary-eyed calling to mind the fear and uncertainty we felt. Knowing not how our lives might be changed forever had the tests not turned out "good." It is understandable that each and every one of us in one way or another is wondering WHAT "TOMORROW" WILL BRING, and what may result in our lives from TODAY.

FAITH COMES BY HEARING

"So faith comes by hearing, and hearing by the word of God" [Rom. 10:17]. What is it that YOU need faith for today? Know that whatever the sorrow, whatever the grief, pain or fear, God is ABLE to surround and sustain you. If you are not yet convinced of this by the trials I have shared, please permit me to tell you other things that I have learned regarding God's grace. He alone has seen my family and I through the course of the past fifteen years. In sharing these things, I pray that your heart and faith will be stirred or inspired? May you perhaps then reach out your hand and allow the Lord to take your hand by faith also? May you then feel His awesome presence in your soul and know that you need never be alone. No matter where you are or what life may bring your way, if you trust God and His promises He will faithfully see you through.

In **May of 1992** my heart was deeply grieved by the sudden death of Grandmother B. She was one of the dearest friends I've known. Very unexpectedly she had become deathly ill. In the early morning hours she was required to be taken to the hospital by ambulance. As life would have it, this day would hold the last memories I have of her. Which consisted of a brief and affectionate exchange we shared on the phone just minutes before she passed away. Thank God, our conversation ended with the expressions, "I love you" as they would be the last words we spoke to each other. Never again would I hear her voice. Not long after we spoke I learned that she had died of a "massive heart attack."

In stillness and silence I stood in the hospital waiting room. I can still remember the numbness I felt throughout my entire body as I heard the doctor state that she had "passed away." I will never forget the stir within me as the REALITY of DEATH surfaced again. There it was, reminding me of how extremely fragile and fortunate we all are, and how often we take it for granted. How many times we overlook the rare and precious blessings that God grants our lives? Vanished in the blink of an eye was the spirit of an important person in my life, whom I loved and adored more than words could express. She had been a friend that I could depend on to love me unconditionally. No matter what—she always was there for me! Those sorts of people simply don't come along every day. I couldn't begin to fathom how I was going to go on living without her. Now all I could do with my beloved grandmother was stand beside her lifeless body and say the Lord's Prayer. Thank God I knew that she had given her heart to Jesus. Because of this, I'll see her again in glory!

As days passed into months, I learned that time alone does not heal a broken heart. It was then that I learned, that much more than time is needed to heal. We need God's tender touch to see us though moments like these in our lives. This was a dreadful "season" for me. There seemed to be no answers to the questions in my mind. It was hard to understand the biggest question of all—WHY? As the days went on, through faith alone I was able to endure those deep and grief filled "valleys." I tell you this because HEALING in my life has only come when I placed my faith in God and trusted Christ Jesus. My grandmother's death was one of the greatest sorrows I have ever known. Yet In the midst of my sorrow I began writing, and poems like this began filling notebook after notebook.

Christene Bolte-Luthey

MEET HIM AT THE CROSSROADS

When you're feeling tempted, lonely in despair
Meet Him at the crossroads He is waiting there.
When the race you're running, never seems to end
Meet Him at the crossroads there you'll find a friend.
When trials flood your heart and mind, as waves upon the sea
Meet Him at he crossroads that is where he'll be.
When in grief you're fainting fast, with not the strength to stand,
Meet Him at the crossroads He will take your hand.
When you feel that no one cares, in pain you're all alone
Meet Him at the crossroads He will lead you home!

C. Luthey

Throughout the following months I would lean upon my heavenly Father for comfort and strength. Although this valley of grief and despair seemed bottomless and broad at times, it soon became a journey where the Lord and I would learn many things about each other. With each and every step we took together, I learned how to abide and trust in Him.

THE VALLEY OF DESPAIR

Dearest Heavenly Father, I come to you in prayer
Walk with me through this valley, of deep and dark despair.
You know my heart, you know my thoughts,
My worries and my fears,
I cast before you humbly these fast and flowing tears.
Unsettled, I am feeling Lord, control I've truly lost
This valley seems to torture me, while in it I am tossed.
I know YOU'VE walked this valley,
So therefore guide my way,
Please grant me strength to journey on
Throughout each passing day.
Until I see this valley end,
Your grace I trust to be
Sufficient; in my weakest hour
As you have promised me.

Christene Luthey

ALL TRIALS have the potential with God to make us stronger. The question is whether or not we will permit them to? This priceless truth I learned as I took God's hand and began to walk with Him though my sorrow. In doing this I also became aware of the blessings that come into view within our hardships. Poems like the few you've just read began to pour out of my grieving heart and onto the pages of my journal. Sheet after was being filled. I wrote constantly about my heartache and love God so mercifully had granted my soul. To my astonishment much of my writing concerning death, grief, sorrow and pain, God would later use to reveal to me the GIFT He had given. It was at this time I came to realize that the Lord might possibly use me to minister to others the power of His Love.

My Grandmother B. went to be with the Lord in His kingdom in May of 1992. By the grace of God I had my first volume of poems published in November of that same year. I could hardly believe God had used the death of my grandmother to inspire me to put in writing many poems that are being read by people in hospitals, prisons, nursing homes, and other organizations. Fortunately, God made use of my grandmother's death to help develop my faith. Only He could have known how much I would have need of it as the days went on.

The year 1993 began reasonably peaceful. Yet within a few short months, beginning with **May**, everything was taking terrible turn for the worst. As life would have it, on the first anniversary of my Grandmother's death, my DAD who was also still grieving the death of his mother (my Grandmother B.) had an accident in his "wood shop." In his spare time he loved to make furniture. This particular day was making an oak picture frame. While working with his table saw he severely cut his hand. Damaging his hand by cutting four of his fingers off. Fortunately he remained conscious and was able to call an ambulance. In talking to the doctors we realized how blessed he was that God had kept him from "passing out." Doctors stated that if he had, he would have bled to death within a matter of minutes.

As the days passed our thoughts were focused on him having his fingers reattached, and regaining the use of his hand. Again, much prayer was needed, however we were asking God for help to manage his pain and to fight off infection. Fortunately, as the grace of God would have it, the month came to a close and he had recovered extremely well.

JUNE 1993 also ushered in a multitude of heart rendering struggles for our family. Just when it seemed as though we were at the peak of celebrating the victory of dad's trial, tragedy like a sledgehammer struck again! Just two weeks into the month, my MOTHER found a "lump" in her breast and was scheduled for surgery. No time was wasted in doing a biopsy. She was diagnosed with breast cancer. There was nothing we could do. I thought this news would destroy my dad, and the thought that she must endure a mastectomy brought horrendous tension to our family.

I will never forget the heaviness of this news, nor the reports, anguish, or terror of it all. Everywhere I turned the reality of our mortality was there. Reminding me of how short and precious life truly is. I couldn't stop thinking about how carelessly we take it for granted. All of the sudden the simplest things in life mean the world to you. The table was now turned. My mother was being prepared for surgery. Now HER life and future were on the line and I was forced to ponder losing her.

I wrestled again with emotions of worry and fear throughout the time of her surgery. I am unable with words to describe the anxiety of that day. No one can begin to identify the chaos a family experiences in a situation such as this, unless you have "been there" yourself? How people survive without Christ in moments like this I cannot understand? It was Christ alone who kept the hearts of my family from being overwhelmed.

All I knew was that God had been with me amidst every trial. Therefore I was going to count on Him again to sustain the hearts and minds of my family. He had promised in His word that He would never leave nor forsake me, and I trusted that He wouldn't. Praying constantly each new day, I surrendered my fears. I knew that this was a battle He alone could win. Again, I placed a life on God's spiritual alter. This time, it was my mother. Thank God I was able to recall the times I had done it before, and gained hope from God's faithfulness. This was the only thing I could do that I knew—would offer me peace. Days seemed to lag on and mom finally received the results of her biopsy. She was told it was a "fast growing cancer," and "needed to begin chemotherapy immediately." To the glory of God, she not only began her six months of treatment, she stepped out in faith to open her own florist shop.

Later in the month of June, I received a phone call. It was my dad tensely informing me that my grandfather had just "passed away." I was absolutely lost for words. Just one year after my grandmother' death, my grandfather also was "gone." Had the Lord not been close to our hearts I am certain we would not have been able to withstand the waves of grief.

JULY 1993 was no less stressful. At some point while mom was undergoing her surgery and chemotherapy treatments, she become deathly ill. Tests revealed she had a STAPHE infection. No day ever seemed to pass without something going wrong. Each hour felt as though it held its own crisis. Yet, I recall writing this prayer for my mother, which comforted me. As you read the following poem I pray it will encourage you? Perhaps you're experiencing something causing you to feel as though there's no hope? Rest assured friend, God knows your trials.

WHATEVER LIFE MAY BRING

Lord, I have known great pain and grief, but this is like no other
To contemplate my precious Lord, the thought of losing my Mother?
I pray for her the courage Lord whatever comes her way
And grace to face each trial Lord, which rises through the day.
Hold tight her spirit in your hand and help her to be strong
Comfort her with your sweet peace that she may carry on.
I know not what to pray or ask, but to trust in YOU
Knowing that whatever comes you will see us through.
Let healing enter in her soul, her body, heart and mind
Lay your hands upon her Lord that health she soon will find.
You are the one who heals the sick, the hurting and the poor
Give to us that healing Lord, that we may reach that shore.
**I can but ask in Faith dear Lord, still knowing you know best
To trust you till tomorrow comes, shall be our hardest test.**
Love us Father grant us hope, though days are hard to bear
Surround us in your tender grace please keep us from despair.
Spread your wings around us Lord, enfold us with your love
Give us sweet assurance, that you hear us there above.
Thank heaven YOU are on the throne, YOU are our victory
**WHATEVER LIFE MAY BRING OUR WAY
LET THAT OUR COMFORT BE.**

Christene Luthey

ONLY FOR A TIME

As I sat alone weeping at the cemetery where both of my grandparents were laid, I began thinking HOW FORTUNATE I was to still have both of my mother's parents. I'd still be able to spend time with them while I was grieving the two I'd just lost. It seemed so hard to divide the loneliness I was feeling. God had called them both "home" so quickly. I barely had come to terms with losing one, and the other was gone also. I will never forget standing there staring at their grave stones, still adorned with fresh flowers. When a vehicle drove slowly by on the paved road behind me. As I turned around to see whom it was getting out and walking toward me, I saw that it was my Grandma K. (Mom's mother).

Gradually she made her way toward me, and gently placed her arm around my shoulders. Striving to remain calm and compassionate she said in a angelic tone, "Honey, remember that we're only here for a little while—then we pass away." "Come." She said, taking me by the hand. "Walk with me a minute." To this day I do not know WHY she arrived at the cemetery, but I do recall praying and asking God if SOMEONE, (anyone) would come along that could UNDERSTAND the awful pain I was feeling inside.

Looking back I believe in my heart that GOD in His infinite wisdom and tender mercy must have provoked her to drive there that afternoon, because she seemed to comprehend very well the sadness in my soul. In fact as we walked slowly she led me to a large heart shaped "headstone" that was to mark HER and my **Grandfather's** graves. As we stood together looking intently at it, she said, "You see sweetheart, this is were Grandpa and I will be buried when it's <u>OUR</u> TIME TO GO."

Holding her hand securely, and tearfully gazing at THEIR names carved in stone, I cried harder still. I didn't want to think about the thought of THEM being gone, let alone ponder it (as it appeared she was). I couldn't conceal my sorrow or the grief that had come to life in the moment. It began spilling out of me like water rushing through floodgates. There I was sobbing louder still. For a while we just stood there embracing each other saying nothing. I am to this day astounded at the total peace and contentment my grandmother displayed. As she tried her best to prepare me for the time when **she** would be "called away."

"Oh gram," I said, wiping the tears from my face, "Let's NOT THINK ABOUT THAT <u>NOW</u>; you and grandpa are going to be around for a long time!" To my surprise she said nothing. Instead she smiled and adoringly embraced me, as we walked back toward our vehicles.

CONSTANTLY AND FAITHFULLY

<u>July,</u> just three days after my mother had been admitted to treat the Staphe infection, I heard an ambulance dispatched to my grandparent's home. Nervous and uneasy I hung onto every word listening to the

paramedics stating they "had a male patient—in cardiac arrest." "Oh, God!" "PLEASE TELL ME IT'S NOT TRUE! " I prayed. Knowing deep in my heart it was GRANDPA. Within a few minutes I found it was true. Upon arrival at the hospital, **another** Grandfather had "passed." He also had swiftly been called away. Such is God's will.

I couldn't believe this was happening. My dad was working out of town and wasn't going to be home until late that evening. "Lord," I asked, "How do you expect me to go into the hospital, and tell mom she just "lost" **HER** father?" I was horrified at the idea. Her condition was serious, and my concern was how this would affect her? I knew I couldn't allow the day to pass without her knowing. How could she ever forgive me for not telling her? How was she going to endure this grief?

It was unquestionably obvious that each and every hour of our lives are <u>uncertain</u>. No one in my family would ever argue that truth! Life, surely was being PROVEN just as the Bible says, that our, **"life is but a vapor."** These circumstances were demonstrating beyond a shadow of a doubt <u>that not one of us may have TOMORROW</u>. Still I pondered, WHY is it that so many of us take each day for granted?

Time followed suit bringing still more heartache, grief and pain. It was as though we were caught in a terrible dream that persistently went in circles. Each new rotation it seemed, we were saying "farewell" to someone we loved. My heart was extremely grieved and with the deaths of my two beloved grandfathers. They were a couple of the most precious men I've known. They'd both been huge blessings to our family. I couldn't imagine life without either of them.

I couldn't escape the words I'd said to my grandmother that "they would be around for a long time." How sadly mistaken I'd been. Returning to the cemetery only<u> month later</u> to stand looking at the heart shaped gravestone at my grandfather's funeral. My words had ironically come back to me as I stood embracing grandma. There we both stood weeping again at the place she had attempted to prepare my heart—for that moment. How absolutely terrible I felt. The beautiful life they had shared as husband and wife for 62 years—was over. It was time to say farewell to her beloved "blue eyed" sweetheart, who'd been the father of their six children. What a testimony I pondered. What an AWESOME portrait of life!

Thank God for Grandma, I thought. She had been such a comfort and inspiration to me throughout the months of May, June and July. Perhaps, *August* would be different? I could only hope? Well, hoping doesn't always make things so. In **AUGUST 1993, Grandma K.** also experienced **a severe**

heart attack, but she didn't pass away as quickly as the others. She instead endured a hard and trying week in the hospital, before she went to her "mansion" in glory. Losing her, the last of my four wonderful grandparents was devastating.

Who would have imagined so much could happen in such a short time? Who could have stopped the pain or eased our sorrow? Who could have granted us peace or given us hope? Who could have kept us from falling apart in the midst of this dreadful nightmare? The answer to all these questions are: **Our Lord Jesus Christ**! Friend, He not only hid us under His wing and sustained us throughout our grief filled days, He also faithfully brought my mother through the deaths of her parents and brought healing to her body.

Do I after all of this, I still believe God exists? Do I trust and believe that He was with us through it all? Do I still feel the same about Him after all we've suffered through? My answer to every one of those questions is, ABSOLUTELY! WITHOUT A DOUBT!! Why, you may ask? Because friend, I have felt His sweet spirit breathe expressions of peace to my soul. His precious words will never be forgotten nor compared to anything else. Like a fresh summer rain that has quenched a thirsting ground, Jesus time after time has converted my deepest despair to HOPE. Even amidst the most seemingly hopeless situations! Christ Jesus has granted me the courage and strength not only to continue on, He also supplied me with the grace needed to PRAISE Him in spite of all sorrow. **"Thanks be to God, who gives us the victory through our Lord Jesus Christ. Therefore beloved brethren, be steadfast, immovable, always abounding in the work of the Lord, knowing that your labor is not in vain in the Lord" [1 Cor. 15:57-58].**

> Do not search this world my friends for peace in your despair
> For it is evident you'll see it's only found in prayer
>
> We shall never comprehend the love of God it's true
> For there is nothing we could know or dare compare it to.
>
> And yet I've found in precious ways He gives to us his hand
> Often far beyond the mind could reach to understand.

Christene Luthey

CONSTANTLY AND TENDERLY

(Tending All Your Care)

I know you cannot see Me, but know that I am there
Constantly and faithfully tending all your care.
Submit your heart and mind today, call on Me for peace
I am more than able child, to cause your fears to cease.
Am I not the faithful one, who sets the captives free?
Did I not on water walk? And part the waves and sea?
Did I not stretch out my hand, to heal the sick and lame?
Remember child, remember, I am still the same!
Yes, I am still the same, it's true, and my power shall not fail
To lift you high above the storm, with grace you shall prevail.
Lift your cares up to me that I may draw you near
Closer still and you will see my love shall conquer fear.
Trust, please trust my tiny one, and give to me your hand
You need only trust in me, though you don't understand.
Fret not my child the knowing WHY, though trials may come your way
Lean upon my promises, to bring you though each day.
The hardest task you shall endure is trusting in my power
And resting in my grace for thee throughout your darkest hour.
I am the Shepherd do not fear, no trial shall conquer thee
I am the great deliverer, let that thy comfort be.
Yes constantly and faithfully tending all your care
Although you cannot see me, believe that I am there.

ChristeneLuthey

Remember in whatever you are going through,
That JESUS can grant strength to hold back fear,
For He has conquered the greatest of all fears: DEATH…

OUR BLESSED HOPE

Because I trust that Jesus lives, I know that I will too
Where there is FAITH, there's always HOPE, enough to see us through.
"Even though he dies," Christ said,

Christene Bolte-Luthey

"If you believe in Me," you'll "live for I am life" he said,
"Through all eternity."
"I am the resurrection." "I give eternal life."
"They shall never perish." "I bear the yoke of strife."
It's not "goodbye" that we shall say
Instead a sweet, "so long,"
Trusting "death was swallowed in," victory's joyous song.

Christene Luthey

A FAITHFUL FRIEND

    In some of the trials I've shared with you, I've felt like a helpless lamb lost in the wilderness. Perhaps you have too? Haven't we all wandered? Haven't we all strayed? Haven't we all felt alone or left behind in this world? Many trials in life leave us trembling and frightened. Many "valleys" seem deep, dark and deserted don't they? More times than I care to admit, I've felt misunderstood. Have you? Haven't we all known the effects of bitterness, and resentment? Throughout life we all experience various trials, and a wide range of emotions don't we? Of course we do!

    We experience voids in our lives that sometimes our dearest loved ones can't fill. There are moments that even the most precious friends we know fail to understand. Yet, there is ONE who <u>can</u> fathom <u>at all times</u> the depth of our being and <u>understands</u> each and <u>every feeling and emotion</u>. His name is JESUS!

JESUS

He has been a faithful friend,
Holding me close through the night
Rocking me gently in the palm of his hand
Until through the darkness came light.

He has NEVER abandoned, nor left me alone
Before I can tell Him, my troubles He's known.

Yet amidst all I have done, throughout the years
He has shown me much mercy and dried all my tears.

So I want you to know Him just as I do.
That you may know then—perfect peace
That the voids deep within that are causing you strife
May be filled with His grace—and cease.

Christene Luthey

A FRIEND IN THE FIRE

If no one else within this world
Could hear my desperate cry
Would you be there? I want to know,
"Oh Yes," Christ said, "I'd die."
I came to bear your burdens
I took the time to pray
Yes, I care sincerely; I gave my life to say,
When no one else within this world
Can hear your desperate plea
Will I be there you want to know?
Yes, you can count on me.
I'll stand beside you in the fire
Yes, unafraid, I'll burn
Despite the raging fires of life
I will <u>never</u> turn…

When the Judgment day arrives
And I stand face to face
With God who searches every heart
WHO shall take my place?
And bear the wrath of God for me
And every grim desire?
JESUS CHRIST, my Lord and King
A friend to share the fire.

Christene Luthey

Jesus said, **"These things I have spoken to you, that in Me you may have peace. In the world you will have tribulation; but be of good cheer, I have overcome the world" [John 16:33].** Friend, whatever "fire" or "valley" you are walking through today, you don't have to feel alone in bearing it. Accept as true that <u>God knows what you are going though.</u> Have faith that <u>He has a purpose and plan to accomplish in your life.</u> <u>Simply trust Him.</u> Do not despair. Our heavenly Father is attentive to everything that happens to us. Even though we may be feeling defeated, destroyed, discouraged, or disheartened, we have God's promise that He'll never leave or abandon us. On the contrary, the Lord will do whatever it takes to see that we are in His perfect will.

<u>The problems you and I are facing don't have to destroy our lives</u>. The Bible says, **"all things will work together for good to those who love God and are called according to His purpose" [Romans 8:28].** Do not be afraid of "shackles" which give the impression that we are bound. Christ Jesus died on the cross to free us from things that bind our heart and mind. Think of trials as the Lord's temporary "pruning." It will shape our character to be more Christ like. Then we will produce "fruit" that is of good use to God and His kingdom.

Friend, whatever trial you're facing, if you take your Bible and begin meditating on God's word, you will find strength, hope and peace. There, God will reveal Himself. Within those wonderful moments you shall increase blessed insights that release answers to the questions you've held in your heart. Some questions that before then has seemed hidden? By faith today I encourage you to call on God for assistance. Even if you're angry with Him, His shoulders are big enough. He loves you, and He knows your pain. This very moment He is anxiously longing for the second you give Him your heart. Keep in mind that our troubles <u>are not meaningless</u> if we allow them with God's "pruning" to free us of impurities and assist in creating the character of Christ. Trust that the same Grace, <u>that saw Jesus Christ through a horrible death on a cross,</u> is <u>available to YOU this very minute</u>. God's word says, **"So I say to you, ask and it will be given to you; seek, and you will find; knock and it will be opened. For everyone who asks receives, and he who seeks finds, and to him who knocks it will be opened" [Luke 11:9-10]. "But let him ask in faith, with no doubting, for he who doubts is like a wave of the sea driven and tossed by the wind" [James 1:6].**

"My brethren, count it all joy when you fall into various trials, knowing that the testing of your faith produces patience. But let patience have its perfect work, that you may be perfect and complete, lacking nothing. If any of you lacks wisdom, let him ask of God, who gives to all liberally and without reproach, and it will be given to him" [James 1:2-5]. Let's take this scripture into our heart that it may be of encouraging and offer wisdom. We KNOW that the testing of our faith will produce <u>patience.</u> Patience in turn will make us complete.

THE HUMBLING STONE

It's hard when on our face we fall and find a HUMBLING stone
Lodged between our heart and mind, then sorrow deep is known.
How tragic is REALITY, when from behind it falls
And brings a loud voice echoing, "YOUR PRIDE" has made these walls.
Then shocked, we sit there wondering, just how we got "this way?"
For little did we realize, the changes day to day?
How cruel the vision of our self, when we TRULY see,
The evil we've created with, the haughtiness of "ME."
How foolish and how vain we are, till we see "pride" as SIN
And we with "pruning" cleanse ourselves, and purify within!

C. Luthey

"**Pride goes before destruction, and a haughty spirit before a fall. Better to be of a humble spirit with the lowly, than to divide the spoil with the proud**" [Prov. 16:18-19].

"**For all that is in the world—the lust of the flesh, the lust of the eyes, and the pride of life—is not of the Father but is of the world**" [1 John 2:16].

WHEN SHADOWS FALL

"**May the Father of all mercies... Comfort us in all our tribulations, that we may be able to comfort them which are in any trouble**" [2 Cor. 1:3-4]. Perhaps you are in a crisis today? <u>I am also</u>. I don't know what you are going through, it may be the loss of a job; the death of a family member, having been told you are ill or someone you love is hurting? These are just a few of the limitless examples that can unexpectedly impact, overwhelm, or immobilize our lives. Any loss or crisis may cause dreadful stress, making us suffer feelings of panic, dread or defeat.

<u>CRISIS IN MY LIFE has NOT ENDED.</u> On the contrary, we have recently known several circumstances that have unquestionably tested our faith and Christian endurance. Between 1993 and now (2001), our lives have known a journey of constant "valley's," "shadows," and "fire." Each of

which have attempted to stop our obedience to God, hinder our trust in Christ, and evaluate our Christian testimony. Before going to Chapter Nine, I'd like to share some <u>recent</u> "tests" of faith. I hope you don't mind? I pray that in bringing you <u>up to date</u>, it will help <u>CONFIRM</u> in your heart that <u>I'm NOT merely "talking" about what I have shared</u>. As we know that "talk; is cheap."

CRISIS AND LOSS

<u>Many things have happened</u> that have affected our family since my grandparents died etc. We have bid "farewell" to a great number of beloved family and friends. Who were dreadfully diagnosed with various illnesses and have gone <u>to be with the Lord</u>. One cherished person for instance in **March of 1999** was my husband <u>Scott's dad, who was diagnosed with esophagus cancer</u>. He suffered terribly the ailing distresses of that horrible disease and its handling before he was mercifully called "home" to live with Jesus.

Again, we had looked at life, and realized that many of us take our health for granted. This dear man whom I adored as my own dad, had just <u>one year previously suffered a severe heart attack</u> that nearly ended his life. He had to undergo five-way by-pass surgery, but came through it well. He had overcome that physical trial and was looking forward to an early "disability" retirement. Suddenly he began to notice he was having difficulty swallowing food. Examinations revealed he had cancer. He was told <u>"he had two months to live; possibly six, if he opted to endure chemotherapy.</u> With much thought he choose to endure the treatments, which prolonged his life—six months.

Then, in **May of 1999** a <u>DRUNK DRIVER hit Scott.</u> This thoughtless person who determined to "drink and drive" under the influence of alcohol, <u>crashed into the vehicle Scott was sitting in</u>. <u>The collision ended up completely "totaling" four vehicles.</u> Miraculously, by the grace and mercy of God, no one was killed, although <u>eleven people</u> (several children) were taken to the emergency room. Scott experienced severe head, neck, and back trauma that have made him unable to work ever since that afternoon. At this present time he has had to suffer and endure "two of three back surgeries" that are planned, which doctors hope will alleviate his continuous discomfort.

This testing was very tough for me because it brought with it anger, resentment and antipathy. Catastrophes such as this we all know could completely be avoided if people did not choose to sin by inebriating themselves and drive intoxicated. Since this accident, Scott is extremely restricted in what he can physically do. Our lives previous to the accident would never again be the same. Now, Scott begins each day struggling with the disheartening emotions that accompany his not being physically able to be the sole provider for our family. Now, nearly two years later, he has to bear pain throughout his body. Today he is not able to enjoy many of the "day by day pleasures" he once did, with our children, family or friends.

Since we are presently in the middle of this "valley" you may correctly sense that even as I write, I fight back emotions of bitterness and anger that are directed toward the person <u>whom brought this misery to our family?</u> We all know this tragedy was unjust and totally avoidable. Yet we also know that Satan would delight in having us wallow in a pond of "self pity." Therefore we have placed our faith in Christ to see us through, and trust God's grace to resist Satan's enticement to "hate" this individual. If we do not abide in Christ we would plummet into utter disobedience, which would give the Devil a strong and powerful grip on our lives. Therefore we must daily surrender this "battle" to the Lord.

In **April of 2000,** the greatest of all trials we had experienced hit our home. The frightful nightmare started with a routine physical exam for our fourteen-year-old son Shane. He was required to have a physical for the fire department, so he could participate as a "Junior Fire Fighter." While the doctor was examining the area around Shane's neck, he discovered an exceptionally large gland in his throat. He stated that Shane should immediately receive a "C.T. Scan." This Doctor being a personal friend of Scott's and mine explained that he was "pretty concerned" and asked his nurse to "schedule an appointment."

The appointment was made without delay and the C.T. Scan was completed. We had not waited two days following that test, when we received a phone call notifying us that <u>"they were reasonably certain that the neck mass was some sort of **LYMPHOMA.**"</u> We then were requested to meet with another doctor almost immediately. There a biopsy could be attained to conclude, "Exactly what form of **CANCER** it was." Diagnosis from the biopsy revealed that <u>Shane had "**Hodgkin's Lymphoma.**"</u>

After a day or two of suffering with broken heartedness and intense contemplation we were bound for Children's Hospital in Pittsburgh Pennsylvania. As we began probing for answers and clarification to this shocking news, Shane began undergoing a sequence of tests and procedures. These brought about the awareness that he was "in the third of four stages."

The cancer was not only inside the lymph glands in his neck; it was also in his spleen. Therefore, as of April of 2000 to this present time we have been persistently traveling back and forth to Children's hospital. There Shane has courageously endured a six-month course of chemo therapy and twelve radiation treatments to his spleen and neck.

Currently although we know that this battle for Shane's health will be an ongoing TEST OF FAITH, we have settled in our minds to optimistically trust God. Despite life's worries and although Shane's future be unknown we are appreciatively praising and thanking God our Heavenly Father, for faithfully and steadfastly holding our precious son and us in the palm of His hand. Believe dear friend, that just as I have repetitively told you throughout these pages, YOU and I <u>ARE NEVER ALONE.</u>

YOU'RE NOT ALONE

Everyone at one time or another you see
Is frightened of something believe and trust me,
And it's not always easy to take terror in stride
I too have known fear, and have at times cried.
I've been in your shoes and I know how you feel
I discern that your doubts are perfectly real.
But today let me share a secret with you
It has helped in my life and it might help you too?
The secret is simple believe me and yet
It's something you cannot and should not forget
That wherever you are and whatever you do
The good Lord above is walking with you.
So whenever a tragedy enters your life
Bringing worries, or tears, maybes and strife,
Stay calm dear friend, consider and say,
I know this will pass and will all be okay.
For it's only with time and years we will see
That memories stay, but the fears will go free.
Just trust in these words and believe I have known
It will help you to KNOW, that <u>YOU'RE NEVER ALONE!</u>

Christene Luthey

I am here to tell you that Jesus Christ our precious LORD and SAVIOR has been at the forefront of this battle and has most assuredly been our "friend in the fire." Each and every step we have walked through this deep, dark, and devastating "valley" **JESUS CHRIST HAS CARRIED US**. With the prayers of our family and friends we shall carry on trusting and believing for Shane's health and total healing in the promises of God.

NOTE: *Thoughts, poems and prayers related to Shane's circumstance I hope to soon share with you in another book I have written from the months of entries and passages I kept in my journal. These go into greater detail regarding his struggles and ours throughout the course of his battle with Cancer.*

Why am I sharing all of these things with you? FOR PITY, <u>Absolutely NOT</u>! I want only to prove to you that amidst ALL that happens in our lives, both good and bad, **God can use every experience we know as an opportunity for us to grow in character and come to know Him on a deeper and more personal level.** I say this because I HAVE experienced crisis in life, but despair and despondence do not have to be the end result of our adversities. Trust me when I say, CHRIST JESUS is a faithful, loving, compassionate friend you and I can count on to see us through WHATEVER situation or circumstance we know.

Although this has been a time of shock and uncertainty for all of us, we know that "it will pass" and we will gradually, regain our strength and bearing so that we may one day encourage others who are struggling with a similar situation. Friend, each day we have sincerely tried with the grace of God to **"walk by faith and not by sight"** with the Lord. Striving to fulfill the call God has placed on each of our lives. This I pray you see can be achieved when we learn from <u>our suffering</u>: compassion, empathy, and sympathy through the trials WE have endured?

THESE TIMES WILL MAKE YOU STRONG

Though days may find you weak and blue, from struggling on your way
Throughout the hours that you must face, in pain from day to day,
Turn to one another when our hopes are fading fast
Together we can both survive, these feelings while they last.
Although we can't perceive it NOW, these trials will be it's true
A block in which we build upon to last our whole life through.
So dry your weary tears my friend, and trust that all will be,
Appropriate, in due time, have faith and you will see!

C. Luthey

Christene Bolte-Luthey

* * * * * * * * *

TRIALS TEACH COMPASSION

Astonishing are the memories, of tests throughout our life
Pondering the valley's deep that come with trial and strife,
Adversities of yesterday, remain although they're years away,
Surmising be it rain or shine, most bruises heal when given time.

Presuming not they'll last forever, Hope is found in each endeavor,
While we strive to best endure, restless seas to reach the shore.
So clear from in those darkened places, Light befalls the gloomy places
And wounds I thought would never heal, taught me how to think and feel.

I've seen and learned so much this way, being "tried" from day to day.
ENDURANCE came through empathy, when problems sought to weaken me.
Trials in life, we can't escape, but character they mold and shape.
Difficulties, all have known, from them you're "blessed" if you have grown.

Then looking at another's pain, we find our suffering not in vain
Then reaching for another's hand, we can truly understand.
And rightly so, they've made me see, some trials in life were meant to be.
Then in another's grief it's true, compassion wells inside of YOU.

Christene Luthey

"These things I have spoken to you, that in me you may have peace. In the world you will have tribulation; but be of good cheer, I have overcome the world" [John 16:33].

WHEN SUFFERING COMES

Dear friend, I want you to know that whatever "SHADOW" has fallen on your life, you need not feel alone in bearing it. Believe with your heart that God knows what you are going through, and trust that He has a purpose and plan to be accomplished in YOUR life. Do not despair. Your heavenly Father is aware of everything that happens to you. Today you may be feeling defeated? Destroyed? Discouraged? Disheartened? Friend, have faith in God's promises that he will never abandon you, because He loves you SO much. Whatever the problem you may be facing today, know that it does not have to destroy you or your life. The Bible says **"all things will work together for good to those who love God and are called according to His purpose" [Rom. 8:28].**

Recall the "inquiry sheets" I spoke of in the *Introduction* section of the book? Throughout the next several pages you will find a few of them. These are sheets I made up using the notes I'VE kept in MY JOURNAL throughout "trials" I've known. The questions are plain yet I've seen how VALUABLE they can be, when USED to help sort out things in your mind. When tragedy strikes, our world is turned upside down. SOMETHING has to get us on track and help us regain our composure. I hope a few of these questions help you do just that! They have been very helpful to me. Log dates and times, you may want to "come back" to it every now and then? One big way these pages were beneficial to me was that: throughout the time I spent pondering and answering these questions, my mind was strictly FOCUSED on that particular issue and NOT USELESSLY DRIFTING with the clouds of fear and sadness that attempted to threaten my judgment. Don't be afraid to write what your heart is feeling, even if you cry doing it? **[Psalm 56:8]** says, **"You number my wanderings; Put my tears in your bottle; Are they not in your book? When I cry out to you?"** *I've given some examples of my entries when we learned of Shane's illness.* I truly pray this helps you?

[1.] What "shadow" or "shadows" have fallen on your life?

Example: My precious 14 year old son was just diagnosed with CANCER… etc.

_____
_____
_____
_____
_____
_____
_____
_____

Christene Bolte-Luthey

When Shadows Fall: A Journey of Faith

[2.] What feelings or emotions are flooding your heart & mind?

Example: I am horrified. I can't believe this is happening

[3.] What <u>*fears or worries*</u> *do you have right now? List them individually*

Example: I'm afraid of what Shane will to go though during his treatments

[4.] How will (or may) this affect your life?

Example: We're going to have be careful about Shane's immune system while he's on Chemotherapy

[5.] What are your <u>concerns</u>? What are the cares on your mind?

Example: SHANE, how will he endure all of this? "Dolly," we'll have to be careful not to neglect her

Christene Bolte-Luthey

When Shadows Fall: A Journey of Faith

[6.] <u>What do I need to do</u> right now regarding this circumstance?

Example: I need to pray and put this in God's hands—then get everyone I know to pray too.

[7.] What **SHOULDN'T I DO** in this situation?

Example: I shouldn't panic or cry too much (it will upset Shane if I do)

[8.] What **CAN I DO** to make this situation **BETTER**?

Example: I can stay positive. I can remain hopeful and I can trust God for Shane's healing.

[9.] What _Can't I do_ because it will make things worse?

Example: I can't be negative. I can't dwell on the cancer or let my fears devastate me

Christene Bolte-Luthey

[10.] What can anyone do to help in this situation? What support do you need?

Example: Someone could maybe help me find information on Hodgkin's Lymphoma. I need to find a place to stay near the hospital while we're in Pittsburgh. I need a map to Children's Hospital and clear directions.

When Shadows Fall: A Journey of Faith

[11.] Who all will be affected by this situation? How can they be helped?

Example: "Dolly," our family and friends. Try our best to keep them all informed as best as possible

_____
_____
_____
_____
_____
_____
_____
_____
_____
_____
_____
_____
_____
_____
_____

[12.] Have you noticed any physical changes since your crisis?

Example: I'm having a hard time sleeping at night so I'm tired early in the afternoon

_____
_____
_____
_____
_____
_____
_____
_____
_____

[13.] *What can you do to help relieve some of the stress?*

Example: I could listen to some uplifting music. Take a long walk or bath. Write… in my journal.

Crisis And Loss

Father of all mercies... Comfort us in all our tribulations, that we may be able to comfort them which are in any trouble" [2 Cor. 1:3-4].

If a "shadow" (crisis) has fallen upon your life then no doubt you are in pain and hurting? I have no way of knowing what loss or tragedy you may be experiencing, the death of a family member, a terminal illness, the loss of a job? These are just a few of the limitless examples that can suddenly and unexpectedly impact, overwhelm and even immobilize our lives. Any *crisis or loss* can cause us shock, stress, and fearful anxiety. Also some uncertainty that makes us feel overwhelmed sometimes with feelings of panic or hopelessness?

Friend, if you are in a crisis, then this is a very critical time in your life. You need to know and understand that for a while it will <u>seem as though your world is out control</u>? Perhaps this might be a serious pivotal or turning point in your life? Whatever your loss or trial, realize that each and every individual responds and reacts differently to their circumstances. Yet I want you to know that whatever situation you're in right now, it does not have to be a time of total despair. Believe that with TIME and PRAYER this adversity will "pass" and God will use your hardship as an opportunity.

"Opportunity for what you might be thinking?" The opportunities to grow in Christ like character and come to know <u>at a deeper, more personal level</u> the God who created you. I pray that I can make these statements to you without sounding "high and mighty"? I say these things only because of the crisis's **I've** known. Many, I have shared with you, some in the past and those in the present. Maybe today you're feeling as though you're being "absolutely crushed" by the weight of your cares? Friend, do not be disheartened. Believe me when I say that I felt as if I was going to die— during the first twenty-four hours of being told that Shane had cancer! Even though I've been a Christian for sixteen years, I couldn't help but collapse in a near by chair when they gave us that terrible news! I was instantly in shock and frightened for "my boy!" I felt as though someone had just shot me in the heart with an arrow!

Friend, know that all of these are NORMAL emotions! I felt this way in April. Perhaps you are feeling or have felt this way? If you are it's because your mind has simply been flooded with torrent of thoughts that are too difficult for your brain to process and bear all at once. That is why we MUST sit back take a deep breathe and exhale slowly every once in a while… Trust me when I say that this moment of shock and disarray will eventually pass. Understand that in your own time, you will gradually regain your strength and bearing.

What has seen me through this ordeal with Shane has been PRAYER, the grace of God, good family and friends… Today in the midst of your trial, know that God is a "refuge" you may seek for comfort and peace. Hide under His wing, there you will find that beneath his feathers is a safe haven in which you may find rest from the "storm." **"He who dwells in the secret place of he Most High shall abide under the shadow of the Almighty. I will say to the Lord, "He is my refuge and my fortress; My God in Him I will trust." Surely he shall deliver you from the snare of the fowler and from the perilous pestilence. He shall cover you with His feathers, and under His wings you shall take refuge; His truth shall be your shield and buckler. You shall not be afraid of the terror by night, nor of the arrow that flies by day, nor of the pestilence that walks in darkness, nor of the destruction that lays waste at noonday" [Psalm 91:1-6].**

Dearest Heavenly Father, you only could know the sorrow within my heart, and the fear in my mind. I seek you today for guidance and peace. Take from me the weight of uncertainty, for it is too much for me to bear. Grant me your strength that I may endure this trial, and hold me tenderly in your arms. Amen

"We are hard pressed on every side, yet not crushed; we are perplexed, but not in despair; persecuted, but not forsaken; struck down but not destroyed" [2 Corinthians 4:8-9].

I don't believe there is quite another emotion that compares to that of being adrift… Do you feel at all like that today? Sometimes when disaster comes it feels like we're helplessly drifting along with our circumstance? If you feel this way, you have only for a time lost your bearing, but God has not abandoned you. If today you feel confused or disoriented by your situation, be encouraged that the Lord is walking with you! He promises to remain steady at your side. **[Matt. 10:29-31] says, "Are not two sparrows sold for a copper coin? And not one of them falls to the ground apart from your Father's will. But the very hairs of your head are all numbered. Do not fear therefore; you are of more value than many sparrows."** Take courage that wherever you go and whatever you do, God is ever near to you. If He knows the number of hairs on our head, he knows the burdens we bear. We need only take his hand by faith and trust Him as the anchor of our soul.

Remember that Jesus is the "rock" we can stand on when the storms of life crash around us! Today if you're feeling aimless and heartbroken, simply take his hand and you will no longer feel that you are drifting along with your problems. He is surely our anchor, refuge, peace and defense. Like a brilliant light shining through the thickest fog, he will fashion our way and supply the quiet haven we are so desperately searching for.

> The eyes of my Savior are on me its true, watching and guiding all that I do
> He's never weary nor far from my side, He listens and whispers, "In me child—abide."
> Therefore no matter what "storm" comes my way, I'm confident Jesus will show me the way
> To act or respond if, I seek first God's will, to follow His footsteps that peace then may still
> The waves that are raging when the clouds block my sight,
> I'll trust HIM forever, my anchor… my light…
> Yes, His eyes are watching and shall not depart
> For there every hour, HE LIVES IN MY HEART!
>
> *C. Luthey*

Lord Jesus, be an anchor for my soul that I may know rest and stability amidst the things assailing me. Grant me safe shelter and peace in your arms. Amen

WHY WOULD GOD ALLOW THIS PAIN?

"Therefore, having been justified by faith, we have peace with God through our Lord Jesus Christ, through whom also we have access by faith into this grace in which we stand, and rejoice in hope of the glory of God. And not only that, but we also glory in tribulations, knowing that tribulation produces perseverance; and perseverance character; and character, hope" [Romans 5:1-4].

When suffering comes we all ask WHY? Why is this happening? These questions are a natural response to affliction and loss. When we're given shocking news whether it is sudden or expected we seem numb for a time. In fact sometimes we find ourselves in a terrible state of disbelief. News of a significant loss immediately causes our throat to tighten and our chest to feel an unexplainable heaviness. Suddenly there is an empty feeling in our stomach and we find it difficult to concentrate on even the smallest things.

Then come the feelings of anxiety, frustration, and hurt. Often when we hurt we search for someone or something to blame. This we do in our despair because we need to lay the fault on something.

In the midst of our anger, denial, distress etc. we strive to make sense of it all, but regardless of our efforts we sometimes fail to understand… That is when we find it hard to believe that God could allow "this" to "happen to us." Then, like a revolving door we may find ourselves saying over and over again, "it can't be true," or "why would God do this to me?" Friend, if it seems you're feeling this way, keep in mind that affliction plagues all mankind. Accidents happen. People become ill and fall victim to disease. Calamities occur, and tragedies overturn our greatest hopes and dreams. Difficulties and pain sometimes make "living" a physical nightmare, and various losses can plunge us into a deep pit of mourning.

NEVERTHELESS, all of the "shadows" I just mentioned need not destroy us. Remember, **God LOVES US and HE DOES NOT MAKE "SHADOWS FALL" ON US**. He has promised though to keep us from despair if we trust HIS WILL and depend on HIS GRACE, MERCY and PEACE.

I realize that it may be very difficult to accept that thought, depending where you are in your "trial." As with ours with Shane, we have suffered a deep and fearsome wound. Therefore as we all know, the deeper the wound the more we suffer. Just as a scab that itches until it's gone, we go through stages before we are healed. Lets you and I take a moment to look at the crossroads we've stood at thus far in our lives. In pondering them perhaps we may see with greater clarity the reality of God and his never-ending faithfulness? Be comforted my friend knowing that although you may be feeling in a daze right now, God will see you through and you will gradually gain more strength and confidence as each day passes. Trust that although you and I cannot always understand why "shadows fall on us," God will use them to reveal and prove Himself—if we let Him? **"For God has not given us a spirit of fear, but of power and love and of a sound mind" [2 Timothy 1:7]**.

The Bible says, **"In the world you will have tribulation…" [John 16:33]** this is true. Yet, Jesus didn't end His sentence there, **"but be of good cheer, I have OVERCOME the world." [John 16:33]**. Friend, Jesus has overcome the world. That means he has overcome tribulation! That is why I say to you HAVE FAITH that you too will overcome whatever trial you are bearing right now. Hold firmly to the NAIL PIERCED HAND OF JESUS! Find courage and hope in these words from **[Romans 8:18]**, "For I

consider that the sufferings of this present time are not worthy to be compared with the glory which shall be revealed in us."

The nail pierced hand of Jesus, is reaching out to you
HE KNOWS WHAT SUFFERING IS my friend; He's tested, tried and true.
There is no fear that he can't halt, no anger he can't cease
He gives only hope and love, perfect joy and peace.
Though "shadows fall" or "fires" rage, or "valley's" wide we bear
If we have faith and look to Him, our sorrows He will share.

C.Luthey

Lord Jesus, you know I am hurting. Help me bear my trials although I do not understand. Enfold me in your loving arms and give peace to my troubled mind. My faith, hope and trust are in YOU. Amen

VESSLES OF HONOR

    Friend, I pray that the inquiry sheets so far have been useful to you? Because I sincerely believe they may be, I wanted to include a few more which God might use to give you understanding as you strive to identify with Christ in His sufferings. Living victoriously in this fallen world will depend on our trusting in Jesus Christ, and believing that God's grace is sufficient for each and every trial. I pray you will make use of the following pages?

    The Christian life is one of true obedience to God and allegiance to Christ Jesus. It demands change in our lifestyle from the culture of the world, and expects sacrifice. Problems don't cease just because we become God's "children." In reality, many times it is the point in which our heartaches and true challenges begin. Yet, if we allow our suffering to daily take us through a process of refining and purifying, God will use our life trials and afflictions to build within us an unshakable Christian character.

    Using time and prayer to gain a Godly perspective on what the suffering in our lives may accomplish for God's kingdom will mean that we must look at and ponder what God is doing in our walk with Him. We must take the time to look at ourselves honestly and see what God is wondrously fashioning in us. The Bible explains this in **[2 Tim. 2:19-21] "Nevertheless the solid foundation of God stands, having this seal: "The Lord knows those who are His," and, "Let everyone who names the name of Christ**

When Shadows Fall: A Journey of Faith

depart from iniquity." But in a great house there are not only vessels of gold and silver, but also of wood and clay, some for honor and some for dishonor. Therefore if anyone cleanses himself from the latter, he will be a vessel for honor, sanctified and useful for the Master, prepared for every good work." In this, we see that we through daily cleansing and purification have the opportunity to become **"vessels of honor,"** whereas we will become **"useful for the Master, ready for every good work."**

What do you think God's purpose is in your life?

Today:

_____
_____
_____
_____
_____
_____
_____
_____
_____
_____
_____
_____
_____
_____
_____

Six Months Later"

_____
_____
_____
_____
_____
_____
_____

Christene Bolte-Luthey

One Year Later

How is God using adversity to strengthen your character?

When Shadows Fall: A Journey of Faith

How can God turn your suffering into something Good?

What "opportunities" can you see in the midst of your crisis or loss?

Had you ever considered at any other time a Biblical perspective of suffering?

Have you ever experienced the presence of God in your life? When? How?

Christene Bolte-Luthey

Can you see any parallel to that which you are suffering now and that which Jesus suffered? Yes or no, explain.

How does it make you feel that Jesus Christ "carried your sorrows?"

When Shadows Fall: A Journey of Faith

How is God making Himself known to you in the midst of your crisis?

Christene Bolte-Luthey

Are you angry with God in any way? Do you blame Him for your adversity?

Why or why not?

How is your life different now? How has your crisis affected the way you feel about yourself, others and God?

How do you think this crisis could bring you closer to God?

Christene Bolte-Luthey

What strengths have you gained from enduring this adversity?

What have you learned throughout this crisis or loss? How have you grown "spiritually?"

What questions would you like God to answer about your trials?

Christene Bolte-Luthey

What is your perspective on adversity TODAY?

When Shadows Fall: A Journey of Faith

How do your thoughts on suffering differ from before?

Christene Bolte-Luthey

What have you learned about Jesus Christ through your suffering and trials?

When Shadows Fall: A Journey of Faith

What have you learned about YOURSELF through your suffering and adversity?

Christene Bolte-Luthey

What have you learned about OTHERS throughout your loss or trial?

Christene Bolte-Luthey

How has this affected the way you see OTHERS who are suffering?

When Shadows Fall: A Journey of Faith

What has encouraged you most throughout your adversity?

Christene Bolte-Luthey

What can you do to encourage others who are suffering?

When Shadows Fall: A Journey of Faith

NOTES:

Christene Bolte-Luthey

Nine
A PORTRAIT OF GRACE

"My Grace is sufficient for you, for my strength is made perfect in weakness. Therefore most gladly I will boast in my infirmities, that the power of Christ may rest upon me. Therefore I take pleasure in my infirmities, in reproaches, in needs, in persecutions, in distresses, for Christ's sake. For when I am weak then I am strong" [2 Cor. 12:9-10].

Though life may crumble around us, and our treasures may be taken
Resting in the arms of God our faith may not be shaken.
For He will never give us a cross we cannot bear,
When we feel as though we "can't" in perfect time He's there.
Knowing every weakness, His spirit sets me free,
Granting me His precious grace and love from Calvary.
There is no trial that can outweigh, God's sweet awesome grace
And in the midst of every storm, is where I see HIS FACE.

Christene Luthey

To face our weakness is the test, that when we know ourselves the best
And once we conquer that great strain, we shall have so much to gain,
Stronger once we've seen our fear, clouds then lift and it is clear.
Compassion, love, forgiveness true, seems to well inside of you.
After I have learned to be, held by grace and then set free.

So it is in God's great plan that we must learn and understand
In each trial that we must face, we must seek out God's will and grace.
This is too a lesson learned, faith is precious, something earned.
Brought on with God's loving hand that we can grow and understand
Tests and trials though harsh and cold,
May with JESUS made us GOLD!

Christene Luthey

BRIDGES TO VICTORY

Being that we are walking daily through a series of countless obstacles we must prepare ourselves for the journey. Understanding completely that we will encounter along the way, ROCKS, STREAMS, VALLEYS, FIELDS, DESERTS, MOUNTAINS, and STORMS. But in due course, if we see our suffering and trials as occasion for God to teach and test us, we will gain knowledge of Christ like perseverance and patience, and faith.

There is no telling what we'll discover, or run into along the way? But to know achievement, we must view adversities as openings for us to know God better. Life indeed is difficult. In fact it's sometimes exceedingly hard-hitting. Each day brings unsure situations, life changing choices and complex crossroads. Often we find ourselves tossed or battered by the storms of life? Yet, we need not despair. We must only persevere. Keeping our eyes on the heavenly goal. Fearlessly trusting God to help us overcome life's trials. In this, we surely will become "vessels of honor." It is through persistence we conquer problems. Along the way we'll produce "fruit" as we learn about ourselves. In the end, we will have gained a deeper trust of our Heavenly Father and experience an extraordinary walk with Him. In this we'll uncover along the way compassion for others who are bearing life's burdens or under spiritual attack. Having laid hold of the grace of God we then will be able to reach out to people with the love of Christ. Then we will see <u>our adversities have turned out to be immense opportunities God may use to demonstrate evidence of His faithfulness, and love.</u>

CONSIDER THE GOAL

Every trial we encounter is testing our faith. Will the stress of our adversity cause us to loose it, or will we unyielding cling to Christ? If we are to achieve the utmost hope of man: <u>Having a personal relationship with GOD through Jesus Christ, we have to learn endurance</u>. That means that we must prevail over life's problems and difficulties. In order to accomplish that, we'll need an experienced coach (Jesus Christ). This "coach" must know the terrain and be capable of showing us the way, because he must have previously run every race and WON.

His counsel then will be worthy of our trust, and he will be able to instruct, assist and prepare us for the stumbling blocks we will come upon as we press toward each goal. He must teach us good habits, and present us with behaviors that will not only ration our strengths, but also perfect our weaknesses. In this, our determination will be strengthened and our character may develop into that of a true, modest WINNER.

Christ, our coach will show us how to gain knowledge from our mistakes, and how to improve ourselves in spite of our weakness. We must listen to to his words of counsel and benefit from his wisdom knowing that his place in life is to pass along the knowledge HE has gained through the lessons he has learned. In this WE too may triumphantly achieve the same victories.

Those of us in life who are sincerely pressing toward the heavenly goal written about in the Bible, must <u>UNDERSTAND COMPLETELY that we will be hard pressed on each and every side,</u> because (Satan) <u>desires to prevent us from achieving the blessed gift of eternal life.</u> Satan absolutely despises individuals who will not give up or yield to life's disappointments, heartaches or despair. That is why you and I as children of God must absolutely and optimistically trust JESUS to turn LIFE'S PROBLEMS into OPPORTUNIES, and LIFE'S TURMOIL into TRIUMPH.

<u>Jesus Christ alone has completed all of the things</u> I have just talked about. He has known victory over each and every situation that was placed before him, and this he did by SURRENDERING HIMSELF COMPLETELY AND UNCONDITIONALLY TO THE PERFECT WILL OF GOD. Therefore, we need not be anxious in any situation because JESUS—has PROVEN HIMSELF FAITHFUL!

GOD'S GRACE IS REAL

Take a minute if you will and imagine viewing a bridge suspended above a cavernous valley. This bridge unites two mountains that are divided by a huge gulf. This bridge is the ONLY route by which you can cross from one mountain to the other. As your eyes begin to scan from the left to the right, you clearly see the solid structure on the left of the bridge. You make out that it is built securely into that side of the mountain. Yet, while impressed by its grandeur, you lose sight of the overpass as you continue scanning. Glancing half way across—you observe a THICK, HEAVY fog. A dark cloud has appeared and has blocked your view. Suddenly, you can't see the other side of the mountain.

Your LIFE depends on CROSSING THIS BRIDGE! What are you going to do? Will you stand at the bridge or will you cross? This is an extremely significant question as the answer you give tells much about your

TRUST and FAITH. We know there are many "bridges" in life we must cross in order to exist and mature, but what I've found is: <u>The strength of our character is manifest when the "shadows" of uncertainty envelopes the bridge that is yet to be crossed.</u>

When we stand at a bridge in life, we only have two choices. We are either going to stand on one side or go forward crossing by FAITH? There are many obstacles in life that block our view of the "other side" to some extent? As I wrote the following poem for a dear friend who was mourning the death of his father, the image of the bridge I've described became extraordinarily clear, and I began to realize that: <u>God allows "shadows" or "clouds" to obstruct our future outcome sometimes, so we will learn reliance upon His GRACE. As it becomes our lifeline we can step out in faith to overcome life's suffering.</u>

KNOW MY GRACE IS REAL

You think that I don't love you? You think that I don't care?
You feel that I am worthless? I am far from fair?
You wonder WHY would one so great refuse to use my power?
To let the anguish and the pain, continue with each hour?
You think that I'm a liar? Whose word is all but true?
For how could such a loving God allow the things I do?
How could I truly care and yet, permit such evil here?
The sickness, murder, death and all the heartache, grief and fear?

But am I really heartless? Did I not feel your loss?
Have I not proved myself to you by DYING on the cross?
Are you yourself Almighty God? Then hold your tongue in pain,
For you can't see the MASTER plan, all anger is in vain.
I see and know all things it's true, although I stay my hand
From crushing evil in its prime which you can't understand.

Yet, **ANY SUFFERING I ALLOW, THE INNOCENT TO FEEL
IS USED TO MAKE MY PRESENCE KNOWN
TO PROVE MY GRACE IS REAL.
FOR GRACE IS ONLY VISIBLE, WHEN PAIN IS EVIDENT
AS TIME BECOMES REALITY—AS IT IS BEING SPENT...**

GRACE is the bridge that spans between the gulf of death and life
Providing an escape for you a route to peace from strive
It seems a cruel barbaric way to join the two and win
Yet with that same amazing grace, I sustained all sin.

All while I was innocent, and had no need to cry
Accepting what life brought to me I then prepared to die.
Refusing not, my place in life, a hard reality
Yet in the end, the "master plan" would be to set YOU free!

God heard the cries of HIS OWN SON, and yet did stay his hand
And with my dying breath it was—ALL that He had planned!
So let God's grace uphold you now, in all you pain today
It IS sufficient, this I know, I rolled the stone away.

So see, you cannot know until, the plan comes into view,
What GOOD can come from suffering and all ONE MAN can do.

Christene Bolte-Luthey

Pondering what I've said concerning bridges in life, and God's goal in striving to prove his faithfulness to us, I am reminded of a memory that vividly exists in my mind. It is of a time and incident I learned the importance of TRUST, and the significance of FAITH at a very early age. The instance went like this: One day when I was about nine, I decided to play in the huge corncrib my dad had built on our farm. All day I'd been in it. Running up and down the towering mounds of corn, swinging hand over hand from cable to cable above the floor. Everything seemed fine until I fearfully noticed that I had swung myself into the center of the crib where no corn was beneath me. To my surprise there was only the base of the crib, and it was a LONG way down! All of the sudden I began to panic. I knew I was going to fall! I could feel the strength leaving my arms and terror filled me. In the midst of my fear I began screaming out, "DADDY!" "DADDY, PLEASE HELP, I'M GOING TO FALL!"

I can still recall hanging from that cold steel cable. Alone. Feeling the devastating sense of horror that had enveloped my body. I remember the burning sharp pain that followed the muscles in my arms, and the dread that came over me as they tightened. It actually caused me to shiver. There I was, vulnerable and afraid. I knew beyond a shadow of a doubt that I was in trouble! As tears began to stream down my face, I could do nothing but nervously contemplate the huge distance that spanned between the floor and me. There I was crying. I knew deep in my heart that falling was inevitable. There was no other way to get down.

It was then I remember bearing in mind the hope I held in my heart that dad would hear me calling. If he did, I knew he'd rescue me! He'd never let me down. So, again, I called, "Daddy, please help!" Sure enough, he heard my voice and responded. Wasting no time, he climbed up in the crib and braced himself below me. With arms extending wide and upward, he said in a reassuring tone, "it's going to be alright." "All you need to do," he said, "is TRUST me!" "Honey," he continued, "just let go!" But I couldn't. I just held fast to the cable. I was too afraid. Fear controlled me, even though I was losing strength every second. Again and again he repeated, "just let go," and promised, "I'll catch you!" "Christene, you just have to TRUST me!" Then, with a lighthearted chuckle he asked, "do you really think I'd let you get hurt?" "Honey, I'd never let you fall!"

The amusing thing was—I had no choice. Yet that didn't seem to prevent me from holding on to that cable as long as I could. I kept yelling, "I'm afraid," and I WAS! Yet the one thing that took precedence over my awful fear, was the FAITH and TRUST I held in my heart for dad and his promises. Throughout my life I had <u>never known him to lie,</u> and he <u>ALWAYS did what he said he'd do. I BELIEVED his love for me was true</u> and I could count on him to not let me down. <u>In fact, I KNEW that he'd probably die before he'd let me get hurt.</u> With those thoughts first in my mind, I finally "let go," and fell unharmed into the safety of his arms. Holding me he said, "I told you—I'd catch you sweetheart!"

If you think about it, every one of us can possibly relate in some way to the TRUE story I just shared? This account I wanted to tell, because in a spiritual way, it illustrates for all that <u>if we haven't "let go" of our pride, and humbly fallen into the loving arms of our Heavenly Father,</u> we too are <u>sure to fall</u>. Believe it or not, until the moment we surrender our lives to Christ, we are spiritually "on the brink" of disaster? "Holding on" with all our might to live and survive on our own. All the while our heavenly Father who loves us, is standing by with His arms wide open to "hold us" if we'd TRUST HIM? Though he encourages us in many ways to believe His word and promises, we stubbornly rely on our own strength. Yet God knows we cannot "hold on" forever… That's why today is a good time to "let go" and trust the One who sent his Son Jesus to die on the cross to prove how much He loves you. Friend, regardless of how many others might have let you down, believe that your Heavenly Father will NEVER abandon you! You can rely and depend on him to be consistently faithful. He has given you his word. Let him prove himself today! Please pray for the courage to "let go" of whatever might be keeping you from a personal relationship with him. When you do, you will come to know calmness within your soul that cannot be explained.

Throughout the times I have felt most alone, weary in life's unpredictable circumstances, I have recalled those around me who have proven their love and faithfulness. Yet NONE can quite compare or compete with that which I have found in JESUS and in the love of God my heavenly Father. When I consider the lonely and fearful feelings we experience in life because we've trusted in our own understanding—I ponder the promise of God's "GRACE. He promises it shall be "SUFFICIENT." This I believe is true, being that by it, JESUS suffered and endured DEATH on a cross. It was only through God's GRACE that Jesus was able to withstand that unfathomable "call" on His life.

This is how we can be certain God is able to see us through every trial we encounter. For what trial or tribulation may we suffer could possibly measure up to the weight of this world's sin? I am sure not one of us will ever undergo any such thing?

Sweet Savior, Sweet Lord, provider of truth, provider of grace and of life
You are the Master of all living things, the Prince that shall conquer all strife.

Lord and Redeemer, my blessed sweet hope, glory and honor to thee,
You have forgiven the vilest sin, setting sin's prisoners free.

You have climbed every mountain. You have conquered each foe
That sought out to kill you oh Lord, winning each battle in meekness and love
Which is why you are so adored.

You have flown like the eagle and touched so the sky, unlike any other has known
You have humbled yourself like a lamb to be slain, revealing the greatest love known.

You only, are worthy of honor and praise, of glory and all we hold dear
For you have upheld the righteous with faith, and captured the power of fear....

Christene Luthey

So if you're in a storm today, where darkness seems to be?
Put your trust in God alone, he'll grant you grace to see.
Slowly turn around my friend he's there to guide your way
Have faith in him and just believe he's with you EVERY DAY!

Christene Bolte-Luthey

THE LORD IS THE SHEPHERD OF HIS PEOPLE

[Psalm 23:1-6]

I am your Shepherd, be not afraid, I shall grant you peace
Take rest in pastures of my precious grace,
And all of your burdens shall cease.

I long so to walk with you by still waters, that I may restore your soul
Walking therein the paths of my glory
Trusting in me be now whole.

Yea though you walk through the valley of death,
Fear no evil there;
For I am with thee always child
I'll keep you from despair.

My rod and staff shall comfort thee
Prepared, I've made a place
Thy cup shall overflow with joy
Come, look upon my face.

> Yes, goodness and mercy shall follow you true
> All the days of your life,
> For those who have loved me, shall dwell in my house
> Away from all sorrow and strife.
>
> *Christene Bolte-Luhey*

CONTEMPLATE THE DREAM

As we continue lets contemplate the dream of victory over all of life's trials, and taking part in the everlasting joy of eternal life. Before we go on, let me ask you this question? Have you decided to be part of Christ's "team?" I inquire about this because if you've said "YES" to Jesus, HE will be your COACH. For HE ALONE is capable and worthy of helping us, **"Work out our salvation" [Phil. 2:12].** He alone has said, **"I am the way, the truth, and the life, no man shall come to the father but through me" [John14: 6].**

Throughout the chapters you've read, I have mentioned many thoughts and Biblical truths that have hopefully made the decision to follow Christ an important and valuable one to you? I sincerely believe this a decision we can't or shouldn't put off. Once a decision to follow Christ is made we must commit to our heavenly goal—heart, mind, body, and soul. **"That you may become blameless and harmless children of God without fault in the midst of a crooked and perverse generation, among whom you shine as lights in the world. Holding fast the word of life, so that I may rejoice in the day of Christ that I have not run in vain or labored in vain" [Phil 2:15-16].**

It was for US Jesus suffered. That we may know victory in the battles we face. Let us remember God's grace saw Jesus through a horrid death, and raised Him from the grave. This is how we can be sure that **"we may take pleasure in all things."** Whether they are good or bad. Trusting God's grace to be sufficient in our suffering, we have the assurance that we will overcome whatever comes our way. How blessed we are to boast such a Savior. How fortunate to have such a friend. One who knows every heartache and pain? A companion who softly whispers to our spirit, "come, hide under my wing." "You need only trust in me." "I will shelter you from life's storms, keeping you safe and warm."

This is what we need to do when the storms of life rage and cause our heart to feel like it's spinning out of control. The first thing we need to do is fall on our knees. Seeking God's help as fast as we can in prayer. It is there that we may call upon him for help to sustain and guard our soul.

PLACE YOUR TRUST IN HIM

When I fail to do my best and worry taunts at me
Let me first surrender Lord, and place my trust in thee.
When I fall beside the way with not the strength to stand
Let me first remember Lord, to quickly take your hand.
When my tears are falling fast, from being troubled so
Let me trust your grace for me, wherever my feet should go.
When I cannot understand, injustice in this world
Let me not loose faith I you that I may be unfurled.
When I feel so all alone, and friends abandon me
Let me come to thee in prayer, and place my trust in thee.
When my heart knows deep despair, nearly at he end
Let me not forget you Lord, my priceless, precious friend.

Christene Luthey

Lord; What a sweet gift you have given to all
Who turn from this world and answer your call.
You shine down with glory like sun on my face
Revealing with splendor God's awesome grace
You warm my heart with a thought or a prayer
Reminding me always that you truly care
Whatever my burden, whatever my fear,
You know the answer, "Dear child, come near."
Beloved Redeemer, Master and friend
Because of you my life will not end…

Christene Luthey

OVERCOMING ADVERSITY

I know many people today are suffering. Many are broken hearted. Many are weary, and living under a heavy spirit of hopelessness. But God wants us to know that we can overcome trials and adversities if we know Jesus and abide in him. Too many of us don't really know him as well as we should?

Rather than trusting and depending upon him for peace and understanding, we trust in THINGS and people. But people and things will let us down. Family and friends are only human. They will fail us. They will struggle also. They cannot be with us at all times. That is why we need God. We need His strength. We need His wisdom. We need His hope, refuge and peace. God alone is capable of being where we need him at any given hour. It's time we understand this truth. Our family, and friends are unable to bear our sorrows. They have limitations.

Yet, Christ on the other hand is NOT LIMITED. When we place our faith and trust in HIM we can rest assured that in every situation and circumstance He will see us through. In Him we have confidence because we are "children" of God. We no longer need bear the bondage sin or its guilt etc., because we've discovered WHO and what the Bible says we are in God's eyes! **"For as many are led by the Spirit of God, these are the sons of God. For you did not receive a spirit of bondage again to fear, but you received the spirit of adoption by whom we cry out, Abba, Father. The Spirit himself bears witness with our spirit that we are CHILDREN OF GOD, and if children, then heirs, heirs of God and joint heirs with Christ, if indeed we suffer with him, that we may also be glorified together"** [Romans 8:14-17]. **"Therefore do not worry about tomorrow, for tomorrow will worry about its own things. Sufficient for the day is its own trouble"** [Matt. 6:34].

We must seek out God and have confidence that our identity is in HIM. Consider this: **"He formed your inner parts; and covered you in your mother's womb. You are fearfully and wonderfully made; your frame is not hidden from him. He knows and understands your thoughts, and is acquainted with your paths and ways. He has laid a hedge behind and before you, and his hand is upon you if you place your trust in him"** [Psalm 139]. You see friend, the Bible says that, **"God created man in his own image"** [Gen. 1:27]. This I why you and I were created, and why God desires a personal relationship with us! God says in **[Jer. 1:5]**, **"Before I formed you in the womb I knew you."** How does that make you feel? Special I hope?

Peace in life many of us forfeit, because we tend to overlook these wonderful things when we're suffering. We'd be wise to write them permanently on the tablet of our heart. Perhaps then we'd remember that God has not left to bear our burdens alone. Jesus is just a prayer away. So let us ponder verses like these when we are perplexed. Being careful to guard our heart against Satan's attempts to rob us of our peace.

I have been a "born again" Christian since 1985. Throughout those years by the grace of God, I have been able to hold fast to God's promises. They have consistently helped me endure every "shadow" that has come my way. It has been encouraging to know that my heavenly Father cares more about my suffering and me than I could ever begin to imagine. This is also true for YOU! **[Psalm 56:8-10]** states, **"You number my wanderings; put my tears into your bottle; are they not in your book? When I cry out to you, then my enemies will turn back; this I know, because God is for me."**

If there is any distance between you and your creator, it will allow the enemy (Satan), to attack your life. You need to fill your heart with God's precious word every day and rely on God's priceless grace to surround and sustain you. Regardless of your injuries, whether they are physical, mental, or spiritual, Christ is able to provide for you the healing we need pull through. Trust and believe that he will not forsake you.

Sometimes we might attempt to apply the "world's" remedies to our pain, and don't consider God's ways of healing our wounds? How then if using the world's cures can we overcome our sorrows, pain, grief or fear? Are we actually looking at what might be generating our suffering? Have we assessed our unhappiness? I sincerely believe that we will not totally live a life filled with total happiness and contentment until we've allowed Jesus to fill the emptiness in our heart. So why do some of us struggle so to live with the void in our soul? Why do some of us deny that it's there? Friend, I'm telling you, JESUS is the ONLY one who can truly mend our scars and relieve our suffering. **"Bless the Lord, oh my soul, ad forget not all his benefits; who forgives al our iniquities, who heals all your diseases. Who redeems your life from destruction, who crowns you with loving kindness and tender mercies, who satisfies your mouth with good things, so that your youth is renewed like the eagles" [Psalm 103:5].**

ONLY CHRIST CAN SAY TO THE WOUNDED

Only Christ can say to the wounded,
I feel the pain you feel
I count the many tears you cry
I know your suffering is real
I too have stayed awake at night
The nights you knew no sleep
It was me who walked beside you there
For I do love my sheep

I feel the fear that grips your soul
Yes every hour I've known
In spite of your great loneliness
You'll never be alone.
I know the wounds within are deep
And peace seems far away,
But I have come to tell you
My love is yours today!
If you will simply take my hand
And seek me with your heart,
Place your faith in me alone
Fear shall then depart.

Christene Bolte-Luthey

ONLY CHRIST CAN SAY TO THE WOUNDED

Jesus isn't afraid to stand with us. He's not afraid of anything. Whether it be suffering or keeping the Devil from tempting us, He will stay at our side. He went to the cross so that we would not have to fear Satan or his accusations. He's not troubled by "life's raging fires," and we don't have to be either. Consider that Jesus has extinguished misery's flames with his blood. Therefore let this knowledge bring you comfort. Jesus Christ has fought every battle known to man and WON! That is why we in Christ may boldly say, **"I can do all things through Christ who strengthens me" [Phil. 4:13].**

No one but Jesus Christ the Messiah, the living Son of God could make the promises he has and keep them. Can anyone else literally feel our pain? Can anyone else experience the fear that grips your heart or mine? Can anyone we know actually walk with us each and every hour? Can anyone we know console us amidst the loneliness we bear? Is there anyone that can promise that we will NEVER be alone? No! Jesus is the only one able to make statements. That is how we can be certain that if we place our faith or trust in anything OTHER than Jesus, we are destined to endure discouragement.

Just as we cannot live without air or water, we cannot live eternally without Jesus. The same is true that we cannot endure the trials of life without the Grace, love or mercy of God. **"Who desires all men to be saved and to come to the knowledge of the truth. For there is one God**

and one mediator between God and men, the man Christ Jesus" [1 Tm. 2:4-5]. I sincerely believe the only cure for our problems today is unconditional surrender to God's will. The less we sin, the greater healing we will see in our nation and ourselves. **"You shall love the Lord your God with all your heart, with all your soul and with all your strength, and with all your mind, and your neighbor as yourself" [Luke 10:27].**

CONFIRM YOUR COMMITMENT

If you are willing to confirm your commitment to God, and are ready to make Jesus Christ the Lord of your life, (or if you already have), be certain that you will be taking the first step on the most wonderful journey you will ever know. Yet this commitment no doubt will require of your life and time, sacrifice, and training in the following areas: Discipline, determination, long hard work, wisdom, perseverance, obligation, responsibility, obedience, and endurance.

If we desire to be winners, we must trust the trainer and commit ourselves to his care and exercise consistency. This requires a solid and determined attitude toward our goal that will fix our thoughts upon victory, not defeat. We must also set our will on crossing the bridges in life that God sets before us, regardless of what it costs. We can do this by faith. Are we willing to make these sacrifices? Have we truly decided to commit our life and will to whatever goals God has prepared for us? If we have then it is time for us to take the step forward toward getting in shape spiritually.

From this day forward we need not walk in darkness ever again. We need to simply begin putting things behind us that have kept us from serving God and moving forward. Put false teachers and teachings behind you. Put bitterness, anger, hatred and resentment behind you. When you kneel before Jesus He will take up your case and carry all the chains that have bound you for so long. Hand them over to him, he wants to carry your burdens. In fact, when you surrender your heart to him, he will make sure that the chains are forever broken so that they never bind you again. Depend on Him and his word to guide you and allow him to direct your paths. In doing this, he will lead you to freedom!

Consider those who had no choice but to rely on their own knowledge and faith in Jesus Christ to see them through life's difficult situations. Two people that have inspired me the most when I am in the midst of a trial are to of God's most faithful followers. Paul and Silas, **[Read Acts 16:16-34]**.

After being beaten and thrown into a cold dark prison they began praying, praising and singing hymns to God. They were not given a hand to hold or a comforting word of encouragement from anyone. They were not granted the opportunity (as they were bound in chains) to attend church services etc. where they might receive the encouragement they needed to withstand their suffering. Yet because they KNEW and had LEARNED to TRUST in the Lord with "all their hear, soul, and mind," they were wondrously and joyously set free from their chains! **"Suddenly, there was a great earthquake, so that the foundations of he prison were shaken, and immediately all the doors were opened and everyone's chains were loosed' [Acts 16:25-26].**

Knowing the power of prayer has on many occasions lifted me above the weight of my cares at the times when I have felt most alone, (Especially when I was stricken with fear—as in the latest trial with our son and his cancer diagnosis.) I truly don't know what I would have done if it had not been for my faith and the comfort I gained knowing that others were praying for us. Today, you might feel all alone too, sort of like Paul and Silas—beaten down by burdens, worries, fears, or chained by your past or the weight of a present situation? Do you feel as though you are living in a prison of your own? If so, I want to tell you again, GOD LOVES YOU and HE CARES ABOUT WHAT YOU ARE GOING THROUGH. Believe my friend that Christ STILL sets captives free! If you can relate to these two men and will place your faith in Christ today, he will be there for you just as he was for them. **"Finally, my brethren, be strong in the Lord and in the power of his might" [Eph. 6:10].**

Jesus is simply waiting for YOU to give him your unconditional trust and for you to let go of your life by placing it in his hands. He then will exchange his life for yours so that you may inherit the promises of God and be given eternal life in Glory. Just come to the cross and humbly ask forgiveness of your sin. Trust Christ as your Savior and believe that He paid the price for your sin. Then the grace of God will fill you with his Holy Spirit that you may by faith be a **"born again child of God."**

GOD LOVES THE SINNER (But hates the sin)

We must separate the two; begin
Ask for forgiveness, yet sin no more
This shall shut and lock the door,
That seems so often open wide

Loosing knots that once were tied
God hates the sin but loves the man
This was in his perfect plan.
Just pray for grace to do God's will
Allowing him—your cup to fill.

C. Luthey

"But God, who is rich in mercy because of his great love with which He loved us, even when we were dead in trespasses, made us alive together with Christ by grace you have been saved" [Eph. 2:4-5].

CONDITION YOURSELF

You will never be ready for the challenge if you do not take measures in conditioning yourself. Conditioning is a critical and important step in each and every life. It is the measure of heart and soul that we put into our goal that will ultimately determine whether or not we survive and overcome the challenges that lay before us. Let us begin our conditioning by wisely applying to our lives a specific amount of discipline. Make working out a schedule a priority in which you will be able to devote a certain amount of time and energy to exercise and reading. Get involved! Be determined to NOT give up or give in, even when the storms of life are raging. Be ready to take the good in life with the bad, and know that you are preparing for the challenges that are just around the bend. The harder you work, the stronger you will ultimately become. The more you give to your conditioning, the more you will be able to draw from when the going gets tough.

Push yourself to withstand the long haul! Be willing to endure. Stretch beyond your present difficulties and yourself. Expect opposition from life and the Devil. Put what you learn into practice! Believe in Christ and his ability to stand with you amidst your injuries, doubts, disappointments, defeats, or despair. Trust that he is able to lift you above all that you may ever face or know in this world. Believe with your heart and soul that if you have made him the LORD of your life, he has not only promised but has signed a contract (covenant) that he will never leave or forsake you.

Place your faith in his will to see you safely across each and every bridge in life and through every storm, regardless of how terrible it may seem.

Although you may (please don't), walk away from Christ throughout the course of your journey, know that HE WILL NEVER LEAVE OR ABANDON YOU! He does not want you to fight your battles alone. He is a faithful friend that **"sticks closer than a brother" [Prov. 18:24].** You must only surrender to God's wisdom and allow him to teach you his ways. It is the only way I know that is guaranteed NOT to fail... The only way you will learn to grow in Christ like character. Remember always my friend, the degree in which you give yourself to God will be the ultimate factor in the battles you win—or loose in life. I know you want victory, as do I, which is why I write these remaining chapters. May the things I have learned throughout the course of our journey thus far inspire you to step out in faith and off of the starting line today. May these thoughts and poems help you to grow in wisdom and knowledge as you strive to accomplish what God has in his perfect will for YOUR life.

Many of the rules have already been presented in the chapters you have read concerning some of the things that are not considered acceptable in the sight of God. May you strive to apply his wisdom to your life and learn to separate yourself from all that would keep you from the glory of God's most precious victories and his richest rewards. Although I have no way of knowing what you may face in the future, or what you may be enduring at this moment, I hope that you find in the following pages TRUTH that will be used to help set you free, GRACE to help you endure, FAITH to build on, and LOVE to see you through whatever comes your way. Remember that God allows (but does not afflict us) with trials in our lives. This he allows only to prove when we are tested that—<u>his will</u> and <u>his alone</u> must ultimately be done.

Ponder in depth your circumstances and your decision before you leap. Be sure to test every action according to God's divine will. God will allow us to be tested to see if we will be OBEDIENT to his word and purpose. Let us in every situation that deals with obedience—consider Christ's test on the eve of his death. Imagine the temptation he might have had to RUN, to escape the pain and torment he knew awaited him. Have WE in any way been tested or tempted to the point in which **"drops of blood have fallen from OUR brow?"** Have we been **"mocked; scoffed at, or beaten; flogged; or led naked to hang publicly on a cross"** before thousands of eyes to suffer and die a horrid death? Absolutely not.

Only JESUS CHRIST was sinless. Only He could be taken so far, and not turn away from his Father's will. By this act of obedience we know that Christ can set us free from all that tempts us to sin against or escape God's will. How obedient will we be to the word of God? Would we suffer unto death? We must stop and consider our ways and decisions, we cannot pick and choose the trials that we will or will not endure. Although we would very much like to. Yet if Christ had only been obedient up to the point of the cross, (and then changed his mind) and not remained faithful to God's calling on his life, <u>the gulf between God and man would not have been bridged and eternal life would not have been offered to us.</u>

Dear friends, I know that I am not the only one to experience trials and tribulations. In fact, I can say with much sincerity that I have known many others personally who have crossed much deeper and wider valleys than I. Many times throughout the years I have searched the word of God for comfort, peace and understanding when trials came my way. I can honestly say that I would NOT be living above the circumstances that have entered my life, IF IT WERE NOT FOR THE GRACE, PEACE, MERCY and LOVE of my Heavenly Father, and the personal relationship I share with JESUS. In order to live above and beyond our adversities we must take steps to **"enter into the rest"** that is spoken about in the book of Hebrews while the Spirit of God is calling. I hope you won't turn away from the truth I've shared with you throughout these pages? I pray you too will allow Christ to see you though the deepest, darkest, dreariest valleys you know in life? He is a faithful loving friend that will never let you down.

NEW LIFE

Lord Jesus when I think of you
I ponder all I've put you through.
All the misery, all the pain,
All the torture, all the shame

Just because you loved me so
You came to "free" to let me go.
Breaking chains that bound my life,
In torment, slavery, sin and strife.

Once I took for granted GRACE
There my soul felt hell's embrace.
Lacking comfort, peace and love,
Everything YOU are above.

Christene Bolte-Luthey

It was coming to the "end" of ME
My eyes were open then to see
The length, the breadth, the depth of YOU
Which made my life—forever new!

C. Luthey

Ten

PRESSING TOWARD THE GOAL

"Not that I have already attained, or am already perfected; but I press on, that I may lay hold of that for myself which Christ Jesus has also laid hold of me. Brethren, I do not count myself to have apprehended; but one thing I do, forgetting those things which are behind and reaching forward to those thing which are ahead, I press toward he goal for the prize of he upward call of God in Christ Jesus. Therefore let us, as many as are mature, have this mind; and if in anything you think otherwise, God will reveal even this to you. Nevertheless, to the degree that we have already attained, let us walk by the same rule, let us be of he same mind" [Phil 3:12-15].

In stillness and silence you speak to me, whispering mercy and grace
There in the Spirit your presence is known, and a shadow appears of your face.

More so the love and the radiance of you, that those who are "busy" won't see
Filling my soul with the sweetest desire, to be closer and closer to thee.

That I may encounter the depth of your splendor, in ways that no other has known
To capture a glimpse of YOU and your glory, to hold fast a gift of my own.

That I may grow nearer to you and your Gospel, in turn then to live as I should
Hoping that others may so then desire, all that is perfect and good.

Oh, sweet Redeemer, Lord, King and Master, place your hand upon me,
Anoint this servant with thy precious love, so that I may work for Thee.

YOU alone Lord have known my sin, and all of the tears I have cried,
Only you deserve my heart, for (my soul) you alone have died.

Christene Bolte-Luthey

ONWARD TO VICTORY

Victory in MY life began by humbly bending my knees and crying out to God. I needed understanding, TRUTH, wisdom and knowledge of HIM. I had had enough of the world's solutions for life's trials and problems. I wanted ANSWERS! I sought to lay hold of that which God had created ME for. I wanted truth in my life that I could stand on. I NEEDED Truth that would make a DIFFERENCE. I wanted truth that would change things. Truth that would not only help and sustain me amidst crisis, but truth that would assist me in overcoming the obstacles I was facing every day.

Throughout life, it seems that we're ALL constantly struggling against one trial or another that sets out to draw our hearts and minds into confusion, control, anger, fear, depression, grief or pain. I don't know of anyone who hasn't (or won't at some point in their life) experience life's adversities and struggle to overcome difficulty. The reasons I believe God allows us to battle these feelings and wrestle with such emotions are "two fold." The first is that we may encounter God's grace, peace, love and hope in our lives. The other is that we might view ourselves as we really are.

In times of trial, I have grown weary, known depression, felt anger, tasted bitterness and trembled in fear. Nevertheless, through CHRIST JESUS who strengthens me, I have endured every storm life has brought my way. There is no reason for even one soul to perish or remain bound in the chains that once linked us to sin and death. Because we know that JESUS CHRIST has broken the ties that Satan used to bind us. JESUS has given us through faith in HIM the power and authority in His name to fight life's battles and WIN. That is why we need not fear the race ahead of us today. We need only guard our hearts and minds as we go along our way. **"And everyone who competes for the prize is temperate in all things. Now they do it to obtain a perishable crown, but we for an imperishable crown. Therefore, I run thus: not with uncertainty. Thus I fight: not as one who beats the air. But I discipline my body and bring it into subjection, lest when I have preached to others, I myself should become disqualified"** [1 Cor. 9:27]. "Therefore we also, since we are surrounded by so great a cloud of witnesses, let us lay aside every weight, and the sin which so easily ensnares us, and let us run with endurance the race that is set before us. Looking unto Jesus, the author and finisher of our faith, who for the joy was set before him endured the cross, despising the shame, and has set down at the right hand of the thrown of God" [Heb. 12:1-2].

RUN THE RACE TO WIN

[1 Cor. 9:24-27]

Let me not forget dear Lord
My aim in life to tell
**To run the race with confidence
And end it just as well.**
Competing for that lasting crown
That no one else may take,
To reach and win the souls of man
For your kingdom's sake.
And not that I may faint nor fall
To not exhaust myself,
Remind me that my aim dear Lord
Exceeds all "earthly" wealth.
Renew me each and every day
With hope and strength and love;
To finish well and please you Lord
Is all I'm dreaming of.

Christene Bolte-Luthey

CHRIST IS THE VINE

We must take heed as we run life's race that PRIDE does not enter in our hearts and deceive us. Do not think that you or I are capable of running the race of life ALONE. When we allow ourselves to trust in anyone (especially ourselves) other than Christ, we can be absolutely certain that we will NOT know victory. It is a foolish thing to think we are able to carry out such a task. Jesus gave each and every one of us these words regarding this saying, **"I am the VINE, and My Father is the vine dresser. Every** branch in me that does not bear fruit He takes away; and every branch that bears fruit he prunes, that it may bear more fruit. You are already clean because of the word which I have spoken to you. ABIDE IN ME and I IN YOU. As the branch cannot bear fruit of itself, unless it abides in the vine, neither can you unless you abide in me. I am the vine and you are the branches. He who abides in me and I in him, bears much fruit; for without me you can do nothing. If anyone does not abide in me, he is cast out as a branch and is withered; and they gather them and throw them into the fire and are burned. If you abide in me and my words abide in you, you will ask what you desire, and it shall be done for you. By this my Father is glorified, that you bear much fruit; so you will be my disciples. As the Father loved me, I also have loved you; abide in my love. If you will keep my commandments, you will abide in my love, just as I have kept my Father's commandments and abide in his love. These things I have spoken to you that my joy may remain in you, and that your joy may be full" [John 15:1-11].

Perhaps we need to ask ourselves the question: AM I ABIDING in CHRIST? Think about it if you will? Could this be why some of us are not "bearing fruit?" We truly need to consider this because of Jesus' words concerning the **"barren fig tree"** (which pertains to you and I and the kingdom of God). Here, Jesus is addressing UNFRUITFULNESS UNDER GRACE. "A certain man had a fig tree planted in his vineyard, and he came seeking fruit on it and found none. Then he said to the keeper of his vineyard, Look, for three years I have come seeking fruit on this fig tree and find none. Cut it down; why does it use up the ground? But he answered him and said to him, 'Sir, let it alone this year also, until I dig around it and fertilize it. And if it bears fruit, well. But if not after that you may cut it down' " [Luke 13:6-9].

Remember were Jesus states that **"he is the vine and apart from him we can do nothing,"** and again that, **"If anyone does not abide in him they are cast out as a branch and is wither and they gather them and throw them into the fire and are burned?"** This lesson of the "fig tree" is a WARNING to every one of us. If we consider ourselves to be "saved," "born again Christians," we might do well to take close look at our lives and ask HOW LONG WILL GOD GIVE US TO PRODUCE FRUIT THAT GLORIFIES HIM? In Jesus' parable the tree had been given three years, but it would not. Therefore it was good for nothing and occupying valuable ground, which could be used for something else. The tree was (because of its unfruitfulness) going to be cut down and burned. But the vineyard keeper had a heart for that tree and sought MERCY for it. He then asked if it could be given another year, because he knew that <u>with effort and attention, it was capable of producing good fruit.</u>

This parable reminds me of JESUS. He has stepped in with his love, mercy, grace and compassion to help us produce good fruit in our lives. He knows that God will one day "cut down" and "burn" the non-producing, withered trees because they are of no use in his kingdom. That may sound harsh, but I believe this parable holds more truth than any of us can afford to disregard. Jesus said, "HE is the VINE." If we are NOT abiding in him, then like it or not, we ARE WITHERING away spiritually!!!! That is the truth, believe it or not! In this present age of grace, Jesus, like the keeper of the vineyard, has asked His Father in heaven to give US another chance to produce good fruit. All we must do is "abide in Him. I tell you no one is more willing than JESUS to give us the attention we require, so that our lives unlike the tree we just read about will NOT come to anything and be thrown away....

If we have sincerely repented of sin and asked Christ to be our Savior, the next thing we need to get to the bottom of are these vital questions: "Have I experienced a TRUE CONVERSION?" HAS MY LIFE TURNED AROUND and AWAY FROM SIN? Have I practiced a true change of heart and mind toward the word of God and the things pertaining to Christ and his gospel? Have I received a hunger and true desire to know Christ personally as my Savior and friend? When we are TRULY "SAVED," God gives us a new birth. A life by which the Holy Spirit takes control and works within us—God's will (and not our own). **"Which were born, not of blood, nor of the will of the flesh, nor of he will of man, but of God" [John 1:13].**

Please hear and <u>do not misunderstand what I am saying here</u>: I am in no way (at any time throughout this entire book) implying that you (or I) by simply "turning over a new leaf" can or will be "saved." This I have found after talking with many "good" people is one of the biggest misconceptions ever—pertaining to eternal life. Not one of us on earth is perfect, nor will we ever be. Even though we strive daily to follow Christ obediently. We at times are going to fail God and ourselves because we are human. Remember, the Bible tells us we **"have ALL fallen short of his glory."** So regardless of how hard we strive to "clean up our lives" we must understand that we cannot enter God's kingdom that way. Why? Because we can never clean up our lives enough for God, **"But we are all as an unclean thing, and all** our righteousness are as filthy rags; and we all do fade as a leaf; and our iniquities, like the wind, have taken us away" [Isaiah 64:6]. When we are TRULY converted by the Grace of God through our faith and Trust in Christ, something super-natural happens within our soul that cannot completely be described. Yet our lives reveal a transformation that is evident and undeniable. This can only be done by the work of God's divine hand. Our heart should confirm within us whether or not God is controlling our lives, or if we are? When we listen to Christ's words we know: **"Do you love me more than these?" [John 21:15]**.

FAITH THAT CONQUERS

Jesus wants our joy to be full! He desires VICTORY for every one of us. Regardless of who we are, were we live, who we know, where we are from, what color our skin is, etc. Because it is written **"Greater love has no one than this, than to lay down one's life for his friends" [John 15:13]**. We may have many friends as we walk though life, perhaps some in very high places? Yet not one will ever compare to Jesus Christ. There is no greater friend any of us could know! He is the one who for OUR victory and the sake of our soul surrendered his life for us, while we were yet his enemies. **"For when we were still without strength, in due time Christ died for the ungodly. For scarcely for a righteous man will one die; yet perhaps for a good man someone would even die. But God demonstrates his own love toward us, in that while we were sinners, Christ died for us" [Romans 5:6-8]**.

Therefore, let us not resist abiding in Christ. He is our only means of Salvation. He is our only hope. He is the only one who can enable us to produce the fruit of the Spirit of God. There is no other way, and by no other means can any of us obtain that which is required by God to inherit eternal life. As we press on toward victory let us understand in greater depth that if we want to receive the prize, we must run the race according to the rules that God has set before us.

Let us not complain, nor become self-centered. Let us not become weary at every turn. Let us not forget it is Christ who can set the pace and see us through the hurdles we have to endure. Never forget the PRICE Christ Jesus paid for you and I. It has allowed us to compete for the heavenly prize. Therefore let us strive with sincere hearts to discipline ourselves until we have learned to follow Christ without reservation, and allow him to bring us to the place where he is able to fashion and fill us with HIMSELF!

Christ for our sake the Bible tells in the book of **[Isaiah 53:7]**, speaking of Jesus: **"He is despised and rejected by men, a man of many sorrows and acquainted with grief. And we hid, as it were our faces from him; He was despised and we did not esteem him. Surely, he has borne our griefs and carried our sorrows; yet we esteemed stricken, Smitten by God, and afflicted. But he was wounded for our transgressions, he was bruised for our iniquities, the chastisement for our peace was upon him, and by his stripes we are healed. All we like sheep have gone astray; we have turned, every one, to his own way; and the Lord has laid on him the iniquity of us all. He was led as a lamb to the slaughter, and as a sheep before its shearers is silent, so He opened not his mouth"** [Is. 53:3-7].

It seems after reading this scripture that our efforts should be humbly spent APOLOGIZING TO THE LORD rather than complaining constantly about everything? Our hearts should break with thanksgiving and tears should flow from the depths of our being, considering the one who DIED for OUR SINS. Don't you wonder sometimes if God might look down upon us and think: where is their gratitude? Let's ponder that a minute. How often have we given thanks to Jesus who in unfathomable agony knew deep within his body the price of sin and spoke these words? **"I am poured out like water, and all my bones are out of joint; my heart is like wax; it is melted within me. My strength is dried up like a potsherd, and my tongue clings to my jaws; you have brought me to the dust of death. For dogs have surrounded me; the assembly of the wicked has enclosed me. They pierced my hands and my feet; I can count al my bones. They look and stare at me. They divide my garments among them, and for my clothing they cast lots"** [Psalm 22:14-18]. Dear friend, could we (in our wildest dreams) contemplate the thought of fulfilling such a great commission? NEVER!

In the midst of Jesus' words, I know that in every situation and every circumstance I may ever encounter, God's grace will be sufficient for me. Because I trust that he has indeed known the pain I am going through. I believe that in every situation he has felt my heartaches and losses, and even more. In spite of being rejected, he died upon he cross for me (and YOU my friend!) That is how I know I could NEVER give Christ Jesus enough thanks for all he has done. I know that if I praised him every known hour of the day, it would not be enough for all he has done for mankind. Before God he as erased (for those who trust in Him) the GUILTY verdict and with the stain of his own blood, written **"innocent"** after our names. If that my friend is not victory, I don't know what is!

A BLOOD STAINED MEMORY

The blood that fell from Jesus' brow, has fallen on my mind
Obedience to this extreme exceeds all words defined.
They've fallen heavy on my thoughts, and burrowed in my soul,
For pondering his love for me, I am not half, but whole.
No ransomed ever held the power, strong enough to free,
The bondage SIN restrained me in, but Grace produced the key.
Today my bloodstained thoughts possess, the deepest thanks I've known
For every drop of blood that fell, from Christ who stood alone,
Resisting not his Father's will, to die in horrid pain
That man live not in "darkness" where, existence is in vain
Oh God, may every fallen tear, make known to me thy grace.
For only blood stained souls shall see, the glory of your face.
Fill my heart with these few words forever let them be
The utmost hope within my mind
This blood stained memory.

C. Luthey

OBEDIENCE TO GOD'S WILL

God will guide and sustain you throughout all of your life if you trust in him. Remember that victory will only come with obedience to God's will. This involves being tested and tried, but do not despair. Keep your heart and your trust in him. Determine in your heart and mind to walk by faith and not by what you see. Especially when you don't understand and you're seeking answers to questions in life. Take all the "whys" and tuck them in the corner of your heart. Trust in God's power. Trust in God's love. Never ever forget that he cared enough about you to lay down his life.

Faith that conquers and leads to victory when we feel discouraged, afraid, defeated and alone comes when we recall moments throughout our lives that we have witnessed the faithfulness of God. When life's hardships attack, think about the times that God has proven himself to you or someone you know. Take for example **David's** faith, his battle, and his victory in the Lord.

"Then David said to the Philistine, you come to me with a sword, with a spear, and with a javelin. But I come to you in the name of the Lord of Hosts, The God of the armies of Israel, whom you have defiled. This day the Lord will deliver you into my hand and I will strike you and take your head from you. And this day I will give the carcasses of the camp of the Philistine's to the birds of the air and the wild beasts of the earth, that all the earth may know that there is a God in Israel. Then all this assembly shall know that the Lord does not save with sword and spear; for the battle is the Lord's and he will give you into my hands" [1 Sam. 17:45-47].

When we learn to unconditionally surrender the battles of life, making them the Lord's, we'll find (like David) that through our faith, the Lord will lead us to victory. David was NOT overcome with fear in the midst of his battle because he humbly surrendered his problem and acknowledged that the **"battle was the Lord's."** He knew that it was GOD and God alone who was able to conquer evil. Yet through David's faith and by his sincere obedience to God's will—**"Goliath fell."**

One thing we must realize about this victory is that David's confession was based on who he was in the Lord. David had access to his needs by faith because he believed that God's power and grace would be sufficient. Believe with your heart, **"I can do all things through Christ who strengthens me"** [Phil. 4:13]. **"For whatsoever is born of God overcomes the world; and this is the victory that overcomes the world, even our faith"** [1 John 5:4]. Understand that it is vital that we rely on the power of God through every trial. Not ourselves. Trusting in ourselves and relying on our own power will lead us to certain disaster, not victory.

Battles in life are only won by spending time alone with God. Knowing what His word says about victory and who you are in Christ. Would a soldier go into battle hungry or forget to take food? Would a soldier stand on the front line without armor, or neglect to take his weapons? Would he step out ignorant of his mission or uncertain of his strategy? Of course not! Why then do WE step out into each day without taking along Spiritual food and armor that God himself has provided for us? Why do we forget God's daily bread that offers us the life, wisdom, knowledge, understanding, and protection we require? We need it not only to withstand the attacks of the enemy, but also for the power to overcome.

I say these things again, because we cannot allow Satan to have any footholds in our lives. Don't forget that he will use any means possible to lure, and damn every soul he can. Remain on guard and take every measure to resist sinning by abiding in Christ. Never forget that we are in a spiritual battle. Times are going to be difficult, but we who are the heirs of Christ need not fear. We have been given God's awesome armor. It has been tested, tried and known to be strong enough to withstand all temptation. Armed with the word of God and abiding in Christ Jesus, we will be better prepared to take a stand against our "adversary."

FOOD FOR THE SOUL

Where do we find food for our soul? In the word of God! It is recorded in the HOLY BIBLE. We can also listen to God through his Holy Spirit. How do you listen for God's voice? Simply begin with surrendering your life to Christ. Give him your heart and don't withhold one thing from his keeping. In this you'll acknowledge that: <u>There is not one thing we have that was not given to us by God. Therefore, there is not one thing we can give back that was not already God's to take.</u>

By this, I mean, (for example): God gave me two children. They were **gifts** God bestowed upon my life. Yet, the fact is-<u>they are not mine to keep one second longer than God has chosen to allow them to be part of my world</u>. They are on "loan", because they were gifts from God to begin with. This truth I have come to understand, when I have had to spiritually "give them both back" to the Lord. As I have shared with you earlier, when it was told us in April of 2000 that our 14-year-old son had Cancer, it was the second time I had placed him on the Spiritual alter in my heart and surrendered his life to the will of God. This I have to admit is probably one of the hardest things any of us will ever have to do in our lives. Yet I know that peace is found when we "give back" to the one who granted life to our loved one—to begin with.

By this I mean we will be blessed if we learn to: **"render to God the things that are God's."** Shall we pay God back by robbing him of that which we owe for his generosity, faithfulness, love and mercy? This is not only true of those we love; it is also true of our money. Rarely, too few of us think about the grace God has granted us that we may even have the pleasure or privilege of working and making the money that buys us so many things. In buying "things" we need to <u>remember not to forget the one who gives us health and life</u>. We need to give back to God our tithes and offerings to show our appreciation, our gratitude and our humility. If we choose to ignore God's blessings, we rob him. **"Will a man rob God? Yet you have robbed** me! But you say, in what way have we robbed you? In tithes and offerings. Bring all the tithes into the storehouse that there may be food in my house, and prove me now in this. God says. "If I will not open for you the windows of heaven and pour out for you such blessings that there will to be room enough to receive it" [Malachi 3:8,10]**. We would indeed be wise to put forth effort to discipline ourselves in this area. **"On the first day of the week let each one of you lay something aside, storing up as he may prosper, that there be no collections when I come" [1 Cor. 16:2].**

When we come to terms with this truth, we are filled with the indescribable peace that is spoken of in **[Phil. 4:7], "And the peace of God which surpasses all comprehension, shall guard your hearts and your minds in Christ Jesus."** Think of having the peace of God dwelling within you. This is something the world has never been able to offer, manufacture or sell, because it's something only God can give. Many people put forth much effort in trying to find peace in the things of this world, but strive to no avail. The word of God says, **"Be anxious for nothing, but in everything by prayer and supplication with thanksgiving let your requests be known to God" [Phil. 4:6].** Why? Because God will then, **"Guard your heart and mind in Christ Jesus!"**

The peace of God is like nothing this world can give. It is a quiet, gentle, perfect sense of contentment that cannot be compared to anything else in this world. This glorious contentment utterly fills you inside. It allows nothing to trouble your soul. Who can receive this peace, only those who have trusted Christ as Savior? **"And all things whatsoever you ask in prayer, believing you shall receive" [Matt. 21:22].**

To press on toward victory, we also need to open the lines of communication between our heavenly Father and us. We must become acquainted with him if we are to live above our circumstances and come to know him well. **"Now acquaint yourself with him, and be at peace; Thereby good will come to you. Receive, please, instruction from his mouth, and lay up his words in your heart. If you return to the Almighty, you will be built up; you will remove iniquity far from your tents. Then you will lay your gold in the dust, and the gold of Ophir among the stones of the brooks. Yes the Almighty will be your gold and your precious silver; for then you will have your delight in the Almighty" [Job 22:26].** The word will become our source of faith, strength and hope. **"These things have I written unto you that believe on the name of the Son of God; that you may know that you have eternal life,**

and that you may believe on the name of the Son of God" [1 John 5:13]. "Your word is a lamp unto my feet and a light to my path" [Ps. 119:105]. If you desire to know God, then you must get serious about spending quality time alone with Jesus. **"Draw nigh to God and he will draw nigh to you" [James 4:8].**

PRAYER is our means of conversation with God. We cannot walk in victory if we do not establish an ongoing prayer life with the King of Kings. Recall reading my description of the "bridge" that spanned between two mountains, and the cloud, which prevented a clear view of the other side? This bridge is not only an example of God's grace; it also reveals to us OUR FAITH as we cross it. Too often we forfeit the greatest blessings and victories in life, because we are simply too afraid to press through the cloud that has enveloped the bridge. When our view of the "other side" is distorted, we turn away rather than TRUSTING God's grace as a guide wire to see us across. We must be: **"Praying always with all prayer and supplication in the spirit, being watchful to this end with all perseverance and supplication for the saints" [Eph. 6:18]. "Now this is the confidence that we have in him, that if we ask anything according to his will, he hears us. And if we know that he hears us, whatever we ask, we know that we have the petitions that we have asked of him"[1 John 5:14-15].**

Don't be deceived, Satan will try his best to convince us that the bridge is impassable, or if possible he might tempt us to delay or cancel our journey? Yet any or all of these examples are tricks the enemy wants to use to hinder our walk of faith with the Lord. Because the Devil knows that to experience victory is to receive "eternal life." Don't be fooled. Satan knows those who claim victory are servants the Lord will call upon and use to further the work of his kingdom. Which is the LAST thing the enemy wants to happen. Remember this when you come to a bridge that needs to be crossed. Don't allow the enemy to tempt or rob you of God's best. Stand firm and be encouraged by this: **"He who is in you is greater than he who is in the world" [1John 4:4].** Don't be afraid of stepping out in faith with whatever you are facing. Take Jesus' hand and know that he will not leave or abandon you. Trust him and he will see you through.

ESTABLISH A RELATIONSHIP

Consider that a relationship with God can be compared to a "marriage." Just as we take a vow and are married, we commit our lives to be faithful to the one we are marrying. So should our hearts be with the Lord. This commitment must be considered SACRED and we must be careful to let no one or no thing part what we share with each other. Just as in marriage we should promise to protect show respect, and give honor to the one we love. In doing this, our relationship will be blessed. Also, as in a marriage we should strive to understand the heart of the person we love and make them a cherished priority in our lives. If we want the marriage to succeed, we will love unconditionally, and never take our loved one for granted.

When we do all of these things with Christ, we will not hesitate to cross the bridges that are set before us on our journey through life. Why? Because the more we know him and understand him, the more we will trust him. The more we trust, the easier it will be to take his hand and walk by faith. Sometimes I believe one reason it's so difficult to cross bridges is we are not able to see the end result. We're simply afraid of the unknown. We don't know what God is trying to accomplish. Therefore we're focused on what we see and don't rely on our faith to see us through.

Often, we don't have the privilege of knowing what God has planned for us. His will is a mystery. Yet, I've found that the deeper our relationship with God, the less apt we are to let Satan deter us from going boldly forward in whatever we are facing. I don't know about you, but I have found that people I spent a lot of time with, I come to know very well. As I get to know them, I have also learned to trust them. As I have learned to trust them, I have been able to take them at their word and place my faith in whatever they have said they would do. This is exactly how it is with Jesus, the more time with him you spend, the more you will love and trust him also!

As I was standing at a (trial) not too long ago I began praying in the midst of it for the Lord to help me understand <u>WHY he always seems to allow clouds (uncertainty), to consume our view of whatever may be on the other side.</u> Humbly I asked him if he would give me any insight or understanding regarding this and the following is what was placed upon my heart as an answer.

Why does God allow "clouds" to consume our view in the midst of a trial? *So that your faith may grow and be strengthened, that you may learn how **not to doubt God's will or his ways**. In doing this, your trust in God will widen and deepen to the point where NOTHING may trouble your heart or mind. In this, you will* *never doubt, but will only believe that God is in complete control and that all will be taken care of in due time, according to God's will. In this, we may know God's peace and learn to fully trust in Him.* **"These things I have spoken to you while being present with you. But the helper, the Holy Spirit whom the Father will send in my name, he will teach you all things, and bring to your remembrance all things that I said to you. Peace I leave with you, my peace I give to you; not as the world gives do I give to you. Let not your heart be troubled, neither be afraid" [John 14:25-27]. "Let not your heart be troubled; you believe in God, believe also in me" [John 14:1].**

We must never, ever forget: that Satan is out to rob, steal, kill and destroy. The last thing the enemy wants is for us to place our complete faith and trust in Jesus Christ as our Lord and Savior. Therefore do not forget that he will use any means available to prey on your every weakness, and try to deceive you in any way he can. He wants more than anything to deter you from crossing "bridges" in life, because <u>he knows that each victory will ultimately reveal to us the faithfulness of God and the Love of Christ</u>. Be certain that the devil knows that those who trust God and overcome life's adversities will walk in the blessed assurance of victory in Christ, and be able to reach out to others <u>helping them in their journey</u>.

TRUSTING ME

    Taking all your doubts and cares
    Releasing them to me,
    Using all my promises
    So that others see—that
    Trusting always
    In my name
    Near to me in prayer—shall
    Grant all you lack within, to keep you from despair.

    Making me your Lord and King
    Entrusting me to do, my will, and still believing, that I shall see you through.
    Christene Bolte-Luthey

"Casting all your cares upon Him; for he cares for you" [1 Peter 5:7].

"Cast your burden upon the Lord, and He shall sustain you" [Psalm 55:22].

"Come unto me, and I will give you rest" [Matthew 11:28].

THE CHALLENGE

If you want to KNOW beyond a shadow of a doubt that you have ABSOLUTELY been "SAVED" and will RECEIVE GOD'S GIFT OF "EVERLASTING (ETERNAL) LIFE," then check yourself by the word of God and God's word below to see if you have truly been "BORN AGAIN" and therefore ADOPTED BY GOD. As you evaluate yourself by God's word through the following, (what the BIBLE states you must do to receive NEW LIFE) you will gain a fullness of spiritual vitality and a life-changing transformation that will bless you beyond that which mere words could ever begin to describe.

I pray with all my heart that by this point you have contemplated many important issues that pertain to life and the fact that there is an infinite gap (gulf) between God and us. If we are ever to approach God (because He is Holy), we must somehow be made holy (just as holy as God is.) Because of the holiness of God, we must have a NEW LIFE in which our SINS HAVE BEEN FORGIVEN and done away with, so that we can be as separated from sin—as God is. Remember that we all by nature are sinful, the word of God says, **"All have sinned and fall short of the glory of God"** [Rom. 3:23].

Therefore, we need the righteousness of God because we know that sin separates us from Him. This is where we may praise God for the **GOOD NEWS of the GOSPEL that CHRIST JESUS DIED for our sins, having taken them UPON HIMSELF and is able to set us apart from them—BY FAITH—BELIEVING THAT JESUS DIED FOR OUR SINS, and that HIS DEATH was in our place and that His payment for our sin is fully acceptable in God's sight.**

If we are to receive the NEW LIFE (Eternal Life) that is the GIFT of God, we must begin with acknowledging our sin. By the grace of God I pray that throughout this entire book the HOLY SPIRIT has convicted our hearts through God's word to correct us, rebuke us, and cause us to consider our sin. If He has done this in YOUR heart, then you will feel severe conviction in the depths of our soul, and realize with fear and trembling that you are in desperate need of a Savior. When God's Holy Spirit makes this known to you, you will have in a spiritual way, come to the "end of yourself." When this miraculously happens you will earnestly **REPENT of your sin**.

When you repent: this means that you must sorrowfully **ACKNOWLEDGE** and **CONFESS** the sadness you feel realizing your sin, <u>not for the consequences of sin</u> but actually—sincere heartfelt sorrow for **YOUR sins**. When this happens you will feel extreme and genuine hatred for them because they separate you from God and His Holiness. In realizing this you will with Christ Jesus' help strive to forsake them always.

Then as you sincerely begin to repent of YOUR SIN, you will feel in your soul the desperate desire and need for **FORGIVENESS**. You must know that <u>there is NOTHING YOU can do to **earn**</u> God's gift of Eternal Life. It is received **THROUGH FAITH** as **God's FREE GIFT** when **YOU BELIEVE in JESUS AS YOUR OWN PERSONAL SAVIOR**. When you receive God's gift of Eternal life though believing in Jesus as your own personal Savior, you can be certain that you are "SAVED or in other words, "BORN AGAIN." This, my beloved friend means that <u>you have been **DELIVERED from the PENALTY OF SIN**</u> and our feelings of guilt, and therefore are no longer separated from God because of sin—but rather as the Bible says, **"adopted"** into the presence of God.

You have in making this step through the leading of the Holy Spirit, been CONVERTED or turned from sin—to righteousness, (from trusting YOURSELF to RELYING ON your heavenly Father. Stepping out and doing these things will mean that you have sorrowfully admitted your sin, repented of it, and desire with Christ's help to turn away from the things in life which separate you from God. You have received the *New Life* that is in Jesus Christ and will from this day on—be spiritually transformed day by day through Christ who is now living and abiding in you. If you have trusted Christ as your Savior, then you are now a **"child of God,"** and are no longer in bondage of sin or its death and destruction. Instead you possess all the rights and privileges of the **"sonship."**

Because of your TRUE FAITH in Christ Jesus and all that he has done and suffered for you; you are now **JUSTIFIED** and your sins have been forgiven. Because you believed you are now able to enter into heaven. Remember always though that you were justified and saved by faith alone, it was not due to any of your works. You received **"SALVATION"** as a GIFT that was acquired only by the holy life of Jesus led and his innocent death.

This was for our benefit and bestowed upon us through God's priceless GRACE.

REJOICE in your assurance of the New Life. Do not doubt your Salvation. You have the PROMISE of GOD, **"In hope of eternal life which God, who cannot lie, promised before time" [Titus 1:2].** God has promised to graciously accept in Christ all repenting sinners, **"To the praise and glory of His grace, by which he made us accepted in the beloved. In him we have redemption through his blood, the forgiveness of sins, according to riches of his grace" [Eph. 1:6-7].** This means that you will one day be with God in heaven, because you are in Christ Jesus.

You as a "born again" believer not only have God's promise of eternal life; you also have the promises of JESUS. He has said that you will not only have life eternal, but an abundant life also. **"Most assuredly I say to you, he who hears my word and believes in him who sent me has everlasting life, and shall not come into judgment, but has passed from death into life" [John 5:24]** and, **"The thief does not come except to steal, and to kill, and to destroy. I have come that they may have life, and that they may have it more abundantly" [John 10:10].** In addition to Jesus' promises, you also have that of the Holy Spirit, to assure your heart of true salvation, **"And I will pray the Father, and He will give you another helper, that he may abide with you forever. [1 Cor. 12:13]** states that it is the Holy Spirit who will place all believing sinners into the body of Christ in which we may have the assurance of being in union with God himself. **"For by one Spirit we were all baptized into one body—whether Jews or Greeks, whether slaves or free—and have all been made to drink into one spirit."**

RECOGNIZE what God and your Lord Jesus Christ have done for you and I. Jesus said, **"I am the resurrection and the life. He who believes in me, though he may die, he shall live. And whoever lives and believes in me shall never die" [John 11:25-26].** Testify to someone today of your decision to follow Christ, do not be afraid to tell the world what God has done for you, **"That if you shall confess with your mouth the Lord Jesus and shall believe in your heart that God has raised Him from the dead you shall be saved. For with the heart a man believes unto righteousness; and with the mouth confession is made unto salvation" [Romans 10:9-10].** Jesus also said, **"Therefore whoever confesses Me before men, him I will also confess before my Father who is in heaven" [Matt. 10:32].**

Know that as you step out in faith, the Holy Spirit is also gradually **SANCTIFYING** those of us who possess a true heart to follow Christ. That means that you and I are daily being made holy in our heart and in our life. This process also helps us produce "fruit" in our lives as we strive to do good works out of love and gratitude to God for his mercy, love and grace. We must realize the fact that even though God will provide in us the power to live the Christian life, we will never become completely "sinless" in this world. Yet we must strive with all our might to **TRY** to do God's will in everything. Please do not misunderstand in any way my precious friend, that even as a "Born Again," Christ "saved" Christian, you are going to struggle throughout each and every day in different instances where you must share your faith with others, resist temptations, or remain faithful to the will of God. In knowing this, please remember that it will be vitally important for you to rely solely on God's power and strength to see you through. We must never trust or depend in our OWN power, wisdom or might as a means to endure each day with its tests and trials. Realize that it is God alone who supplies each and every one of our needs, **"And God shall supply all your needs according to His riches in Glory by Christ Jesus" [Phil. 4:19].**

DEVELOPE PRAYER LIFE. Begin today learning how to grow in the new life that God has given you. Let the first step be that of realizing the importance of PRAYER. It is and forever will be your means of talking and listening to God. You will talk to him with your lips and with your heart. Let your prayers sincerely contain:

Adoration and **Praise:** Acknowledging God, His Holiness, Grace and Goodness

Thanksgiving: Giving God our appreciation for His mercy, which will keep us in a state of genuine humility for his countless blessings, love and kindness toward us.

Confession: Of our sins and guilt before God. Freely admitting our sins without excuse, and expressing Godly sorrow, and asking for forgiveness because of our deep regret

Petition: That we may by faith, in the name of Jesus, ask God to cleanse us from all sin, and grant us wisdom that we may be delivered from all evil in this world.

Do not forget to humbly pray the **Lord's Prayer** in addition to your own prayers found in the book of **[Matthew 6:9-13].** If you are able, when you pray, try to kneel, sit or stand with your hands folded, as kneeling displays an attitude of humiliation, especially when we are confessing our sins to God.

Also remember that we should always pray in Christ's name. Remember that we have the promise that whatever we ask in His name will be given to us. **[John 16:23]**. Let us always be quick to pray, **"not my will, but Thine, be done"** as Jesus, prayed, **[Matt. 6:10] & [Matt. 26:39]**. Have faith when you pray that God always answers the prayers of believers. The Bible says that if we ask anything according to his will he will hear us. **[1 John 5:14], "Now we have this confidence that we have in him, that if we ask anything according to his will, he hears us."**

Know that Spiritual growth and maturity are impossible without prayer. Also, begin worshiping God, honoring him either through public or private services, **"Where two or three are gathered together in my name, there I am in the midst of them" [Matt. 18:20]. "When you stand praying, forgive, if you have ought against any: that your Father also which is in heaven may forgive your trespasses" [Mark 11:25]. "Your father knows what things you have need of, before you ask Him. After this manner therefore pray, Our Father which art in heaven, Hallowed be Thy name" [Matt. 6:8-9]**.

STUDY GOD'S WORD daily; and faithfully learn to apply it obediently to your heart and life. Reading the word of God is very important. Ask the Spirit of God while you are studying to meet your needs as you read. Think carefully about the meaning and implications of what the word of God is saying to your heart. Read and examine the Bible repeatedly and extensively. Try not to be distracted when you are meditating on God's word. Read the Bible faithfully and obediently, remembering that it is Spiritual food for your soul, and it will keep you from sinning.

Rely always on God's word to help fix your mind on God, and provide the daily sustenance needed for your spiritual life. Depend on God's word to continually provide you with guidance, and instruction for every aspect of your life. Meditate upon the word of God day and night (at all times) and it is promised that God will guarantee prosperity and success in the new life he has given us. Also, understand that in reading God's word we must remain obedient to it. Obeying what God's word indicates to us that we should do in each and every situation. By being obedient to God's word we may expect to be treasured by God, blessed, avoid evil, be given safety, know freedom from fear and anxiety, bear fruit in our lives that is pleasing to God, receive the promises God has given us, continue in the abiding love of Christ, dwell in God's love, and gain entrance into heaven.

Remain committed to God and his will. Commitment is the foundation to living a life that is dedicated to Christ. If we are to avoid being conformed to this world then we must strive to be transformed by God's word. This can only be accomplished by dedicating our lives as a living sacrifice to God's perfect will. Commit our Salvation, works, and goals to God as Jesus did while he was on earth. Last, let us in the hour of our death, commit our souls to God with perfect peace and confidence in the blessed assurance that any and all commitments to the Lord will accepted and honored. **[1 Cor. 15:58], "Therefore my beloved brethren, be steadfast, immovable, always abounding in the work of the Lord, knowing that your labor is not in vain in the Lord."**

Use the Spiritual Gifts God has bestowed upon you. Spiritual gifts are those gifts God has given you by the Spirit of God to accomplish God's purposes in the world and for the uplifting of the body of Christ. The Bible states that every believer has been given spiritual gifts **[Romans 12:5],** and the gifts belong to God and are given to us so that we may use them for the Glory of God **[1 Peter. 4:11]**. God has given us these gifts that we may serve God and our fellow believers with them. These gifts are useless and considered worthless if we don't put them to use in the service of God. Therefore let us strive daily to consider our gifts and use them wisely to do that which God has intended so that the body of Christ may maintain strength, health and vitality throughout.

GIVING: Let us all ponder the gifts of God through giving. When we give cheerfully on the first day of the week, we are obediently honoring God with that which he has given us. Failure to give back to God is a serious matter (and I believe we covered this earlier in the book). A person who fails to honor God with his money actually robs God, **[Mal. 3:8]**. Giving to God helps support his children who are in need, and promises provision for those who are serving him. Therefore, let us honor God with our new life by cheerfully giving back a portion of what he has given us, for it is the key to spiritual growth.

WORSHIP: The Bible teaches that God alone is worthy of our worship. **[Ps. 29:2]**. True worship which is valued and found pleasing to God involves, reverence, public expression, and service. When we worship God we must reverence him with honor and respect. We must submit ourselves in humble obedience to surrender our thoughts and emotions to God as Christ Jesus did and said we must do. Jesus told us in **[John 4:24]**, that we are to worship God **"in spirit and truth."** The term spirit speaks of the personal nature of worship. The word "truth" speaks of the content of worship. God is pleased when we worship him, because in doing so, we understand and honor the true nature of his character.

In worshiping God in a public expression we are showing others that we want to thank God for his blessings, and doing it privately is not sufficient. As we worship in service to God, we are displaying with humble and joyful hearts our sincere obedience to him. If we are to remain true, steadfast, sincere and humble before God, let us remember these things. Dwell on God's word and sing his praises. Lift high God's holy name, and don't forget the grace we've received through faith in Jesus Christ our Lord. Let us worship and thank him daily for the high price he paid for your soul and mine. **"These things I have spoken to you, that my joy may remain in you, and that your joy may be full" [John 15:11]**.

Believe in God, share what you have, and give what you can both of your money and spiritual gifts. Love everyone without hope of any appreciation being returned to you, and you will be blessed. Do things out of love for one another, not for thanks or praise, in doing this you will never be discouraged, and will be less apt to give up on doing that which you know is good and right in the sight of God your heavenly Father. Again, give graciously, just as our Lord has given to us. Don't look for rewards here on earth, trust that the greatest you can receive will be given when Christ returns in Glory and distributes his rewards according to that which we deserve.

RESOLVE ALL STRIFE: Make peace with God and everyone you know. Forgive all of your enemies. Strive to love all unconditionally regardless of those who do wrong, hurt or fail us. Seek peace and harmony with all people, in spite of their failures and faults. Live according to God's word, **"God is faithful, by whom you were called into the fellowship of His Son Jesus Christ our Lord. Now I plead with you, brethren, by the name of our Lord Jesus Christ, that you all speak the same thing, and that there be no divisions among you, but that you are perfectly joined together in the same mind and in the same judgment" [1 Cor. 1:9-10]. "And do this knowing the time, that now, it is high time to awake out of sleep; for now our salvation is nearer than when we first believed. The night is far spent, the day is at hand. Therefore let us cast off the works of darkness, and let us put on the armor of light. Let us walk properly as in the day, not in revelry and drunkenness, not in lewdness, lust, not in strife and envy. But put on the Lord Jesus Christ and make no provision for the flesh, to fulfill its lusts" [Rom. 1311-14].**

Guard your heart and protect your soul by keeping in constant union with Christ Jesus. Constantly seek God's will and his face. **"Let us draw** near with a true heart in full assurance of faith, having our hearts sprinkled from an evil conscience and our bodies washed with pure water. Let us hold fast the confession of our hope without wavering. For He who promised is faithful. And let us consider one another in order to stir up love and good works, not forsaking the assembling of ourselves together, as is the manner of some, but exhorting one another, and so much the more as you see the day approaching" [Heb. 10:22-25].

WALK IN THE SPIRIT: Dear friends in order to walk successfully with God we must learn to "walk in the Spirit." To begin walking in the Spirit, we need to <u>continue in the attitude of our CONFESSION of sin</u>. In doing this our heart will not lose its sorrow for sin or the desire to turn away from it. This is somewhat keeping our thoughts of repentance present in our mind. The Bible tells us of some specific times that we should walk in the spirit in an attitude of confession. One is before the close of each day, **"Be angry, and do not sin, do not let the sun go down on your wrath"** [Eph. 4:26]. And also before the Lord's Supper, **"Therefore whoever eats this bread or drinks this cup of the Lord in an unworthy manner will be guilty of the body and blood of the Lord. But let a man examine himself, and so let him eat of the bread and drink of the cup. For he who eats and drinks in an unworthy manner eats and drinks judgment to himself, not discerning the Lord's body. For this reason many are weak and sick among you, and many sleep. For if we would judge ourselves, we would not be judged. But when we are judged, we are chastened by the Lord, that we may not be condemned with the world"** [1 Cor. 11:27-32]. As we walk in the Spirit, let us understand that we will need to confess our sins either privately **[1 John 1:9]**, with someone of whom we have sinned against **[Matt. 5:23]**, or publicly **[Matt. 18:17]**, if our sin has been of a public nature.

As we walk in the Spirit, <u>we must also YIELD to the will of God</u> to be used for his service. Scriptures tell us that we are to yield ourselves, body and mind, **"And do not present your members a instruments of unrighteousness to sin, but present yourselves to God as being alive from the dead, and your members as instruments of righteousness to God"** [Rom. 6:13]. **"Therefore submit to God. Resist the devil and he will flee from you"** [James 4:7]. **"I beseech you therefore, brethren, by the mercies of God, that you present your bodies as a living sacrifice, holy, acceptable to God, which is your reasonable service"** [Romans 12:1].

This yielding ourselves, body and mind, we are willing to allow God to do some specific thing in our life. We are surrendering our will and dedicating ours to that which He commands. We are told, **"do not conform to this world" [Rom. 12:2],** because this world is opposed to God and if we do NOT yield ourselves to His will, then we're following our own. As we learn to yield our heart and life to God, we will also be "renewing" our mind day by day. This renewing will occur as we go to God in prayer and meditate on his word. As we yield ourselves and everything in our life, we will be slowly transformed, and brought to the place where we think much more like God, **"And be renewed in the spirit of your mind, [Eph.4: 23].** Do not misunderstand, this "renewing" and transformation will not happen overnight, it is a <u>lifelong course of action</u> that will not be completely finished until we are with Christ, **"Being confident of this very thing, that He who has begun a good work in you will complete it until he day of Jesus Christ" [Phil. 1:6].** Nevertheless, learning to yield ourselves along life's journey will most assuredly bring us much peace and joy in that we are striving to have the mind of Christ.

Also as we go forward walking in the Spirit, <u>we must surrender to the FILLING of the Spirit</u>. To walk successfully in the Christian life, we must be "filled" with the Spirit, which is to also be controlled by the Spirit. For us to "be filled" by the Spirit we must do that which I have already mentioned, (confession of sin and yielding to God). As we choose to obey God in doing these things, we will be filled with the Spirit and enabled to begin manifesting character that similar to Christ Jesus.

By this I mean that as we learn to surrender ourselves in greater depth to the will of God and dedicate our lives to his service, we will begin to demonstrate more and more the Christlike personality God so desires for each and every one of us which is described in **[Gal.5:22-25], "But the fruit of the Spirit is love, joy, peace, longsuffering, kindness, goodness, faithfulness, gentleness, self-control, against such there is no law. And those who are Christ's have crucified the flesh with its passions and desires. If we live in the Spirit, let also walk in the Spirit."**

May we request daily, that God will through the wondrous work of his Holy Spirit, encourage each and every one of us to desire wholeheartedly the beautiful traits that Christ Jesus established, that we may day by day be transformed and become more like Him. As we walk in the Spirit, let us not forget that we are not walking alone. God knows our strengths and our weaknesses and if we trust him daily, he will help us accomplish all of these things.

We Are Not Alone

As we face problems and trials in life, let us always remember that we are not alone, we have as "born again" Christians the Holy Spirit to comfort, strengthen, guide and protect us. **"You shall not be afraid of the terror by night, nor of the arrow that flies by day, nor of the pestilence that walks in darkness nor of the destruction that lays waste at noonday"[Psalm 91:5-6].** Whether our difficulties in life are of physical or spiritual nature, we must take courage in knowing that God will strengthen us and help us grow in faith and knowledge as we with Christ Jesus—face and conquer them. As we grow, we will bring glory to God for He will demonstrate amidst our trials his faithfulness and prove that his grace is sufficient for each and every one of our needs. **"My grace is sufficient for you, for my strength is made perfect in weakness. Therefore most gladly I will rather boast in my infirmities, that the power of Christ may rest upon me" [2 Cor. 12:9].**

As we begin our new life, we need to know that we are undoubtedly going to come up against problems with sin, temptation, struggling to know what the will of God is in our lives and require the strength to do it. We will also at times experience heartache and suffering. Do not be deceived, our lives will not (just because we are "Christians") be void of tribulation. Many times throughout our Christian journey we may find ourselves feeling doubt, fear, disappointment, and concern, but when these things happen we through our faith and trust in God may rest assured that we are not alone. God will see us through whatever it is that we are having difficulty with, **"Because you have made the Lord, who is my refuge, even the Most High your habitation, no evil shall befall you, nor shall any plague come near you dwelling; for He shall give his angels charge over you to keep you in all your ways" [Ps. 91:9-11].**

Facing Problems

One of the biggest problems we will encounter in our new life is SIN. We already know what it is and why we don't want to be a part of it. What we need now is to focus on how to become aware of it and in what ways we can resist it. The best way we can resist sin is to be cautious of places, situations and times in which we may be open to temptation. The only way we can <u>avoid temptation</u> is to progressively grow in Christ Jesus. As we grow in Christ, our mind will be filled with the thoughts and ways of the Lord and we will not be as vulnerable to temptation.

Keep in mind that which we have already discussed regarding "self-will," it is a serious sin against God and we must watch ourselves daily so that we do not fall into this temptation. Remember that it was THIS sin that led Satan to fall, **[Is. 14:12-14]**. We have become familiar with reading, that the world holds many temptations for us. We have learned that the world opposes God, his values, his statutes, his word and his ways. The world values all the things that are opposite to God's will, therefore we must not let the attractions of this world lead us astray in our walk with the Lord.

Temptation to sin also as we have read before, cannot only approach us though the things of this world. Satan too will try his best to hinder the work and will of God in our lives. Do not ever forget my friend, who Satan is and how much he hatefully opposes everything that God wants for us in our Christian life. He along with his angels—will stop at nothing to hinder the will of God in our lives, **"until he is cast into the lake of fire" [Matt. 25:41; Rev. 20:10]**. He will blind our minds, **"Whose minds the god of this age has blinded, who do not believe, lest the light of the gospel of the glory of Christ who is the image of God, should shine on them" [2 Cor 4:4],** he will try to take the word of God from our heart, **"Those by the wayside are the ones who hear; then the devil comes and takes away the word out of their hearts, lest they should believe and be saved" [Luke 8:12],** and attempt to control us, **"But Elymas the sorcerer for so his name is translated withstood them, seeking to turn the proconsul away from the faith." [Acts 13:8].** It is good to study and recognize the ways the devil will try to deceive us and cause us to sin. You can read about the ways he wants to destroy your life in some of the following scripture verses: **[Rev. 12:10 / 1 Pet. 5:8 / 1 Thess. 2:18 / 1 Cor. 7:5 / 2 Cor. 11:14]**

As Christians our response to Satan is to first recognize his power and his deception. In doing this, we are to hold fast persistently to the faith, and refuse (resist) to go along with him. **[James 4:7]** states, **"Therefore submit to God. Resist the devil and he will flee from you."** We cannot and must not give Satan opportunities to bring destruction on our lives. Be certain that the only way to fight Satan is to stand fast in your Christian faith and receive the word of God into your heart so that you will not be misled or deceived. Witness to those you know and love who have not received the new life, and compassionately strive to snatch them from the blinding lies of Satan's control in their lives.

Dear friend, remember in whatever you endure throughout your life, this blessed promise from God's Holy and precious word: **"And we know that all things work together for good to those who love God, to those who are the called according to His purpose. For whom He foreknew, He also predestined to be conformed to the image of His Son, that He might be the firstborn among many brethren. Moreover whom He predestined, these He also called; whom He called, these He also justified; and whom He justified, these He also glorified. What then shall we say to these things? If God is for us who can be against us? He who did not spare His own Son, but delivered Him up for us all, how shall He not with Him also freely give us all things? Who shall bring a charge against God's elect? It is God who justifies. Who is he who condemns? It is Christ who died, and furthermore is also risen, who is even at the right hand of God, who also makes intercession for us. Who shall separate us form the love of Christ? Shall tribulation, or distress, or persecution, or famine, or nakedness, or peril, or sword? As it is written: For your sake we are killed all day long; we are accounted as sheep for the slaughter. Yet in all these things we are more than conquerors through Him who loved us. For I am persuaded that neither death nor life, nor angels nor principalities nor powers, nor angels nor things present nor things to come, nor height, nor depth, nor any other created thing, shall be able to separate us from the love of God which is in Christ Jesus our Lord"** [Romans 8:28-39].

Understand that temptation is not "sin." We do not sin until we yield to it. Although we will face many crossroads in life where we may be tempted to sin, we DO NOT have to succumb to the desire, remember, "resist him and he will flee from you." Being a child of God, you may say to the devil with confidence, **"I have not a high priest which cannot be touched with the feelings of our infirmities; but was in all points tempted as we are, yet without sin. Let us therefore come boldly to the throne of grace, that we may obtain mercy, and find grace to help in our time of need"** [Heb 4:15-16]. **"That the trial of your faith, being much more precious than of gold that perishes, though it be tried with fire, might be found unto praise and honor and glory at the appearing of Jesus Christ"** [1 Peter 1:7].

When we are tempted to sin, recall the Lord's strength when he was tried. Never lose sight of the race that has been set before us and make every effort to run and win. Do not become disqualified amidst the race by pleasing the devil, in doing this we will grieve the heart of God. We must renounce evil always that we may remain blameless and pure until the time when the Lord returns. Let us do as we are told and, **"Pray without ceasing, in everything give thanks; for this is the will of God in Christ Jesus for you. Do not quench the spirit. Do not despise prophecies. Test all things; hold fast what is good. Abstain from every form of evil. Now may the God of peace Himself sanctify you completely; and may your whole spirit, soul, and body be preserved blameless at the coming of our Lord Jesus Christ. He who calls you is faithful, who also will do it"** [1 Thes. 5:17-22].

Abiding In Him

When we do the will of God we are abiding in Him. In this we will not only grow Spiritually, but we will also produce much good fruit, which is pleasing to our heavenly Father. **"But this I say; He who sows sparingly will also reap sparingly, and he who sows bountifully will also reap bountifully. So let each one give as he purposes in his heart, not grudgingly or of necessity for God loves a cheerful giver. And God is able to make all grace abound toward you, that you always having all sufficiency in all things, have an abundance for every good work"** [2 Cor. 9:6-8].

ALL REAP WHAT THEY HAVE SOWN

The weeds and thistles, briars and thorns, shall all be thrown away
Tossed into my wrath of fire known as judgment day.
The sickle then will separate the stalk from which has grown
So too shall be the wheat and chaff, all reap what they have sown.
Those who sow a love for "self" will surely weep hard tears,
Seeing Me before them stand; they shall regret those years.
Those who sow a love of want; shall also weep in pain
Seeing all their things destroyed, their labor was in vain.
Those who never took the time to take another's hand
Shall receive no mercy then that THEY shall understand.
LIFE is living all to give. To serve another free,
Taking nothing in return, the way it is to be.

Christene Bolte-Luthey

To stand beside a weary heart, whose hopes were bruised and lost
To bear another's burdens; regardless of the cost.
To do the things I ask of you, that my will may be done,
I ask no greater thing from you—than to walk with Christ My Son.

Chistene Bolte-Luthey

THE KEY

How you choose to live will show
Just how much your "fruit" will grow.

Those who will not follow me
Will forfeit peace, eternally.

Close the door in Satan's face
Let his hatred have no place.

Within you or your spirit there
Place all battles in my care.

I will ransom those in chains
And there shall be no more remains.

Those who trust themselves right now,
Will in misery ponder—How?

When they are left behind to dwell
In what shall be a living hell.

All because they would not see
My grace, my way, my will, the KEY.

Christene Bolte-Luthey

Let us from this moment on, not only receive the grace of God into our heart, but let us also pass the knowledge of it on to others so that they may receive Christ and lay hold of the power, promise and peace that is in him. May He be our beloved example to follow in each and every situation, every circumstance, every temptation and every trial. For in him all hope is found.

"Now the God of hope fill you with all joy and peace believing, that you may abound in hope by the power of he Holy Spirit" [Romans 15:13].

Believe it or not, each and every day of our life, we are being tested and tried by our circumstances and crossroads we choose as to whether we will choose to follow God in obedience to his will, or go with Satan and love the world. We no doubt are on a journey that will ultimately demonstrate, and determine where our heart is. Are we going to rebel and follow the devil, or are we going to surrender in humble adoration to the will of God and accept whatever comes our way? God has granted each of us a choice as to which we will go. Every time we turn around we will find ourselves standing at the crossroads of decision. I hope and pray that you and I will be wise and allow the Holy Spirit always to lead, guide, and direct our paths?

WHATEVER THE CUP THAT I MUST DRINK

Whatever the cup that I must drink
Grant me Lord thy grace
To worship with a thankful heart,
And state my cares with praise
For I know neither what lies ahead,
Nor what this day will bring
I can only trust in you with all and everything.
Help me live throughout my trials,
In your perfect ways,
That I may glorify you Lord
All my earthly days.
None will ever know the pain
Which you endured for me
It's that the memory of your love
Which sets my spirit free
I keep you in remembrance Lord
Because I love you so
Whatever the cup that I must drink,
May that in suffering show.

Christene Bolte-Luthey

Christene Bolte-Luthey

THE CHARACTER OF CHRIST

If we are to walk in victory we must lay hold of the Character of Christ Jesus and know the core of his life and ministry so that we are not deceived. Let us review that which was written in the word of God so that there is no mistake. Remember that there is only one way into heaven. Jesus said, **"I am the door; by me if any man enter in, he shall be saved" [John 10:9]. "He that enters not by the door into the sheep fold, but climbs up some other way, the same is a thief and a robber" [John 10:11].**

Beware! Do not be deceived! <u>Thinking right</u> does <u>not</u> save us. <u>Denying self</u> does <u>not</u> save us. Denying the existence of sin does not save us. <u>Turning over a new leaf</u> does <u>not</u> save us. Service or <u>works</u> do <u>not</u> save us. We are not saved through personal sacrifices either. Let us understand that these examples are all empty substitutes for salvation. Never forget <u>Jesus alone can provide TRUE Salvation.</u>

Jesus throughout his life and ministry challenged each heart to **"follow him,"** saying, **"I will make you fishers of men" [Matt. 4:19].** Because, **"all have sinned and come short of the glory of God" [Rom. 3:23].** Jesus came to fill a human need, **"I come not to call the righteous, but sinners" [Luke 5:32].** Providing salvation, He came to be the sinner's substitute, **"the good shepherd gives his life for the sheep" [John 10:11]. "Who His own self bare our sins in his own body on the tree, that we, being dead to sins, should live unto righteousness; by whose stripes we are healed" [1 Peter 2:24].** Jesus came to do what no one else can or ever could do, **"I am the way, the truth, and the life; no man comes to the Father but by me" [John 14:6].** In this way, Christ offered to us Salvation, **"For by grace you are saved through faith; and not of yourselves; it is the gift of God" [Eph. 2:8].** To the man who accepts Salvation through his blood, **"He that has the Son has life; and he that has not the Son of God has not life' [1 John 5:12].** Jesus came to provide total assurance to sinners who placed their trust in Him, **"Thy sins are forgiven, go in peace" [Luke 7:48-50].** Read also: **[Romans 3:24 & Colossians 1:14].**

Again I want to remind you that there is a HUGE difference between KNOWING GOD, and knowing *ABOUT* God. When we stand before Him what we've "heard" about him will NOT enough for him to welcome us in to his kingdom, make no mistake. **"And when he putteth forth his own sheep, he goes before them and the sheep follow him; for they know his voice. And a stranger will they not follow, but will flee from him; for they know not the voice of strangers" [John 10:4-5].**

ABIDE IN CHRIST

Abide in me,
Abide in me,
And I shall always set you free.

Trust my power,
Trust my will
And I shall always quench and fill.

Follow me
And you shall see,
Thy soul—rejoice in victory!

Christene Bolte-Luthey

THE GREAT COMMISSION

"And Jesus came and spoke unto them saying, all power is given unto me in heaven and in earth. Go ye therefore, and teach all nations, baptizing them in the name of the Father, and of the Son, and of the Holy Ghost; teaching them to observe all things which I have commanded you; and, lo, I am with you always, even unto the end of the world. Amen." [Matt. 28:18-20]. Let us today put on the full armor of God in the name of Jesus and in the authority he has given us through His Holy Spirit, receive the calling of the greatest commission ever given to mankind. "But ye shall receive power, after that the Holy Spirit is come upon you; and you shall be witnesses unto me both in Jerusalem, and in all Judea, and in Samaria, and unto the uttermost part of the earth" [Acts 1:8].

To fight life's battles and claim victory in Christ, we must put on the full armor of God spoken of in the book of Ephesians, **"Finally my brethren, be strong in the Lord and in the power of his might. Put on the full armor of God, that you may be able to stand against the wiles of the Devil. For we do not wrestle against flesh and blood, but against principalities and against powers, against rulers of the darkness of this age, against spiritual hosts of wickedness in the heavenly places, therefore take up the whole armor of God, that you may be able to** withstand in the evil day, and having done all to stand. Stand therefore, having **GIRDED your waist with TRUTH**, having put on **the BREASTPLATE of RIGHTEOUSNESS**, and **having SHOD YOUR FEET** with the preparation of the **Gospel of peace.** Above all, taking the **SHIELD OF FAITH** with which you will be able to quench all the fiery darts of the wicked one. And take the **HELMET of SALVATION**, and the **SWORD of THE SPIRIT**, which is the WORD of God; praying always with all prayer and supplication for the saints" [Eph. 6:10-18].

Remember that the standards of the world do not and will not ever apply to "Born Again" Christians. God has his OWN set of standards we are to follow and obey. We must strive to live our lives beyond reproach by confessing our sins before God daily. As we repent then of them and seek forgiveness, we will be preparing for the fight in which Satan is waging war against us. Do not allow Satan to use your sins against you. Make it a habit to place this Spiritual armor on you each and every day. In doing so, you will find it much easier to identify temptation, resist sin, and fight evil.

The **BREASTPLATE OF RIGHTEOUSNESS:** In order to receive Biblical Righteousness that is pleasing to God, we need to begin living upright lives with the help of the Holy Spirit. When we place this breastplate upon ourselves by Faith, we are protecting our heart against the temptation to sin. In order for this to be effective, we must be willing to live a righteous life before God and the world. Let us be excellent witnesses of the Christian faith. We should make a resolution to assess ourselves each day. In faithfully doing so we will persistently cleanse our lives, that they may be seen as pleasing to God. Let us try hard to check the way we live by the word of God and allow its wisdom to bring formation and godly character to our life and home.

The **GIRDLE OF TRUTH**: Because we have learned that Jesus IS truth, we must search ourselves on a daily basis to see whether or not our lives are reflecting the instructions and commission He has established for us as His followers. We absolutely cannot be living Luke-warm Christian lives. God will not tolerate it. If we are not living in truth we must seek out God's word for direction and spend more time with him in prayer. When we are submissive in doing so solutions for our lives will be made more apparent and bring organization to the lives we lead. Do not think my friend that you will be able to fight Satan in any battle and win if you are not abiding in

Christ Jesus and walking obediently in God's will. To combat Satan in anything, we must be walking honest lives in the sight of God. If we are not, it will not take long to figure out that you are fighting the battle on your own. God will not support anyone who is obviously sinning; it would be contrary to his Holy Word. On the other hand, if you are walking in the light of truth, and in the will of God, you can be confident beyond a shadow of a doubt that God will defend and preserve you completely. Think about THAT extensively before you deal with the enemy.

Picture this; you need God to sustain you in a battle that Satan has just brought on your life. You decide to brawl with him and find that you are losing. You can't understand why and seek God for validation but hear Satan in the midst of your gloom mocking your transgressions and laughing at you for not walking in obedience to God. Satan too knows that God will not and cannot excuse your sin, and therefore will not back you until you have acknowledged it and sought after his forgiveness. If we are to anticipate God's support in the battles we face in life, then we cannot live and walk in darkness. Especially AFTER we have received the blessed light of the truth.

When we walk in obedience to God we bear the Girdle of Truth which will brace and uphold us—whatever our circumstance. Trust and believe that the enemy knows that too, which is one of the reasons he receives so much enjoyment when we sin. He knows that our defiance to God's word will get in the way of our confidence and assurance as we experience battles with him.

The **SANDALS OF THE GOSPEL OF PEACE**: We must know and understand the word of God and what the Gospel of Peace entails. As we become more and more familiar with its significance we will be better equipped to share the Good news that has granted US the New Life we know in Jesus Christ, so that others too through our testimony may come to receive it also.

When we put on the Sandals Of The Gospel Of Peace, we are preparing ourselves to go out as Jesus Himself commanded to preach and teach the *Good News* to the ends of the world. These spiritual sandals grant us through the Holy Spirit, power and mobility to go forth boldly to proclaim the truth that God's sinless Son Jesus Christ has come to bring peace, hope and life to the souls who receive Him into their hearts. Let us remember always that God's word is "quick," and "powerful." Our testimony with the Holy Spirit's help can be used to deter Satan from trying to destroy those in the world who are still dead in sin. Through our witnessing others too may discover the truth that is in God's word and receive eternal life.

Let us always run the race to win, and not be on the "defensive" when it comes to dealing with Satan and his plots to ruin our lives. We must always take the "offensive" position using God's powerful word and the authority we have in Jesus' name to charge evil, making the battle "the Lord's," in doing so, we will in our race remain triumphant. If we do not make each and every battle "the Lord's," we will never know the thrill of victory. Our goal in every position must always be to not only cross the bridges in life ourselves, but also to reach back when we have crossed and <u>take the hand of someone else</u> so that <u>they may cross also</u> and come to know the love and faithfulness of God in their lives.

To become more effective and fruitful in our Christian lives we must "suit up" for the spiritual battles that attack us every day. Not only do we need to suit up, we must learn the deceiving tactics Satan uses to oppress and manipulate our lives. We do not want at any time in our New Life to become disqualified by not running the race according to the standards and principles God has set for us. If we are to be winners in the sight of God, we must consider seriously the commission Christ has placed before us and resolve in our hearts and minds whether or not we are willing to fight for the kingdom of God. Remember always to never give up. Call upon Christ to help you at each and every hurdle, lap or turn. The success of our race depends on our endurance and desire to "run the race to win," that we might one day hear Jesus say, "Well done my good and faithful servant."

The **SHIELD OF FAITH:** Is the armor that we use to "extinguish the fiery darts of the evil one." The question is, do we know what the enemy is and what strategies he uses against us? Are we at all familiar with Satan's weapons? Let us think about a few of them for a moment, and ask yourself how many of these we have allowed Satan to use through our life lately? We can begin with everything God hates. The Bible tells of **"six things the Lord hates, yes seven are an abomination to Him"** [Prov. 6:16]. **"A proud look, a lying tongue, Hands that shed innocent blood, A heart that devises wicked plans, feet that are swift in running to evil, A false witness who speaks lies, And one who sows discord among brethren"** [Prov. 6:17-19].

In addition to these Satan uses many of the SINS below to attack and demolish our lives. So the next time we discover ourselves trapped in one of these sinful traps, let us swiftly repent and ask God to forgive us for permitting the devil to get in the way of our New Life and growth. Let us quickly distinguish and refuse to go along with all of these knowing that Satan can and will use each and every one of them if we allow him to, to stop, rob, and hinder our Christian faith. ANGER, BITTERNESS, CRITICISM, DISCOURAGEMENT, DEPRESSION, DOUBT, DISOBEDIENCE, DISSAPPOINTMENT, DESPAIR, FEAR, FATIGUE, FAILURE, GREED, GRIEF, HYPOCRISY, ILLNESS, LONELINESS, JUDGING, MURDER, OPPRESSION, RESENTMENT, PAIN, PERSECUTION, PREJUDICE, SIN, SUFFERING, TEMPTATION, TRIALS, WEAKNESS, and so on.

Why does Satan attack us with these things? Because he knows very well that if we do **not allow sin** (in forms such as these) to have any place in our heart or life, then we WILL walk victoriously with Christ and obtain our heavenly rewards. Therefore the Devil wants to do all he can to keep us from pressing forward toward our heavenly objectives. The Shield of Faith that God has given us is not only to guard our heart, but also to repel the "fiery darts" that Satan launches at us.

This priceless shield is that of faith which is the **"substance of things hoped for, the evidence of things not seen" [Heb. 11:1].** When we spiritually place this Shield of Faith over our heart we will have supernatural confidence in the battles we face because we may then rest in our faith of GOD'S unfathomable power and ultimate control to see us through everything we may encounter. In faith, we have total assurance that God will be in charge of anything that comes our way, in spite of what we may believe is going on around us. Through faith we know that God will in every situation work all things for our good. All we have to do when the storms of life are raging is to prayerfully listen carefully to what God's word has to say about our situation and determine in our mind that we will not waver in our walk with him. Why? Because we know deep in our soul that in our submission to God, he will complete that which he has purposed in our lives for his Glory.

We must only place the shield of Faith over our heart and allow God to fight the battle for us. In doing this, we must "let go" of our problem and believe that in laying down my cares, I will not be tormented or afraid of whatever has come my way. I must rely on the promise that because I am placing my trust in Almighty God he will keep me from despair.

Above all things, the Shield of faith will help ground each and every dart that Satan may intend to use and bring me harm. Faith will undeniably conquer and defeat every battle we may face. Just to mention a few, depression, discouragement, sickness, etc. Because we trust in God's word when it guarantees us God's awesome power, provision, healing and authority in all that we may encounter. When adversity comes my way, I need more than ever to take the Shield of faith and allow it to quench the fiery dart of DOUBT. This is one of the most reliable "darts" Satan uses on those of us striving to achieve a fruitful walk with Christ. When this happens, remember this, **"A double-minded man is unstable in all his ways."** Do not allow yourself to become "double-minded," Satan if he can, would love nothing more than to uproot your faith, and steal it from your heart. Do not take him for granted. Do not sin and give him an opening (through doubt in God) to do any such thing. As a replacement when you feel doubt's attack on your heart and mind, go right away to God in prayer and lay your trouble at his feet. As you hand it over to him you will feel doubt's grip on you begin to slip away. Surely there in the midst of God's grace and mercy you will experience FAITH again because God will restore what Satan tried to steal from you.

The **HELMET OF SALVATION:** Because our head can be very open to injury during an attack we must always remember to wear the Helmet of Salvation. God has supplied us with this spiritual helmet so that our head is kept from harm. With this piece of armor we will be not be influenced by the devil to quit, stand still, retreat, run away, cower, or turn away from that which God has called us to do for His glory. When we take this piece of protection and use it to guard our mind, we will stand firm in God's word and not be persuaded in any way to turn from that which God has inspired us to complete.

With the helmet of Salvation guarding our mind, we will not lose sight of our goal, nor the hope and trust we have in Christ Jesus. We will not be taken back by the lies of the enemy, nor deceived because our mind will be set on the unchangeable word and promises of God. We will hold fast to the blessed guarantee that we are "born again—children of God." Trusting that God will never leave or forsake us, we are able to say in each and every crisis that <u>I am no longer a prisoner in chains, I have been set free by the sinless blood of the Lamb</u>. Therefore, I no longer allow the things of this world to control or manipulate me. I have decided once and for all time, to trust Christ Jesus—the Redeemer and blessed Savior of my soul. As the word of God says, I can say resisting the enemy in all things, **"I have been crucified with Christ, therefore I no longer live, the life I live—He now lives in me!"**

My mind in this armor is totally and unconditionally focused on my SALVATION and I am not going to in any way give myself over to think like the world. I will not worry when the winds of life blow hard against my house, for I will know that my heart has been sanctified and my soul has been renewed by the work of the Holy Spirit. Even though the Bible says that Satan is **"the accuser,"** and **"the enemy of my soul,"** I will wrestle him (making each battle the Lord's) and win. For the forces of darkness cannot stand in the pure and brilliant light of God's truth and glory. I will use the Good News God has given me to wage spiritual warfare on the father of all lies, and stand in the authority that Christ has given me in His name—and overcome the works of the enemy in my life.

The **SWORD OF THE SPIRIT:** The sword of the Spirit is the word of God. In each and every situation, circumstance, temptation and trial, we must always stand against the enemy just as Christ Jesus did—with the words, **"It is written."** Remember that God's word is **"sharper than a two-edged sword."** We can never fight Satan with our own strength, because he will always win. Any attempt to fight the enemy under our OWN power or authority is destined for catastrophe. When war is waged upon wickedness and evil, the only way to overcome it and win is with the ANOINTED WORD OF GOD and in the precious name of Jesus Christ.

Just as a soldier prepares for battle, dressing in protective clothing so must we in the armor that has been provided for us by God. Also, we must arm ourselves with spiritual weapons for the battles we face. Our weapons consist of the knowledge God has given us in his Holy word. These to name a few are: FAITH, HOPE, LOVE, UNDERSTANDING, and WISDOM. Learn what the Bible says about each and every one of these. Write them on the tablet of your heart and proceed boldly without fear, because the enemy cannot withstand the word of God. It is his disadvantage and his ruin.

We must be sure to keep a watchful eye out for the enemy. Be aware of our surroundings. Watch in all directions of your life, and remember NOT to allow Satan to get a "foothold." **"Come out from among them and be separate, says the Lord. Do not touch what is unclean, and I will receive you. I will be a Father to you, and you shall be My sons and daughters, says the Lord Almighty"** [2 Cor. 6:17-18]. **"For to this you were called, because Christ also suffered for us, leaving us an example, that you should follow His steps: Who committed no sin, Nor was guile found in His mouth. Who when He was reviled, did not in return; when He suffered, He did not threaten, but committed Himself to**

Him who judges righteously" [1 Peter 2:21-23]. "And who is he who will harm you if you become followers of what is good? But even if you should suffer for righteousness' sake you are blessed. And do not be afraid of their threats, nor be troubled. But sanctify the Lord God in your hearts, and always be ready to give a defense to everyone who asks you a reason for the hope that is in you, with meekness and fear" [1 Peter 3:13-15].

"You therefore, my son, be strong in the grace that is in Christ Jesus. And the things that you have heard from me among many witnesses, commit these to faithful men who will be able to teach others also. You therefore must endure hardship as a good soldier of Jesus Christ. No one engaged in warfare entangles himself with the affairs of this life, that he may please him who enlisted him as a soldier. And also if anyone competes in athletics, he is not crowned unless he competes according to the rules. The hard working farmer must be first to partake of the crops. Consider what I say, and may the Lord give you understanding I all things" [2 Tim. 2:1-7].

PRAYER AND PETITION: If you desire to resist and fight the devil the best way to wage warfare upon him, is to praise God and worship him in the spirit of thanksgiving and honor. Believe me when I say that prayer and petition activate this blessed armor. When we learn to adore God in the Spirit, the armor of God becomes a mighty force in withstanding and repelling the enemy's deadliest arrows, **"When you pray, enter into your closet and when you have shut the door, pray to your Father which is in secret; and your Father which sees in secret shall reward you openly"** [Matt. 6:6]. "If you abide in me, and my words abide in you, you shall ask what you will and it shall be done unto you" [John 15:7].

When Shadows Fall: A Journey of Faith

ALMIGHTY ARMOR

Dress me in your armor Lord, that I may face this day
Without hesitation, dearest Lord I pray
The **Helmet of Salvation**, that I may resist sin
The **Breastplate of Righteousness**, restoring me within,
The **Girdle of Truth** to guide my way, being not deceived
Hearing not temptation, but only truth received.
Prepare my feet with **Sandals of peace**, your Gospel quick to tell
And also place your **Shield of Faith** upon me Lord as well.
The **Sword of the Spirit**, give to me, to quench the fiery darts
Do this Father as I pray, before the battle starts.

Christene Bolte-Luthey

Christene Bolte-Luthey

Eleven
POEMS TO INSPIRE YOUR HEART

OUR
LOVING
SHEPHERD

Poems Of

Faith & Hope

Jesus said, "I am the good shepherd; and I know my sheep, and I am known by my own. As the father knows me, even so, I know the Father; and I lay down my life for the sheep."
John 10:14-15

When Shadows Fall: A Journey of Faith

MY SHEPHERD, SWEET SHEPHERD

Dear father I'm weary with life and its trials
And I do not know what to do
I don't understand, and I don't have the answers
So give me your hand, see me through…

Lead me and guide me keep me, sustain me
Hold tight when you see I may fall
And father, remind me as often as need be
That YOU are the SHEPHERD OF ALL!

MY SHEPHERD, SWEET SHEPHERD
Who walks through each valley
Guiding with thy tender care…
Leading me onward through all the darkness
Keeping my heart from despair…**(PSALM 23)**

Oh, HOW could I manage how could I linger
Without YOUR dear hands on my life?
Oh, I could not bear it, Sweet savior I'd drown in
The worries of trial and strife…

It is YOU my SUSTAINER my STRENGTH, my PROTECTOR
My BUCKLER, my SHIELD, and my SWORD
YOU are my REFUGE, FAITHFUL and LOVING
TRUE, and LASTING…my LORD…**(PSALM 91)**

Christene Luthey

"I will say of the Lord, He is my God, in whom I trust. Surely he will save you from the fowler's snare and from the deadly pestilence. He will cover you with his feathers, and under his wings you will find refuge; his faithfulness will be your shield and rampart. You will not fear the terror that flies by day, nor the pestilence that stalks in the darkness, nor the plague that destroys at midday" Psalm 91:2-6

Christene Bolte-Luthey

LET CHRIST IN YOUR HEART

Within the heart of every man
There dwells a certain place
Where emptiness abides unless
It's filled with love by grace.

Perhaps you've noticed something friend
Lacking in your soul?
A need to feel accepted?
And wish you could be whole?

You're not quite sure of what it is
That you are longing for?
But quietly you wish for it
And peace you do implore?

Recognize that you are lost
And floundering in sin
Repent; and Christ will enter—Your heart
And live within.

He's waiting for your yielding
Unto his perfect will
To come abide within your soul
Himself—your void to fill…

*"For the wages of sin is death,
but the gift of God is eternal life
in Christ Jesus our Lord." [Romans 6:23].*

MY GARDEN OF "GETHSEMANE"

Plunged within a valley
I did not understand,
I cried at first in anger there
It was not what I had planned.

Trembling I was quite afraid
Of being alone in life;
And soon became aware that ALL
Were darkness, grief and strife?

The battle then was pure control
My heart had paid the cost
Losing in the end I found
All I had "gained," I LOST!

Finally bending knees once locked
I BOWED before the lord
Alone I laid my burdens down
To one (till then) ignored.

"I commit this FALSE control
Into YOUR steady hands;
Yielding from this moment on,
To all thy word demands.

Be it joy or trial Lord
Let me follow thee
Faithful to my father's will
As in "GETHSEMANE…"

C. Luthey

"*Then Jesus came with them to a place called Gethsemane, and said to the disciples, "Sit here while I go and pray over there." And He took with Him Peter and the two sons of Zebedee, and He began to be sorrowful and deeply distressed. Then He said to them, "My soul is exceedingly sorrowful, even to death. Stay here and watch with me." He went a little farther and fell on His face, and prayed, saying, "O My Father, if it is possible, let this cup pass from Me; nevertheless, not as I will, but as You will" [Matthew 26:36-39].*

GOD'S EVERLASTING SOVEREIGNTY

Today I saw God's glory
Shining out for all to see
It's radiance shone with splendor
In a cloud which swept by me.

As I watched with eyes of wonder
At the sky so broad and blue;
I imagined me beholding
His majesty so true.

It was grand and oh, so perfect
That no mind could understand;
It was filled with DEPTH unequaled,
As it overlooked the land.

And the brilliance shining from it
Was more than I could bear?
So I turned my eyes then from it
As I became aware,,,

That we often take for granted
The richness of His GRACE
As I conceived in pure despair
The glory of His face.

For exalting from the heavens
I saw alive today
God's everlasting sovereignty
In such a subtle way.

C. Luthey

Christene Bolte-Luthey

I PLEDGE TO YOU MY HEART

Today I stand before you Lord
Humbled by your love
I'm blessed beyond mere words can tell
By grace from up above.

You've brought me to REPENTANCE
In each and every way;
Now, I will gladly serve you
Each hour of the day.

I take this step by faith and trust
To seize this moment sweet;
For all you've done for me oh, God
Please make my walk complete.

I've searched my heart and pondered deep
The storms that brought me near;
Depression, doubt, and emptiness
Anger, grief and fear.

It was only when I longed for peace
To soothe my aching soul;
I found that you could fill the voids,
That made me new and whole.

I've learned so much about MYSELF
Which truly helps me see
Faith, hope, and love are real
Such truth DOES set you free

C. Luthey

Jesus said, **"If you hold to my teaching, you are really my disciples. Then you will know the truth and the truth will set you free"** *[John 8:32].*

THE GOOD SHEPHERD

Magnificent you are oh Lord
In all your perfect ways;
You grant us love and grace divine
And fill our "earthly" days.

Who can know how GREAT you are?
I could not comprehend
Your magnificence is greater Lord
And does not know an end.

Infinity is NOTHING when
I ponder who YOU are
You created heaven and earth
You light the brightest star.

You cause the earth to move each day
You know the oceans deep
And still within your HOLINESS
You tend to all your "sheep!"

You feed the humble and the poor
You love all without shame
If we could only be dear Lord
A people without blame.

Create a chain that time can't break
Of hearts that love you true
Make us strong and grant us grace
To work on earth for YOU!

C. Luthey

"I am the good shepherd. The good shepherd lays down his life for the sheep. The hired hand is not the shepherd who owns the sheep. So when he sees the wolf coming, he abandons the sheep and runs away. Then the wolf attacks the flock and scatters it. The man runs away *because he is a hired hand and cares nothing for the sheep. I am the good shepherd; I know my sheep and my sheep know me—just as the Father knows me and I know the Father—and I lay down my life for the sheep. I have other sheep that are not of this sheep pen. I must bring them also. They too will listen to my voice, and there shall be one flock and one shepherd. John 10:11-16*

THE PUREST LOVE

Like the dew that has fallen and rests on the green;
Your LOVE is the PUREST my eyes, Lord have seen.

Like the clear and clean morning of August—September;
Your heart is as warm as a glowing red ember.

Like the sun that shines down at the brink of a day;
Your spirit comes calling to counsel my way.

How blessed I am father for thy faithfulness;
Granting wisdom and power for souls in distress.

Thank you for sunshine that brings HOPE anew
Like its glory and radiance I'm reminded of YOU!

C. Luthey

**"But God demonstrates his own love toward us,
in that while we were still sinners, Christ died for us." [Romans 5:8].**

Christene Bolte-Luthey

GOD'S ABOUNDING GRACE

Do not search this world my friend
For peace in your despair;
For it is evident you'll see
It's only found in prayer.

We shall never comprehend
The LOVE of God it's true
For there is nothing we can know
Or dare compare it to.

And yet I've found in precious ways
He gives to us his hand
Often far beyond the mind
Could reach to understand.

C. Luthey

"As you have therefore received Christ Jesus the Lord, so walk in Him rooted and built up in Him and established in the faith, as you have been taught, abounding in it with thanksgiving." [Colossians 2:6-7]

THE DEPTH OF YOUR GRACE

I love thee Lord Jesus my MASTER and KING
Thou hast caused me to praise thee
You make my heart sing.

All heaven and earth shall bow at they face;
For none can quite fathom
The depth of thy grace.

I lift up before thee my life and my days
For YOU Lord are worthy
Of all of my praise.

Sweet Savior, Redeemer
Lord; whom I love,
Touch with thy splendor
This soul from above....

C.Luthey

Christene Bolte-Luthey

MEET HIM AT THE CROSSROADS

When you're feeling tempted lonely in despair
Meet him at the crossroads he is waiting there!

When the race you're running seems to never end
Meet him at the crossroads there you'll find a friend!

When trials flood your heart and mind as waves upon the sea
Meet him at the crossroads that is where he'll be.

When in grief you're fainting fast with not the strength to stand
Meet him as the crossroads he will take your hand.

When you feel that no one cares in pain you're all alone
Meet him as the crossroads he will lead you home!

C. Luthey

"For He himself has said, "I will never leave you nor forsake you"
Heb. 13:5

HUMBLED BY YOU

Lord, I am humbled by the dawn
That greets with morning light
And dew that glistens on the ground
To my heart—it is delight.

For when I think of YOU,
I see everything you've made
And within ALL and EVERYTHING
The splendid part you've played.

Who but YOU could tell the sun
To light the bluest sky?
Who but YOU could grant the birds
Grace enough to fly?

Who but YOU could "save" a soul?
With just a tender touch?
You are priceless, this is true,
That's why you're loved SO MUCH!

C. Luthey

"Of old You laid the foundation of the earth, and the heavens are the work of Your hands." Psalm 102:25

Christene Bolte-Luthey

LOVE IS

(1 Corinthians 13:4-8)

LOVE: suffers long…
LOVE too is kind
It is remarkably tender and blind.

LOVE: does not envy…
Or boast itself
Instead, LOVE is patient and waits on a shelf.

LOVE: Acts NOT rudely…
And seeks NOT its own;
It is NOT provoked to evil—it's known.

LOVE: does not glory…
In things that are wrong
But only in TRUTH rejoices in song.

LOVE: bears ALL things…
Believing all things
It HOPES and ENDURES WHATEVER life brings.

Regardless of conflict…
This promise prevails
God's word is true that: LOVE NEVER FAILS!

C. Luthey

"Love is patient, love is kind. It does not envy, it does not boast, it is not proud. It is not rude, it is not self-seeking, it is not easily angered, it keeps no record of wrongs. Love does not delight in evil but rejoices with the truth. It always protects, always trusts, always hopes, always perseveres. Love never fails" 1 Cor. 13:4-8

THE PROTECTOR OF OUR WAY

I am the protector of thy way
Seek my will each passing day.
I shall give you grace to be
Sufficient child to set you free.

Let me hold you let me care.
Know that I am ALWAYS there
Close enough to touch your hand
Wise enough to understand.

Peace I give, so real to you
Strength enough to see you through;
All I ask, all I require
Please let ME be your one desire.

Let me hold each second fast
Let me not be chosen "last."
Let me walk with you—my FRIEND
Let your FAITH on ME depend!

C. Luthey

"And he said to me, My grace is sufficient for you, for My strength is made perfect in weakness." Therefore most gladly I will rather boast in my infirmities, that the power of Christ may rest upon me. Therefore I take pleasure in infirmities, in reproaches, in needs, in persecutions, in distresses, for Christ's sake. For when I am weak, then I am strong" 2 Cor. 12:9-10

Christene Bolte-Luthey

SURRENDER UNCONDITIONALLY

I feel the WAR between us WON
Before You Lord, I am undone.
Stripped of power. Stripped of my will.
Empty, so you now may fill,

This vessel with your precious wine,
My ways, and thoughts no longer "mine."
Lead me guide me in your ways,
Feed me TRUTH throughout my days.

Make me strong enough to do
Everything that pleases YOU.
I SURRENDER ALL TO THEE
In faith oh Lord, UNCONDITIONALLY!

It's what you've wanted for so long
I feel the joy within this song!
Oh, how sweet surrender brings
FREEDOM to the sparrow's wings.

That I may soar again with might
For you have blessed, and granted flight.
Fly now sparrow—EAGLE BE,
Christ thy strength shall carry thee.

C. Luthey

"Praise the Lord, O my soul, and forget not all his benefits, who forgives all your sins and heals all your diseases who redeems your life from the pit and crowns you with love and compassion, who satisfies your desires with good things so that your youth is renewed like the eagle's." Psalm 103:2-5

GIVE EACH DAY TO ME

Inside your heart are many things
You cannot understand
It seems that NOTHING in this world
Turns out the way you planned.

Why must life be so unfair?
So senseless and unkind?
As you live and face each day
These questions fill your mind.

I know the path you're walking…
I know the pain you bare
I know you feel alone and tired
I sense your every care.

I know your deep depression…
Your anger and your pain;
I know you feel that every turn
Seems to end in vain.

BE STILL and know that I AM GOD…
Be quiet hear MY voice
COME and cast your cares to me
You must make a choice.

My yoke is light come wear it
By giving in you'll see
Each problem you SURRENDER
Shall surely set you free.

Be patient and believe it's true
I see and know all things
TOGETHER we can face the trials
Each tomorrow brings…

C. Luthey

Christene Bolte-Luthey

"Come to Me, all you who labor and are heavy leaden, and I will give you rest. Take my yoke upon you and learn from me, for I am gentle and lowly in heart, and you will find rest for your souls. For my yoke is easy and my burden is light."
Matthew 11:28-30

NEW LIFE

Lord Jesus when I think of you
I ponder what I've put you through
All the misery,
All the shame,
All the torture,
All the pain.

Just because you loved me so
You came to "free" to "let me go."
Breaking chains that bound my life
In torment
Slavery
Sin
And Strife.

Once I took for granted GRACE
There my soul felt "sin's" embrace.
Lacking comfort,
Peace and love
Everything you are above.

It was coming to the "end" of "me"
My eyes were open then to see
The length
The breadth
The depth of YOU
Which made my life forever NEW!

C. Luthey

"Therefore, whosoever humbles himself as this little child is the greatest in the kingdom of heaven" Matthew 18:4

Christene Bolte-Luthey

IN HIS ARMS

(I Long to Be)

If you listen you can hear it
It though it's subtle, it is there.
His sweet voice is softly calling
ALL TO COME TO HIM IN PRAYER.

There he answers those who seek him
With their heart and trust his love;
Through their faith he will carry
The BELIEVERS home above.

It's so simple yet so many fail
To hear his loving call;
Unaware that without him,
They will fall,

And not much longer will he GRANT
Time to "choose" our destiny
This decision will determine
WHERE you spend ETERNITY.

He is calling, HAVE YOU ANSWERED?
Saying, "yes dear Lord take me;"
"When you come with trumpets sounding,"
"In your arms I long to be!"

*"Verily, verily I say to you,
he that hears my word and believes on him that sent me,
has everlasting life,
and shall not come into condemnation;
but is passed from death unto life"
John 5:24*

FREED BY MERCY

Glorious Master,
Savior and friend
You are the Redeemer
The beginning and end.
I've been freed by your mercy
I've been loved through your grace
I'm at peace in the splendor
Of your warm embrace.
Not once have you faltered
Not once have you lied
You've remained ever constant
And close at my side.
How wondrous your power
How awesome your love
That you would touch man
With your hand from above.
Filling in spaces
Where voids use to be
By lifting up Christ
On the cross so to see
That anyone willing to place faith in you
Would be "born again"
And sanctified, new…

C. Luthey

Christene Bolte-Luthey

HOLD ON TO EACH TOMORROW

May these words bring comfort
When your hopes are fading fast?
When your heart no longer feels
The darkened days will pass.

No one knows the grief you bear
Because you have your pride;
Remember though you have a friend
In which you CAN confide.

Keep in mind HE knows your cares
It's true he sees it all
Trust that he is waiting there
To catch you if you fall.

We are not invincible
Sometimes we lose our way
Struggling with the trials we face
Throughout each passing day.

Hold on to each tomorrow
The light will soon shine through
Bringing with it peace of mind
To calm and comfort you.

C. Luthey

"Be anxious for nothing, but in everything by prayer and supplication, let your requests be known to God; And the peace of God which surpasses all understanding, will guard your hearts and minds through Christ Jesus" Phil. 4:6-7

WALK BY FAITH

Fear not when you feel all alone
For I am always near.
Trust in Me, I'll take your hand
Until the skies are clear.

Be not afraid of shadows dark
They hold no harm for you.
You need only **"walk by faith"**
Until you see the blue.

Hold high your head be confident
This battle you have won.
For I am with you all the time
You shall not be undone.

LIFE is hard; you'll have bad days
When you will want to hide
Remember though my hand dear child
I'm standing at your side.

Let me be a friend to you
I'll fill the voids you feel
I'll be your shelter in the storm
I'll be your comfort real.

Let go of doubts
Release your fears
You have strength unknown
Hold tight my hand I'll show you grace
That comes from Me alone.

WE shall conquer everything
That comes your way, you'll see
Just take my hand and walk by faith
And victory, yours shall be!

Chris Luthey

Christene Bolte-Luthey

LOVE'S STAIN

Oh merciful Master,
Lord God and King
You are the ruler
Of all living things.

Lead me and guide me
In your Righteous ways
Carry my burdens
All of my days.

I love you more dearly
Than any can know
Though you are aware
For you fashioned my soul.

Give to me life
That I might then see
At the end of my time
Eternity…

Ransomed forever
From sin and it's chain
I'll bask in the glory
Clothed in Love's stain.

The stain, which has blotted out
"Iniquity,"
That I may forever
Abide Lord with thee…

C. Luthey

SURRENDER

(Now is the Hour)

Look at you with
Confusion in your eyes
How much longer will you live
In clouded skies?

Aren't you weary from life's trials?
Hard and rough?
Aren't you TIRED?
Haven't you had ENOUGH?

Let me tell you
I have walked that desperate trial
Seeking refuge in MYSELF
To no avail;

I was lonesome,
Searching for some sympathy
When a voice softly whispered,
"ONLY I CAN SET YOU FREE!"

JUST SURRENDER!
I will shield you in the storm
TRUST IN ME
I will keep you safe and warm
JUST SURRENDER!!
And I will make things right
I AM THE WAY,
And I'M THE GUDING LIGHT…

C. Luthey

"For by grace you have been saved through faith, and that not of yourselves; it is the gift of God, not of works, lest anyone should boast"
Eph. 2:8

Christene Bolte-Luthey

LORD JESUS, I PRAISE YOU

Lord Jesus I praise you
For: Dying for me.
For: Shedding your blood
For: Calvary…

For: The suffering you knew
To set my soul free,
No other has done so for me…

Lord Jesus I praise you
For: Rising again.
For: Ascending to Glory
For: Being my friend.

For: Breaking the chains
That Hope would not end,
No other has done so for me…

Lord Jesus I praise you
For: Leading the way
For: Giving me life.
For: Truth every day.

For: Denying yourself
Out of sweet empathy,
No other has done so for me…

Chris Luthey

CHRIST MY SAVIOR

It's true, it's true I saw His face
On Calvary where He took my place,
I saw Him there in agony
Where for my sins, He died for ME!
I couldn't bear to see his pain
But greater still, to know the gain
Was mine—to hold sweet victory,
IF I believed, He'd set me free…

The tears, the blood, the sin, the shame
I knew I'd never be the same,
For greater love I could not tell
Would ransom me from sin's sad hell.

Would I stay, would I believe?
Would my soul—Christ receive?
Would I trust in Him who died?
Who through God's grace was glorified?

True my heart must ponder deep
These questions yet, before I "sleep"
For this I know the soul shall be
Kept in one eternity.
Either hell where sadness reigns
Or glory where there are no chains.

The hour nears my heart may sleep
Who then my soul shall hold and keep?
In peace my answer friend shall be
My Savior—CHRIST—eternally!

C. Luthey

Christene Bolte-Luthey

HOW IS IT

How is it unto me dear Lord
That you would show thy face?
How is it unto me dear Lord
That I should know thy grace?
How is it unto me dear Lord
A sinner through and through
Should know the sweetest joy within
To have a friend like YOU?
How is it you would die for me?
In horrid pain and still
Embrace a heart that knew you not
And clung unto my will?
How is it you should even care?
To save my soul from hell?
How is it dearest Lord and King?
Thy love too great to tell.
How is it you would summon me
To share your home in Glory?
How is it you would "graft" me in?
To God's most splendid story.
These questions fill my heart and mind
How is it you loved Me?
To leave your glorious place on High
To die on Calvary's tree?
I could go on with these
For questions fill my soul
And yet when pondering all of this
I just in awe "let go."
And think with heartfelt thanks that I
Am blessed to be your friend
How is it?
It's the gift of Grace
The greatest God could send!

C. Luthey

GIVE ME WINGS

Dear Savior sweet, I love you so
It's true you know me well
The depth of what I feel for you
Mere words could never tell.
You've given me a life that's full
You've granted many things.
Not much more from you I'd ask
But—to one day give me wings…

Wings to fly up to your home
Where glory grand does shine
To see your face and touch your hand
To sense your grace divine.
For that would be the greatest gift
I ever had received
Except dear Lord the moment when
In faith I first "believed."

Oh what splendor, oh what joy
In that vast instant Lord,
Shall be the day I meet with you
Where you are most adored.

C. Luthey

Christene Bolte-Luthey

OUR SHELTER IN THE STORM

Poems Of Courage & Strength

"For he will deliver you from the snare of the fowler
and from the deadly pestilence; He will cover you with his pinions,
and under his wings you will find refuge; His faithfulness is a shield
and buckler.
You will not fear the terror of the night nor the arrow that flies by day"
(Psalm 91: 3-5)

When Shadows Fall: A Journey of Faith

HIDE UNDER HIS WING

Oh, child of mine; so deeply distressed
Come close beside me, I'll give thee rest.

Only the "pruning"; hurts for awhile
But soon comes the bloom, bringing a smile…

I hold the righteous; safe in my hand
It shall be they; who inherit the land.

I know how you feel; I too have known pain
Yet we both KNOW; it was NOT in vain.

As I too have suffered the grief of contempt;
Mocking and hatred in days that I spent
Doing the will of my Father it's true
And that is just why, he'll see YOU through!

So lift up your eyes; and dry all your tears
Let me now carry the weight of your fears.

There is NOT one thing; I have not known;
I am the keeper of my very own.

No weapon shall prosper; against you I say
HIDE UNDER MY WING; I'll protect you today.

Ride on my feathers; rest now in me
Know that in time truth all shall see.

It cannot be hidden; forever it's true
Although it "SEEMS" that way now to you.

C. Luthey

"You are my friends if you do whatever I command you. No longer do I call you servants, for a servant does not know what his master is

doing; but I have called you friends for all things that I heard from My Father I have made known to you. You did not choose me, but I chose you and appointed you that you should go and bear fruit, and that your fruit should remain, that whatever you ask the Father in my name He may give you. These things I command you, that you love one another."
[John 15:14-17].

A PORTRAIT OF GRACE

Though life may crumble around us
And our treasures may be taken
Resting in the arms of God
Our faith will not be shaken…

For he will never give us
A cross we cannot bear
When we feel as though we "can't"
In perfect time—he's there…

Knowing every weakness
His spirit sets me free
Granting me his precious grace
And love from Calvary…

There is no trial that can outweigh
God's sweet—awesome grace;
And in the midst of every storm
Is where I see his face?

"Peace I leave with you, My peace I give to you; not as the world gives do I give to you. Let not your heart be troubled, neither let it be afraid."
John 14:27

Christene Bolte-Luthey

MY ONLY PEACE

Words escape me; I know not what to pray
Only for peace, grace and strength
To see me through this day.
My heart today is troubled, not knowing what I'll find
Therefore precious Jesus, please guard my heart and mind.
Wrap me in your presence,
Please let me feel you near
Embrace this frightened child I ask
Take away all fear.
You are my only refuge Lord,
Amidst the trials of life
You are my only hope and peace
You rescue me from strife.
Be with me as you've promised
Let this comfort be,
I know that you my dear sweet Lord
Will not abandon me.

C. Luthey

"If anyone desires to come after me let him deny himself and take up his cross daily, and follow me. For whoever desires to save his life will lose it, but whoever loses his life for my sake will save it." Luke 9:23-24

THE WAY, THE TRUTH, THE LIFE

"I am the way, the truth the life,"
This you know is true
Each and every step you take
I shall walk with you.

Be not afraid of ANYTHING
This world may bring your way
For I shall grant your every need
Throughout each passing day.

Do not worry, dread or fear
Take refuge under my wing
Forgetting not my strength and power
For I know everything…

Take my sweet peace into your soul
And trust with all your heart
I shall not leave—I'm always near
We shall never part!

"Therefore we do not lose heart, even though our outward man is perishing, yet the inward man is being renewed day by day. For our light affliction, which is but for a moment, is working for us a far more exceeding and eternal weight of glory, while we do not look at the things, which are seen. For the things which are seen are temporary, but the things which are not seen are eternal"
2 Corinthians 4: 16-18

Christene Bolte-Luthey

CAST YOUR CARE UPON HIM

Whatever you must struggle through
Have FAITH and just BELIEVE
I know your every doubt and fear
My peace I give, receive…

Let not your heart be troubled
Let me hold you near
Calming every anxious thought
Drying every tear.

Cast thy concerns upon ME please
Your shoulders are too small
Have faith that in my love for you
I will not let you fall.

Trust in what you know of me
To be forever true;
Draw nigh to ME amidst the storm
And I'll draw nigh to YOU!

C. Luthey

"Draw nigh to God and he will draw nigh to you" James 4:8

"Cast your burden on the Lord, and HE will sustain you" Ps. 55:22

"Come unto me… and I will give you rest" Matt. 11:28

MY PEACE IN EVERY STORM

Guard my heart and mind oh God
Keep me far from fear
Let me know WHATEVER comes
That you are ever near.

All my hopes and dreams rely
On YOU and you alone;
For in the midst of every storm
You're the peace I've known.

Forever I shall trust in thee
To be my strength and guide;
Therefore Lord surround my heart
Close to me—ABIDE....

YOU are the LIGHT that makes my way
Bright and ever true
That conquers fear and darkness
Making all things new...

C. Luthey

"Therefore, having been justified by faith, we have peace with God through our Lord Jesus Christ, through whom also we have access by faith into this grace in which we stand, and rejoice in hope of the glory of God. And not only that, but we also glory in tribulations, knowing that tribulation produces perseverance; and perseverance, character; and character, hope. Now hope does not disappoint, because the love of God has been poured out in our hearts by the Holy Spirit who was given to us"
Romans 5:1-4

Christene Bolte-Luthey

THE VALLEY OF DOUBT

Let not my DOUBTFUL mind dear Lord
Continue on its way
Please grant me strength to disregard
All it has to say.

Let your SHIELD OF FAITH repel
These thoughts confusing me;
Keep my eyes upon YOU Lord
Not the "waves" and "sea…"

See me through these storms of doubt
Placing trust in you;
There I know my comfort lies
And worries shall be few…

Doubt, I know, displeases you
Forgive me please—I ask
Grant me courage dearest Lord
To carry out my task…

I need you in this valley Lord
Stay forever near
Surely FAITH will conquer all
And make my path quite clear…

C. Luthey

Jesus answered them saying, **"Assuredly, I say to you, if you have faith and do not doubt, you will not only do what was done to the fig tree, but also if you say to this mountain, be removed and be cast into the sea, it will be done. And all things whatever you ask in prayer, believing, you will receive." Matthew 21:21-22**

THE VALLEY OF DISAPPOINTMENT

Dear Lord I need your shoulder
On which to lay my head;
As DISAPPOINTMENT I must bear
From something someone said.

I need for you to hold me
Tenderly in your care;
As LIFE with its disappointments
Are often and unfair…

I placed a limit on a dream
And then it came and went
Broken I am weary Lord
As time is quickly spent…

Please help me carry on I ask
And where I'm empty fill
Take my hand and lead me up
This disappointing hill…

I know ALL things "work for good"
To them that seek your plan;
So keep me in your perfect will,
I need not understand…

C. Luthey

"And we know that all things work together for good to them that love God and to them that are called according to his purpose."
Romans 8:28

Christene Bolte-Luthey

THE VALLEY OF DESPAIR

Dearest Heavenly Father
I come to you in prayer
Walk with me through this valley
Of deep and dark despair…

YOU know my heart YOU know my thoughts
My worries and my fears;
I cast before YOU humbly
These fast and flowing tears…

Unsettled I am feeling now,
Control, I've truly lost
This valley seems to torture me
While in it I am tossed.

I know YOU'VE walked each valley
So therefore guide my way
Please grant me strength to journey on
Throughout each passing day…

Until I see this valley end,
Your grace I trust to be
Sufficient; in my weakest hour
As YOU have promised me…

C. Luthey

LET CHRIST HEAL YOUR SCARS

I know of a heart that hungers for bread
For the bread to sustain its life;
Yet caught in a web of confusion
It is bound up in worry and strife.

So many things to "let go" of,
It's hard because of pain
You shall not "lose" be not afraid
You have so much to gain!

Let ME come into your heart.
Let ME warm thy soul
For I alone can heal your scars
I can make you whole…

I'm waiting wanting desperately
To feel you near to ME:
Lay hold of LIFE and you will know
Peace eternally!

C. Luthey

"Therefore I take pleasure in my infirmities, in reproaches, in needs, in persecutions, in distresses, for Christ's sake. For when I am weak, then I am strong"
2 Corinthians 12:10

"Now to him who is able to do exceedingly abundantly above all that we ask or think, according to the power that works in us."
Ephesians 3:20

Christene Bolte-Luthey

LORD HELP ME FACE

(WHATEVER COMES)

Be not far from me dear Lord
That I not fall away.
Hold on; do not let go, I ask,
Guide me through this day.

For I am weak, but YOU are strong
You are my only prayer.
Uphold me with Thy steady hand
Keep me from despair.

Let not my faith falter now,
Help me trust in thee
Knowing not the answers Lord
Your grace must set me free.

I know I must surrender Lord
"YOUR WILL ON EARTH BE DONE;"
I pray you give me COURAGE then,
To face—WHATEVER comes!

C. Luthey

NEARER TO ME

No pleasure comes from suffering
I know the grief you bear
But do not be discouraged
I'll take away your care...

If you did not experience
That which now you know;
HOW—dear child, I ask of you
Could you in spirit "GROW?"

Some things I do "permit" in life
That you my child—may see;
Each and every trial and tear
Has brought you closer to me.

You'll never be alone because
You see we are, "ENTWINED;"
In spirit, heart, and so much more
Body, soul and mind...

"These things I have spoken to you, that in me you may have peace. In the world you will have tribulation; but be of good cheer, I have overcome the world"
John 16:33

Christene Bolte-Luthey

LET HIM CARRY YOU

I have so much to offer you…
You have so much to give
Come into My resting place…
I'll teach you how to LIVE!

Hear the plea unto your heart…
To let ME be your friend;
I am a "rock" amidst life's storms…
On which you can depend.

Now other has more love for you…
Nor longs to hold you near;
No other can erase your pain
Nor wipe away all fear.

I am your Savior in ALL THINGS…
So let me carry you
You need never walk alone…
As a friend I'll see you through.

Let Me PROVE myself today…
Simply take my hand
Step by step my precious child…
You shall understand.

C. Luthey

When Shadows Fall: A Journey of Faith

COME AND REST

In many ways you've seen me
And know that I exist
Upon thy face—quiet subtly
I have often kissed.

But sometimes when I reach for you,
You turn and walk away
You do not understand my love
Or things you've heard me say…

I want so much to feel you near
To fill you're every need
To counsel you until you KNOW
You surely will succeed.

All hopes, all dreams, all promises
Are found in ME alone
All others child will fall and fail
But here my grace is shown.

Trust in me to hold you through
The deepest, darkest night;
I'll be your Shepherd and your strength
You need not fear—or fight…

C. Luthey

Christene Bolte-Luthey

HE IS THE DOOR

(TO HAPPINESS)

Inside I know you're fearful
Not knowing what to do
This I offer you today
That it may see you through.

In life we've all made some mistakes
Some bring us grief and pain
But know that IF you're WILLING
You have a lot to gain.

Just take your hurt and sorrow
Lift it to the ONE:
Who KNOWS your EVERY HEARTACHE?
See, healing has begun.

Leave the past behind you
And see what is in store
For those who TRUST in JESUS
You'll find HE IS THE DOOR.

The door that leads to refuge
Within the storms of life;
He is the door to God's sweet peace
He'll calm the winds of strife.

He is the door to VICTORY
ALL battles he does win
He's the KING of all creation
But you must LET HIM IN!

Let him, He will guide you
To life: the BEST you've known
He never will forsake you
He makes YOUR TRIALS HIS OWN.

C. Luthey

SWEET SAVIOR

Sweet Savior, Sweet Lord
Provider of truth
Provider of Grace and life
You are the master of all living things
The prince that shall cease pain and strife.

Lord and Redeemer
Blessed Sweet Hope
Glory and honor to thee
You have forgiven the vilest sin
Setting all prisoners free.

You have climbed every mountain
And conquered each foe
That sought to kill Thee O Lord
Winning each battle in meekness and love
Which is why you are so adored.

You have flown like the eagle
And touched so the sky
Unlike any other has known
You have humbled yourself like a lamb to be slain
Revealing the greatest love known.

You only are worthy, of honor and praise
Of glory and all we hold dear
For you have upheld the righteous with faith
And captured the power of fear!

Chris Luthey

Christene Bolte-Luthey

ENFOLDED IN GOD'S GRACE

Lift your eyes to me in prayer
Do not give in to fear
My grace is far outreaching
Don't forget that I am near!

I will never leave you
Nor forsake you to the end
Believe in me amidst your trial
I am a PROVEN FRIEND!

Don't dwell upon your troubles
I know the road you take
I will lead, and guide you
I know each step you make…

Little lamb let me enfold you
I'm your shelter from the storm
Come nearer, I will hold you,
And protect you from all harm…

C.Luthey

"Beloved, do not think it strange concerning the fiery trial which is to try you as though some strange thing happened to you, but rejoice to the extent that you partake of Christ's sufferings, that when His glory is revealed, you may also be glad with exceeding joy" 1Peter 4:12-13

TRUSTING IN GOD'S POWER

In the midst of every storm
Give to him your hand
For he can still the wind and sea
With just a slight command.

Cast your cares to heavens realm
And let Him dry your tears
He has not forgotten how
To calm the greatest fears.

Trust in Him when this He says
"I too have witnessed pain;"
And though His cross was hard to bear
His "cup" was not in vain.

So let your faith go on dear one
For all the world to see;
God is faithful this I know
He sets the captives free!

When you're in desperate need of hope
Let Jesus be your LIGHT
His love will keep you ever hour
And through the darkest night.

C. Luthey

"But the lord is faithful; he will strengthen you and guard you from evil"
2 Thes. 3:3

"If we confess our sins, he is faithful and just, and will forgive our sins and cleanse us from all unrighteousness" 1 John 1:9

Christene Bolte-Luthey

CHRIST BROKE SINS CHAINS

No other heart has needed you more
Than I have precious Lord
And that is why with every thought
You are so adored.

You broke the chains that bound my soul
Eternally to sin
Darkness pain and agony
And torture deep within,

You took my shame upon yourself
And bore my wretched fee
You never sought to turn away
For love refused to see,

All the reasons I deserved
To suffer for my wrong
Instead you came to die for me
That I know victory's song…

Chris Luthey

I PLACE MY TRUST IN THEE

When I fail to do my best
And worry taunts at me
Let me first surrender Lord
And place my trust in Thee…

When I fall beside the way
With not the strength to stand;
Let me first remember Lord
To quickly take your hand…

When my tears are falling fast
From being troubled so
Let me trust your grace for me
Wherever my feet shall go…

When I cannot understand
Injustice in this world;
Let me not lose faith in you
That I may be unfurled…

Chris Luthey

"The saying is sure and worthy of full acceptance. For to this end we toil and strive, because we have our hope set on the living God, who is the Savior of all men, especially of those who believe"
1 Timothy 4:9-10

Christene Bolte-Luthey

YIELDING TO THE "CUP"

Lord, I see you in the garden
And picture you alone
Unlike any heart or mind has ever thought or known.

Trembling in the darkness
No one at your side
But trusting in Your Father's care all your fears confide.

Sweating drops of blood amidst
The place in which you prayed
Yielding only to the "cup" God in love displayed.

And kneeling humbly Lord I guess
You had bowed your knee
For grace from God to carry on your priceless destiny.

To live in true obedience
Regardless of your pain
Unto your Father's perfect will that LIFE was not in vain.

C. Luthey

IF I COULD HAVE ONE THING IN LIFE

If I could have one thing in life that no one else possessed
I'd want the knowledge of God's grace for conquering each test.
This knowledge would be priceless beyond the mind could measure
    Far exceeding anything a man conceives as "treasure."
For it embraced my precious Lord and saw him through the sorrow
Of sin and death yet conquered them that we may live tomorrow.
    Free from all that causes fear; instilling joy inside
    For where He is—peace and joy, tenderly abide.

C. Luthey

Christene Bolte-Luthey

HOLD TIGHT YOUR FAITH

Often we are given tests
Though life we must endure
Abiding certain obstacles
Though weary and unsure…

The measure of our CHARACTER
Judges WHO we are
Influenced by the strain we bear
As we travel far.

Do not lose hope of dreams you've shared
And planned to see come true;
Hold tight your faith that in due time
Each one will follow through…

"I have fought the good fight. I have finished the race I have kept the faith. Finally, there is laid up for me the crown of righteousness, which the Lord, the righteous Judge, will be to me on that Day, and not to me only but also to all who have loved His appearing" 2 Timothy 4:7-8

TRIALS TEACH COMPASSION

Astonishing are the memories
Of trials throughout our life;
Pondering the valleys deep
That comes with pain and strife.

Adversities of yesterday
Remain although they're years away
Surmising is it rain or shine
Most bruises heal when given time.

So clear from in those darkened places
LIGHT befalls the gloomy places
And wounds I thought would never heal
TAUGHT me HOW to THINK and FEEL.

Trials in life we can't escape
But CHARACTER they mold and shape
Difficulties; ALL have known…
From them you're BLESSED if you have GROWN.

Then looking at another's pain
We find OUR suffering NOT in vain;
Then reaching out to take a hand
We can truly understand…

And rightly so, they've made me see
Some trials in life are meant to be
Then in another's grief—it's true
COMPASSION wells inside of YOU.

C. Luthey

Christene Bolte-Luthey

YOU'RE NOT ALONE

It's not always easy to take fear in stride
I too have been frightened
And many times cried…

I've walked some deep valleys and know how you feel
I know that your sorrow…
Is perfectly real.

But please let me share this secret with you
It has helped in my trials
And it might help you too.

Wherever you are and whatever you do
The good Lord above…
Is walking with you…

So whenever a storm enters your life
Bringing worries, or tears
Maybes and strife,

Stay calm, and trust HIM remember and say
"I KNOW IT WILL PASS"
"It will all be Okay."

Believe in these words and trust I have known:
It will help you to know
THAT YOU'RE NEVER ALONE…

C. Luthey

**"Let your conduct be without covetousness, and be content with such things as you have. For he himself has said, I WILL NEVER LEAVE YOU NOR FORSAKE YOU. So we may boldly say, The Lord is my helper; I will not fear.
What can man do to me? Hebrews 13:5-6**

GOD GIVES STRENGTH TO THE WEARY

I have redeemed your soul
With faith you'll never die
You've been bought with a great price
So spread your wings and FLY!

Fly high above the mountain-tops
Fly over rocks and trees
Fly over valleys deep and wide
Fly over lakes and seas…

Trust in Me and in My power
I'll forever lift thee up
Press toward the goal with joy my child
Whatever the "storm" or "cup."

Fly like the EAGLE strong and proud
Of WHO—in Christ you are
Protected by God's loving hand
You shall journey far!

C. Luthey

"He gives power to the weak, and to those who have no might he increases strength. Even the youths shall faint and not be weary, and the young men shall utterly fall, But those who wait upon the Lord shall renew their strength; They shall mount up with wings like eagles, They shall run and not be weary, the shall walk and not faint" *Isaiah 40:29-31*

"Let the words of my mouth and the meditation of my heart be acceptable in Your sight, O Lord, my strength and my redeemer." *Psalm 19:14*

Christene Bolte-Luthey

THE JUST SHALL LIVE BY FAITH

The glory of life when ALL is done;
Shall be in CHRIST… the BATTLES WON.

Letting FAITH our substance be
The door that opens HEAVEN for thee.

Faith is precious…ever growing;
New each day…while never knowing
WHAT this moment may reveal
Yet teaching us, God's GRACE is REAL!

That is why the JUST lay hold
OF FAITH as though it were pure gold
It is the key to heaven's door
Where one may live forever more…

"Now faith is the substance of things hoped for, the evidence of things not seen…Through faith we understand that the worlds were framed by the word of God…But without faith it is impossible to please him: for he that cometh to God must believe that He is, and that He is a rewarder of them that diligently seek him" Hebrews 11:3,6

"By grace are ye saved through faith; and that not of yourselves; it is the gift of God; not or works, lest any man should boast" Eph. 6:14,16

LET GOD HOLD YOUR TOMORROWS

Each and every day we live
We're facing TRIALS it seems
But in the midst of all our woes
We can't discard our dreams.

Sometimes that's what we want to do
We suffer and we fail
We struggle and we seem to drown
Through life to no avail,

Life ISN'T EASY, isn't FAIR
And often isn't kind;
But IS without a doubt I've learned
A priceless state of mind.

For when we've faced with tragedy
Heartache, loss or fear;
Throughout those valleys deep and wide
Our CHARACTER is clear.

I could have quit so long ago
Within the trials I've known
But this I've found will see me through
GOD and God alone!

So if you've never trusted CHRIST,
I'm asking now you do
Then when you haven't strength to stand,
He will CARRY you!

C. Luthey

Christene Bolte-Luthey

THIS TOO SHALL PASS

Although your hopes may all seem lost
Do not give in to fear
For brighter days wait just ahead
The darkened days will clear.

Remember you are NOT alone
Turn to those who care
Should your heart grow weary when
LIFE does not seem fair.

Seize the faith within your heart
To face each trial and know;
Christ is watching every step
His word has told you so.

I hope and pray these words can be
Of courage, love and peace;
I wish your pain and discontent
Then, to quickly cease.

C. Luthey

"Rejoice in the Lord always. Again I will say, rejoice! Let your gentleness be known to all men. The Lord is at hand. Be anxious for nothing, but in everything by prayer and supplication, with thanksgiving, let your requests be made known to God; and the peace of God, which surpasses all understanding, will guard your hearts and minds though Christ Jesus"
Philippians 4:5-7

When Shadows Fall: A Journey of Faith

(This poem was inspired when a drunk driver killed a dear friend)

SUSTAIN ME WHILE I SLEEP

Lord, please hear my desperate plea
And grant me sleep tonight
Still these restless feelings
Until the morning light.

I need your strength to carry on
Do not abandon me
With your help I trust in time
I'll set these feelings free.

Please dry each lonesome tear I cry
When memories cause me pain
And fill me with contentment
Though anger causes strain.

Please take these mournful feelings
Which cause my soul to grieve
Release the helpless sorrow
And force all hatred to leave.

As I close my eyes to rest
I pray dear Lord you keep
Close at my side throughout the night
Sustain me while I sleep…

C. Luthey

"God is not the author of confusion, but of peace"
1 Corinthians 14:33

"Peace I leave with you, my peace I give unto you; not as the world gives, give I unto you. Let not your heart be troubled, neither let it be afraid"
John 14:27

Christene Bolte-Luthey

OUR SAVIOR LORD AND KING

Poems Of Blessing & Encouragement

"We have this as a sure and steadfast anchor of the soul, a hope that enters into the inner shrine behind the curtain, where Jesus has gone as a forerunner on our behalf, having become a high priest for even after the order of Melchizedek"
Hebrews 6:19-20

I'LL NEVER BE AFRAID

In the midst of your despair
Lift your hands and say a prayer
God will hear if you obey
Trust in Him, His word and say—

"I BELIEVE that God is TRUE
Watching everything I do
Sleeping never—Holding me
Loving, Guiding, Faithfully!"

"In His ways I shall abide
Keeping Him close at my side
He's my shepherd, Lord and King
Joy that makes my poor heart sing…"

"I shall never be afraid
Of darkness, Death, or gloomy glade;
For walking with me night and day
Is Christ, "The TRUTH, the LIFE, and the WAY!"

C. Luthey

Christene Bolte-Luthey

THROUGHOUT EACH TRIAL

(Please Help Me Grow)

Though rivers of worry around me flow
Deep within my heart I know

You are near to comfort me
Peace you give to set me free.

You are true unto my fears
You shall wipe away my tears

Trusting only in your grace
I shall behold your resting place.

There my heart shall know sweet peace
And worried feelings then shall cease

Grant me Father strength to be
Faithful: true unto thee.

Help me stand amidst this rain
Lead me guide me through all pain

Help me trust your perfect will
Lead me guide me love me still.

How I love you this you know
Throughout all this please help me grow.

C. Luthey

When Shadows Fall: A Journey of Faith

(Written after we learned of Shane's cancer)

WALK BY FAITH AND NOT BY SIGHT

God only knows what lies ahead
His will I trust be done
I do believe amidst all fear
This battle shall be won.

I am just a soldier here
Fighting with myself
The war within of Spirit & flesh
Is one of awesome wealth.

To walk by faith and by sight
Is very hard to do
When darkened clouds befall your way
Obscuring every view.

I need only take God's hand
Resisting not his way
For it is best no matter what
My thoughts or fears might say.

I will trust in what I know
That God will see me through
He is a faithful, loving friend
Tested tried, and true!

C. Luthey

Christene Bolte-Luthey

(Written after learning of Shane's cancer)

WE CAN'T ESCAPE OUR TRIALS

Gone are the days of careless thinking
That you just journey on your way
Stop and take a good look around
We're ALL facing battles each day.

Some are of sickness, some harbor pain
Some carry fear or regret
Whatever the burden our heart must carry
We are wise if we don't forget

God watches all, and knows where our heart is
Do we love ANYTHING more than HIM?
If we do, we must change before it's too late
For that we all know is a sin.

We can't escape our trials
They'll follow us where we are
Although we try our best to ignore them
They'll follow us near and far.

We can but trust in God our father
Whatever—comes our way
And choose to do His will and love him
Each hour of every day…

C. Luthey

When Shadows Fall: A Journey of Faith

(Written after learning of Shane's cancer)

JESUS OUR SUSTAINER OF HOPE

Father of TRUTH
Provider of LIFE
Lead us in the paths of your righteousness.
Let not our feet be moved from thy will
That we may know perfect peace,
And rest in the assurance of your grace…
Creator of LOVE
Sustainer of HOPE
Walk beside us and carry our burdens.
We surrender them all to your will.
That our faith may shine like the sun
And bring glory, honor and praise to your name.

Holy FATHER
Blessed REDEEMER
You have allowed this "cup" to come to our family
Show us the way to drink of its flavor.
And let us not be overcome by its bitterness.
Grant us divine pleasure in all things
So that those around us may be strengthened
And be encouraged to seek You in their lives.

Tower of LIGHT
Anchor of PEACE
Shine forth with glory to direct our way
Let us never be afraid, knowing you are with us.
Throughout all our days, you are faithful and true.
All honor be to you on high!
Let us sing praises of your wondrous love
And lift up your Holy name.
Forever and ever you are the one true living God
Who gives all, helps all, and strengthens all
Who place their trust in you.

Chris Luthey

Christene Bolte-Luthey

BELIEVE WITH YOUR HEART

Believe with your HEART…That God's word is TRUE…
And the secrets of life…shall be open to you…

Believe with your HEART…That Christ died for YOU…
Your life will be changed…your soul made anew…

Believe with your HEART…That CHRIST IS GOD'S SON…
And the battles of life…and all trials shall be won…

Believe with your HEART…in the power of Prayer…
Trusting in FAITH…God knows every care…

Believe with your HEART…That Christ is THE WAY…
Trusting God's GRACE…Each step of the way…

Believe with your HEART…Christ conquered the grave…
Trusting in FAITH…From JUDGMENT He saves…

Believe with your Heart…He's coming again…
Trusting In FAITH…Rewards issued then…

Believe in your HEART…That God's heart is known…
Trusting in FAITH…In HIS SON ALONE!

Believe in your HEART…That CHRIST is the "door"…
Trusting in FAITH…you'll wonder no more…

Believe in your heart…that God lives on High…
Trusting in FAITH…that you'll never die…

It's simple and yet **FAITH** holds the KEY…
To ALL you BELIEVE…And ETERNITY!

Chris Luthey

LET CHRIST CALM YOUR FEARS

Like water that evaporates
Amidst a clouded sky;
Life it seems is fading fast
And we all wonder why?

Perhaps it is the weight we bear?
Perhaps its how we "row?"
We struggle hard to swim the tide
While Tossed hard to-and-fro…

Battered by the winds of change
That hit us unaware
We falter falling victim to
Heartache and despair…

But if we seek the One who said,
Unto the sea, "BE STILL!"
And trust His power—in the storm
He will guide our will…

Just as the wind then ceased to blow
There came a blessed "calm;"
Lay hold of faith, and do not fear
He holds you in His palm!

"And a great Storm arose, and the waves beat into the boat, so that the boat was already filling. And he woke and rebuked the wind, and said to the sea, PEACE! BE STILL! And the wind ceased, and there was a great calm" Mark 4:35-41

Christene Bolte-Luthey

YOU STAND ALONE

God in Heaven…
When I take in the freshness of your spirit
There is no doubting your existence…
As clean as the MORNING dew
That has fallen Upon the Earth,
You are True…
Without spot—Blameless—Pure—
You are unlike any other.
You, O God Stand alone.
Perfect…
And I rejoice deep within my spirit
Trusting always in your word,
And in your heart,
Your promise
To keep forever
Those who love You.

Chris Luthey

Let not your heart now trouble you
Trust in God, he'll see you through.
He shall send you comfort there
Whenever you should feel despair.
Rest and then lay down your fears
Surrender all your cares and tears.

"It is of the Lord's mercies that we are not consumed, because his compassions fail not. They are new every morning… Therefore I will hope in him. The Lord is good unto them that wait for him" Lam. 3:22-25

HOPE IS FOUND IN FAITH

All hope is found in faith alone,
To see us safely through;
The valleys deep and wide with pain
Until we're made anew.

For faith gives light where darkness hides
In corners of each thought
Granting joy are memories
Which at no price may be bought.

Take courage weary wanderer
God knows each step you take
Find refuge in His promises
Your trust he won't forsake.

Take hold of peace and let it be
The gift that helps you on
Place your heartaches in God's hands
His grace will make you strong.

Be not discouraged; be of cheer
Knowing God is true
Hide under his warm wing my friend
He'll calm and comfort you.

Do not be frightened, or alarmed,
By burdens you must bear
Within the mist of all your grief
He hears your every prayer.

Healing will with patience come
With every passing day
You have the shepherd at your side
Just let him lead the way.

Chris Luthey

Christene Bolte-Luthey

"For we were saved in this hope, but hope that is seen is not hope; for why does one still hope for what he sees? But if we hope for what we do not see, then we eagerly wait for it with perseverance" Romans 8:24

LAY HOLD OF GOD'S PEACE

Lay hold dear one of God's sweet peace
All your fears in Him shall cease.
Is there on earth a friend so true?
As Christ the One who DIED for YOU?
Trust Him always this I say
He shall guide you—come what may.
For true, He loves His precious sheep
Throughout life's trials—He'll bless and keep.
Rest; and reach for GRACE to borrow;
And HOPE will shine, beyond your sorrow…

"He is my refuge and my fortress: my God; In Him will I trust. Surely he shall deliver me from the snare of the fouler, and from the noisome pestilence…His truth shall be they shield" Psalm 91:2-4

"Which hope we have as an anchor of the soul, both sure and steadfast" Hebrews 6:19

Christene Bolte-Luthey

PURE PERFECTION

Trust God with
Your WHOLE HEART...

BODY
MIND and SOUL...

THIS IS PURE PERFECTION
The TRUE and PRICELESS GOAL...

The goal in which the doors of heaven
Shall open wide for thee
Embracing you in
LOVE and PEACE
Throughout ETERNITY.

C. Luthey

(Inspired by the death of my grandfather)

LOVES SINCERE EMBRACE

The angels stood at heavens door
Their arms were open wide
Waiting so impatiently
To welcome you inside.

For through the years you spent on earth
They've watched you from above
Working hard to build a life
Based on faith and love…

And though the angels begged each day
To bring you HOME at last
The Lord said "no" to each request
And so the years went past.

But NOW the Lord has called you home
With love's sincere embrace;
For in His heavens high above
Not one could take your place…

C. Luthey

Christene Bolte-Luthey

(Inspired by the death of my grandfather)

THE EVERLASTING CHAPTER

Hold tight your thoughts of YESTERDAY…Yet LOOK AHEAD to see
The GRAVE can't hold my spirit there… For God has set it free!
No longer must I bear the pain… Within this "earthly" shell;
Sickness lost its grip on me… For God decreed me WELL!
A place has been "prepared" for me… One where I may rest;
You all know my prayers were heard… For I had done my best.
So do not stand and weep for me as if I knew no glory
DEATH (on earth) Turn page and see…
NEW CHAPTER, On with story!!!

Upon my call to heaven's gate,
I heard the angels singing
A song was being sung for me…
And crystal bells were ringing.
When I looked up a banner flew…
With WELCOME written on it
And JESUS sang my life to me…
Delivered in a sonnet!
And just as He had finished that…
Loved ones I had missed,
Embraced me with resounding joy…
As on my face they kissed.
No shoes were placed upon my feet…
Yet they were given care…
Then I was lead to fields of green…
To fill my senses there…
Then I was lead on further yet…
To know my SWEETEST dream;
To sit beside MY precious LORD…
Along a timeless stream…
And here I'll rest ETERNALLY…
For I have found true peace;
Within the twinkling of an eye…
All earthly care DID cease.
So please remember when a tear…

Escapes your lonely heart
Though separated (For a time)
We shall never part.
Fear not THIS chapter when it comes…
It's GOD who writes the story…
FAREWELL until HE summons me…
To meet YOU here in GLORY!!!

Chris Luthey

Christene Bolte-Luthey

A SONG OF VICTORY

Because I TRUST that JESUS LIVES **(1 Cor. 15:12-28)**
I trust that I will too:
Where there is faith, there's also HOPE
Enough to see us through.

Let the PROMISE Jesus gave
To us so long ago;
Bring sweet peace into each heart
As we of "earth" let go…

"Even though he dies," Christ said, (John 11:25)
"If you believe in me,"
You'll **"live for I am life,"** He said
"Through all eternity…" (2 Cor. 4:18)

"I am the resurrection." (John 11:25-26)
"I give eternal life," (John 10:28)
"They shall never perish" (John 3:16)
"I bear the yoke of strife."

"I am the God of Abraham" (Matt. 22:31-32)
Let peace complete your story
The spirit now at HOME is well (Phil. 3:17-21)
"Clothed in heaven's glory." (2 Cor. 5:1-4)

It is NOT "good-bye" that we shall say
Instead a sweet "So long;"
Trusting "Death was swallowed" in (1 Cor. 15:15)
VICTORIES joyous song…
C. Luthey

PEACE AMIDST THE STORM

Christ knows the questions in your mind
They're written on His heart
Why are YOU left here on earth?
While loved ones must depart?

There are few who walk so far
And yet still seek His face
This I'm sure is evidence
Of his abiding grace...

Lift up your head for He has much
In store for you to do;
Fret not the WHAT'S, the HOW'S and WHY'S
He will guide you through...

Reach out in faith and take His hand
He is a trusted friend
His peace and hope are yours today
And they shall never end...

Like you He's known true anguish deep
He bore a horrid, "cross,"
He prayed, "His Father's will be done,"
Regarding not His loss.

Recall him drinking from the "cup"
Which He alone could take?
That's how you know in every trial
He'll stay—and NOT forsake!

C. Luthey

Christene Bolte-Luthey

IN THE WILDERNESS

So many things in life you've faced… So many trials you've known
So many threads of twine and wire…you have sadly sewn…
No other heart has known YOUR pain…nor ever felt your loss;
Except the one who gave His life…by dying on the cross…
He's felt your deepest agony…He's known your greatest fear
He's logged inside His book; it says…your each and every tear…
He's struggled with temptations…He's carried weight unsaid
All to offer hope and life…to lift YOUR weary head.
In all that you are going through…He is a friend who'll stay
He'll love and guide you tenderly…each hour of the day…
He'll never leave your side it's true…He'll walk with you each mile
While you are in the WILDERNESS, he'll train you all the while…
He'll teach you HOW to TRUST HIM…To get you through each hour.
And yet unveil in His sweet way…His awesome mighty power…
He'll teach you TO SURRENDER…everything on earth…
Your life, your world, your family…and give you "SECOND BIRTH."
This birth (I've learned) is death of "SELF"…a shedding of YOUR will…
That He ALONE controls your life…and the way you think and feel…
This truly is a wondrous thing…we cannot understand…
I just know it HAPPENS…The MORE you take his hand!
The more you take His hand by FAITH…And TRUST his will by grace
The more He will unto His Friends…Reveal—His blessed face…
Those and ONLY those who've walked…these valleys deep and wide…
Can say with true conviction… "The LORD IS ON MY SIDE!"
For this they know with PEACE quite sure…He IS a FAITHFUL FRIEND
Whose love enfolds you tenderly until your journeys end…
And then throughout Eternity…In Glory you shall reign…
And know beyond all doubt my friend…our trials were NOT in vain…

Chris Luthey

When Shadows Fall: A Journey of Faith

(Inspired by the death of my grandmother)

LIFE ETERNALLY

Though Sorrow shows its depth to me
When I think of you
For tears of peace and pain exist
Caught between the two…

Fond memories—Are all I have
To ease this troubled heart
I pray that God will hold me
The time we are apart…

The peace of God I've felt within
Knowing you are free
His grace HAS given me the HOPE
OF LIFE…ETERNALLY!!!

"In hope of eternal life which God, who cannot lie, promised before time began, but has in due time manifested His word through preaching, which was committed to me according to commandment of God our Savior" Titus 1:2-3

"However, for this reason I obtained mercy, that in me first Jesus Christ might show all long suffering, as a pattern to those who are going to believe in Him for everlasting life" 1 Timothy 1:16

"But has now been revealed by the appearing of our Savior Jesus Christ who has abolished death and brought life and immorality to light through the gospel"
2 Timothy 1:10

Christene Bolte-Luthey

A TIME TO GRIEVE

There is a time we must allow
For tears to freely flow;
As GRIEVING is a NEEDED time
For hearts and minds to grow.
When we lose a part of us
It's hard to say, "good-bye;"
Being strong seems what to do
And yet we need to cry.
With our tears we cleanse our heart
As rain restores the land;
Tears are something everyone
Should know and understand.
A grieving heart expresses LOVE
As only tears can do;
In times of loss we sometimes fail
To bear our feelings true.
The time for moving on is such
That each of us must face
It's personal and quite unique
Regarding room and space…
Then the past won't hurt as much
Recalling given years;
Like rain it's true NEW HOPE IS BORN
As FREEDOM flows in tears.

C. Luthey

"You number my wanderings; Put my tears into your bottle; Are they not in your book? When I cry out to you, then my enemies will turn back; this I know because God is for me" Psalm 56:8-9

SOME WISHES CAN'T COME TRUE

I wish that I could love you
At lease a THOUSAND years:
Yet, when those years had passed away
I still would cry these tears...

I wish I had a THOUSAND years
To hold you tenderly;
Yet if I did I still would say,
"It's not enough for me!"

I wish I had a THOUSAND years
To sit and talk with you;
Yet if I did I couldn't say
ALL I wanted to...

THAT is WHY the LORD ABOVE
Carries out HIS WILL:
It's CLEAR that I, would NOT LET GO
Your place NO ONE could fill.

And it would be UNFAIR to YOU
To wish you HERE with ME:
When you can be in PARADISE
Through all eternity!

Sincerely, I have LEARNED today
Thanks I never knew
I'm PRAISING God for wishes NOW
He kept from coming true.

C. Luthey

Christene Bolte-Luthey

HEAVEN IS AS CLOSE AS THE HEART

Today as I sat thinking it was clear…
Recalling precious memories I have held so near.
I looked toward the spacious sky…with hope that I might see
Something up there in the clouds, wanting there to be…
A message, or some unique sign that I could clearly say,
I saw you or I heard you there for I needed so today!
For awhile I gazed into the white… Drifting on the blue
But clouds could NOT in any way, still my thoughts of YOU.
So then I paused and closed my eyes, to SAY A LITTLE PRAYER,
In seconds to my soul's delight, you would meet me there!
For as I PRAYED, I found within, the truest greatest part
Heaven is a sacred place, deep inside the HEART!
It's the wondrous feelings; you and I have shared,
Moments known together that cannot be compared.
It's the treasured gentle touch, a sweet and warm embrace
It's the tender character seen within your face…
As I closed my eyes to pray, I could clearly see
Heaven ISN'T in the clouds, it DWELLS INSIDE OF ME.
What sweet comfort, what sweet peace, GOD supplied today,
How thankful, now I am it's true, that I took TIME to PRAY.
Without a doubt, I know it's true; DEATH could NEVER PART
LOVE nor JOY nor HAPPINESS It's WRITTEN in the HEART!
TODAY, I opened HEAVENS Gate, Whispering a PRAYER
I used the key and sure enough, YOU were waiting there.

"For Your mercy reaches into the heavens and your truth unto the clouds. Be exalted Oh God, above the heavens; Let your Glory be above all the earth" Psalm 57:10-11

WE'LL MEET AGAIN ONE DAY

From "earth" I have departed now
That life has passed away
Grieve NOT my dearest family
WE'LL MEET AGAIN ONE DAY!
Let sorrow not o'er take your hearts
For truly I am home;
A place has been prepared for me
Where only angels roam.
If thoughts of WHY should fill your mind
Let this your answer be;
Almighty God did hear my prayer
And set my spirit free!
Unfailing His perfect love,
His mercy and His grace
Have lifted me to PARADISE,
That of no other place.
So let your tears be few dear ones
Let memories fill your heart
With this I will remain with you
And we shall never part.
As certain as we all are born
We ALL must, "pass away,"
But JOY is found in THIS dear ones,
WE'LL MEET AGAIN ONE DAY!
Then not again, will we exchange
"Good-byes" for we shall be;
TOGETHER ever more, it's true
Throughout ETERNITY!

Chris Luthey

Christene Bolte-Luthey

WHEN SOMEONE BECOMES A MEMORY

No longer may I touch your face
Or hear you call my name
Since the Lord has CALLED YOU HOME
Nothing is the same…

Though I have said "farewell" to you
It's hard to LET YOU GO
The pain within from missing you
GOD could ONLY KNOW…

For LIFE it seems will be TOO LONG
If we must be apart:
That of you, which shall remain
Now dwells within my HEART…

For precious thoughts are all I have
Of days I spent with you
Yet I trust to draw from them
STRENGTH to see me through…

For when someone you love becomes a MEMORY;
The memory becomes a TREASURE
One you hold eternally and CHERISH it FOREVER!

C. Luthey

"*Then they cried out to the Lord in their trouble, and he saved them out of their distresses: Psalm 107:19*

UNTIL YOU HEAR GOD'S CALL

Although my time on earth is through
And I must depart from here
Remember what I loved the most
And do not shed a tear.

For I will watch from up above
And wait at heaven's door
Until we meet AGAIN dear ones
To live forever more.

Yes, parting will be sad, it's true
But still you must GO ON
Find the strength you need and then
Continue to be strong.

Relive the memories of my past
Do not forget my name
For if you leave the past behind
I've lived by life in vain.

Words alone cannot express
How much I loved you all
Many God watch over each of you
Until YOU hear God's call…

C. Luthey

"Our Savior Jesus Christ; who gave himself for us, that he might redeem us from all the iniquity, and purify unto himself a peculiar people"
Titus 2:13-14

Christene Bolte-Luthey

(Inspired by my grandmother who was a registered nurse shortly after her death)

GRANDMA'S ROCKING BABIES

DEATH is very hard to bear, especially when you're eight…
Questions of the heart and mind…Surface when it's late…
So it was for one sweet girl…who called me in the night
"Mama, can we talk a while…Maybe till it's light?"
"What's the matter, angel babe, can't you go to sleep?"
"No!" she answered, "Mom, I can't" And she began to weep.
Please explain WHY Grandma died, Why'd she go away?"
"Couldn't Jesus leave her, just another day?"
"I know that she's in HEAVEN now, and doesn't have a care;
But what I really want to KNOW is WHAT SHE'S DOING THERE?"
Oh dear lord, answer this, OUR QUESTION please I pray,
What IS Grandma doing up above today?
Then, as though I felt His touch…worried feelings ceased,
This answer filled my heart and soul, flooding it with Peace.
Well, sweetheart, this I feel with no uncertain maybes
Jesus NEEDED Grandma there, to ROCK THE LITTLE BABIES.
Since abortions came to be, heaven's full above
With tiny little angels sweet requiring lots of love.
And before I spoke another word we embraced each other
The tears we shared that moment, were truly like no other.
Then with eyes of JOY, not strife, She said,
"I know it's true, JESUS REALLY NEEDED HER,
MORE THAN ME AND YOU!"
"I'll bet she's telling stories mom, laughing all the while;
Up in heaven's rocking chair, making children smile!"
"Yep, that's what Grandma's doing, with no uncertain maybes
Cause Grandma WAS her HAPPIEST, when she was rocking babies!"
Then NOT again would WE cry out in fear of any night,
For DEATH is easier to bear, Since LOVE turned on the LIGHT!

Chris Luthey

When Shadows Fall: A Journey of Faith

OUR SOURCE

OF

GRACE & PEACE

Meditations

Devotions & Prayer

"My Grace is sufficient for you, for my power is made perfect in weakness. I will all the more gladly boast in my weaknesses, that the power of Christ may rest upon me"
2 Corinthians 12:9

Christene Bolte-Luthey

TRUE EXISTENCE

As best I can with human mind
The heart of God my soul does find
To be gentle…
To be kind…
The depth of grandeur so defined.
True it is with thoughts of Him
Earthly things grow dark and dim
To be empty…
To be grim…
He holds a matchless diadem.
Should my days be short or long?
I'll abide in Him, my song
To be faithful…
To be strong…
Amidst life's trials which come along.
Lord, this my true existence be
A binding of my soul with thee
To be happy…
To be free…
And walk with you eternally.

Chris Luthey

THE SACRED RIGHT OF WAY

No human mind can touch you
No human mind can see
No human thought can comprehend
The heart and soul of thee…

For flesh is such a fleeting thing
Perhaps—Gone tomorrow?
Time within this earthly shell
We use; we beg; we borrow…

Only that which in the soul
Exists throughout all time
May reach and know the core of YOU
Sincere and so sublime.

The spirit knows and testifies
Of that which eyes can't see
Your grace, your strength your eloquence
Your priceless majesty…

So fitting you had rightly planned
That flesh which fades away
Would never gain or understand
The sacred "right of way."

It's only granted to the heart
That yields unto the "cross"
Believing in Christ's innocence
Of sin and all it's cost.

C. Luthey

Christene Bolte-Luthey

GOD'S TRUE TABERNACLE

(In the wilderness)

"The Most High God does not dwell
In temples made by hand."
Amidst His awesome splendor
Not a stone could stand…

"Heaven is My throne," he said
"My footstool" is the "earth."
"What house could you build for me?"
What shall you say it's worth?

"My hand has made all things," He said
What is my resting place?
Look deep within your heart and see
I dwell alone in grace…

It's grace that shall sustain you
In times of want and need;
Grace and grace alone can save
A soul from death and greed.

Therefore come; please take my hand
Walk with me alone
I'll show you where I live my child
In the HEART, not wood and stone…

C. Luthey

"Our fathers had the tabernacle of witnesses in the wilderness, as he appointed, instructing Moses to make it according to the pattern he had seen. But Solomon built Him a house. However the Most High does not dwell in temples made with hands, as the prophet says: "heaven is my throne, and earth is my footstool. What house will you build for me says the Lord, or what is the place of My rest? Has my hand not made all these things?" Acts 7:44-50

"God, who made the world an everything in it, since He is Lord of heaven and earth, does not dwell in temples made with hands. Nor is He worshiped with men's hands, as though He needed anything, since He gives to all life, breath, and all things"
Acts 17:24-25

Christene Bolte-Luthey

THE JOURNEY

This life is but a journey
Throughout the vast unknown
A road of winding ups and downs
But you are not alone.
The reason why you "stumble" so
At each and every turn
Is this, and only this my child
You will not yield to LEARN.
I HAVE SO MUCH TO TEACH YOU.
My will, my thoughts, my ways
I have so much to share with you
To lighten up your days.
You have not fallen down so low
That I can't lift you high
For more than all you've ever done
I took the cross to die.
Do not be led astray by words
From any who might say
You've "fallen short" of love and grace
For I tell you this today.
I love you more than you could know
I've granted you your life
I've given you my best and yet
You give in to strife.
Take heed unto these words and see
If peace you do not find
I calmed the restless oceans
I can ease your troubled mind.
Come to me as one I've called
To be my very own
I'll take and bear your burdens
All you've ever known.
Trust that I turn not away
From any who should care
To come to me with brokenness
I'll end your deep despair.
Crossroads come and crossroads go

When Shadows Fall: A Journey of Faith

Decisions you will make
LIFE with good and bad you'll see
Are choices you must make?
Let me be your confidant
Your steady constant friend
I'll never leave your side it's true
Throughout your journey's end…

Chris Luthey

Christene Bolte-Luthey

LORD JESUS, MAKE ME MORE LIKE YOU

Let me come to you in prayer
Laying down my every care.
That burdened not I may seek
Strength and courage when I'm weak.

Help me follow every day
Thy will, thy statutes and thy way.
Let me never this world love
But keep my thoughts on those above.

Help me overcome each fear
Help me keep my conscience clear.
Let me harbor not one goal
Which might harm or plague one soul.

Fill me rather with your self
That I may know true lasting wealth.
In all of this I ask you too
Lord Jesus, make me more like YOU!

Chris Luthey

"Until we are ready to place ourselves wholly in God's care;
True understanding will be hidden behind a veil.
For only in brokenness can we honestly come to the Son of God
And receive forgiveness and pardon for sin.
By faith alone can we step beyond the earthly realm of disbelief
To discover the magnificence of TRUTH..."

C. Luthey

LIFE AND THE VINE

    Silly are the thoughts of man senseless are his ways
    If Christ is not his one true aim all his earthly days.
So far from him this world has gone so far we cannot see
We're being broken from the "vine" and losing life you see.
  Has He not said, "we must abide" in Him—to get along?
  Yes, we must cling to Him it's true, in order to be strong.
  The manner here, which separates is simply "wasting time"
We're "too busy" doing this or that whilst breaking from the vine.
    Rather all should tend to it with passion, zest and zeal
"Pruning" and "maintaining" it then "FRUIT" it shall reveal…

C. Luthey

Christene Bolte-Luthey

STILL MUCH TO LEARN

What manner of persons we ought to be
In light of the sin debt from which God did free.
We show no remorse. No sorrow, nor shame?
We by no means change, but stay just the same.
What shall God do with a world seeing not?
Christ's suffering and that of the price we were "bought."
Oh, this generation, has still much to learn
How to repent, and how so to yearn
For God and his ways, his statutes and grace
If we seek to enter—His blessed Holy place.

C. Luthey

PERFECT LOVE

It was such a gift to give to man
PERFECT LOVE was in God's plan.
Unto us he gave HIMSELF,
PERFECT LOVE and untold wealth.
For you and I he gave his soul.
Yielding all that we be whole.
Could we ever comprehend?
That GOD would DIE to be OUR FRIEND?
No human mind would grasp how deep
The love of God for us His "sheep."
He is infinitely wise.
He's pure and hallowed no disguise.
Where he lives I cannot tell
But in the souls of "sinners" made well.
In this I feel secure within
For PERFECT LOVE erased my sin.

Chris Luthey

Christene Bolte-Luthey

THE PROMISE

As I watched the sun rising this morning
With a brightness dawning anew
My heart was filled with hopefulness
And Lord, I thought of you.
Though life may often look "cloudy"
Or winds of change toss us round
The grace you grant my precious friend
Will keep my faith safe and sound.
If I just believe like the sunrise
Whatever this life here may bring
Like winter with it's passing season
There's always the promise of spring.
So therefore Lord I ask of you
Let your words comfort me still
Grant me comfort, peace and strength
As well as courage to trust in your will.

Chris Luthey

When Shadows Fall: A Journey of Faith

(This poem was written shortly after learning of Shane's cancer)

OUR SUFFERING IS NEVER IN VAIN

I never knew love's depth
Nor felt it gripping fears
Until I learned that you were ill
Which brought both pain and tears.
For you I've loved since life began
And from my womb you came
Your soul and mine for quite some time
Together have danced and sang.
How sharp this sword that's cut my heart
How threatening is its edge
How cruel and cold its icy blade
How wide is "cancer's" wedge.
No pain (but torture) could compare
To this deep hurt inside
Mortality we cannot ignore
From it we cannot hide.
How blunt, how harsh this world can be
We'd crumble with life's pressures
If not for CHRIST and God's sweet grace
And loves abounding treasures.
Thank God for HOPE through CHRIST our Lord
In him our strength we gain
Following where he leads we know
Our suffering is never in vain…

Chris Luthey

Christene Bolte-Luthey

MY HEARTS DESIRE

I long to take the hand of one
Who does not know the way?
And lead them to the Savior's arms
That they go not astray.

I long to sit with someone sad
Whose tears are falling fast?
And share the love of God with them
Who pardons from the past.

I long to stand beside the one
Who wants only to die?
And share with them the peace of God
Which grants them hope to fly.

I long to walk with someone who
Has known a broken heart
And share with them the healing grace
God's Holy words impart.

My hearts desire is but to serve
As Christ has asked me to
That you may see in me—His love
In all I say and do.

Therefore if it is that I
May serve my master here
I humbly offer you my hands
Without a doubt or fear.

In this may God be glorified?
And these once grieved find peace
As in the name of Christ we see
The Love of God released.

Chris Luthey

When Shadows Fall: A Journey of Faith

LORD I'M HUMBLED BY YOUR LOVE

Life is so hectic we sometimes forget
Just why it is we live?
To worship, honor and praise thee O Lord,
To walk in your spirit and give.

It's hard at times to do all those things
Although my heart longs to see
One day without blemish, without regret
When I'm all that you want me to be.

I'm so far from perfect, so very far
I'm humbled—you love me at all....

Oh, let me not fall, dear Savior and friend
Guide me each step that I take
Please lead me and grant me the wisdom to live
For thy blessed Glory and sake.

You know very well this heart deep inside me
Have mercy upon my soul
Forgive my transgressions, and grant me thy grace
That I be made righteous and whole.

Chris Luthey

Christene Bolte-Luthey

THE SONG OF A BREEZE

How fresh the breeze that blows this hour
Caressing in a way
The wind chimes as it passes through
Thus causing it to play.

Touching somewhat tenderly
The bell, which moves the string
Each gust of air creates new notes
And urges it to sing.

What a pleasant thing to hear
From that which can't be seen
A romance and ballet of sorts
Beneath the limbs of green.

Where from, does blow this freshness?
Where goes it now from here?
Onward still to yet bestow
Its mystery far and near.

Only God knows of these things
I question not His art
All I know for certain is
He creates with heart.

Today I've heard a miraculous tune
A breeze made melody
Just God confirming to my soul
He's ALWAYS there for me…

Chris Luthey

MORNING

I often think of "Eden" when I see early morn
And smell the freshness of the earth
Creation—true is born...
The foggy mist that covers all, between the sky and earth
Rising slowly up toward God
Unveils a new day's birth...
Untouched, as yet by anything, but sounds which fill the air
Of mourning doves and chirping birds
Who sing without a care...
How beautiful these morning hours, grant a scene for me
Displaying God's depiction
Of how our lives could be...
If only we would follow HIM obeying as we should
Like morning we would come to know
All that's pure and good...
So morning is, as "Eden" was, a time of peace and grace
When quietly a soul may seek

God's sweet, loving face...

Chris Luthey

Christene Bolte-Luthey

Devotions and Prayers

The Crimson Stain

Most merciful Father, master and King
You have taught me to walk in your will
Is the greatest pleasure known
There amidst your holiness, I see my failures and faults
The facts that "accuse" me,
I am but a "sinner" saved by your love and precious grace.
There is none to compare to you.
You are wondrous in my sight.
Your Crimson stain is all I see sweet Jesus
When I dwell in prayer with thee.
Crimson… Crimson… Crimson…
The priceless color of LOVE…
Even the sweat that fell from thy brow was crimson.
Crimson drops of love blotting out my sin in God's hallowed book.
Oh what mercy you have shown to me.
So much greater than I have ever thought possible
Sanctifying my life with your own blood.
All glory belongs to you. O Lord of Lords, you are worthy of praise.
Oh if not for the "saving" crimson stain…
The blessed stain that made me "whiter than snow."

C. Luthey

(A few Prayers written after learning of Shane's illness)

Dearest Father in heaven,
What do you want me to do?
I want only to do your will
For it is perfect and right.
I surrender all unto thee,
All that I have, all that will ever be.
Holding back nothing,
I open my heart and hands to you
May you use my life for that which you have predestined?
Nothing is mine to keep.
Like your servant Job dear Lord,
Should you choose to take everything from me?
I would love and worship you still.
All I ask of thee amidst these uncertain "storms"
Is to hold me gently in your arms and never let me go.
Carry me wherever you are
And let me feel your loving presence in my soul
Have mercy upon all those I love,
And please spare them from physical pain.
Please do not let (Shane) suffer…
I can only request this of you,
Knowing that ultimately your will shall be done.
(Regardless of my desires.)
Help me trust when I am frightened.
Help me follow you when I do not know the way.
Take my hand in yours
And guide me through the rough and rocky places.
Help me to not be afraid.
I am not strong enough to face this battle alone.
Grant my heart peace
When the sea of uncertainty is rushing in
And flooding my thoughts with fear.
Grant me wisdom
When I must face decisions
And make your will clear. Amen

Christene Bolte-Luthey

Dearest Father in heaven,
How I long for you to speak to my heart in this situation.
I need to hear from YOU concerning this matter.
Please comfort my soul.
You know every thought that passes through my mind
Every feeling that crosses my heart.
Lead me and guide me in your will
Do not let us take the wrong paths.
Forbid it to happen.
Let me not take one step in the wrong direction
Let me not stray from that which you have chosen for my family and me.
I love you more than anyone or anything I have ever known.
You know and have examined the inner depths of my being
And you know my love for you is true.
I fully, unconditionally surrender to your divine plan
And seek only your perfect will for my life and our family.
Grant me the grace and courage to withstand life's difficulties
That daily surrounds me, for they seek to devour my faith.
My assurance, my trust, my hopes are all found in YOU.
Let me not be removed from the foundation you have set me on.
Keep me holding on to the "rock" of my salvation. JESUS… Amen

(During Shane's Illness)

LET FAITH GROW

No life that's lived that knows any fears
   Has ever begged or shed sad tears.
No life that's lived that's known no pain
   Has ever lost its pride—to gain.
   This lesson I have learned and say
Praise and thank God for each new day
   For he alone can see you through
Life's journey and its mysteries anew.
   Alone: you dare not walk my friend
   Your ways and path on him depend
   Frail are we—lost sheep who need
   A loving Shepherd to succeed.
   Follow where he leads and know
His will is perfect—just let faith grow.

Chris Luthey

Christene Bolte-Luthey

> "No life is lived without some grief
> No life is blessed without fears
> No heart is complete without misery and pain
> No heart is wise without tears.
> For only through grief, heartache and woe
> Does a person learn WHO they are?
> Vulnerability seems to show us our dreams
> And prompts us to reach for a star.
> In reaching we find that we can't help ourselves
> We need someone greater than "we"
> And in admitting our weaknesses, finally then
> Our eyes become open—to see..."

C. Luthey

Almighty God, Have mercy upon me

Count not my sins against me,
But rather forgive me of my faults and failures
That I might find favor in your beloved eyes
And not vengeance.
Spare me oh merciful master
From your righteous judgment.
Keep me safe from harm
I sorrowfully repent oh Lord of my half-hearted attempts
At being the Christian you desire me to be.
Forgive me for not upholding your statutes, your laws, and your ways.
I am ashamed of my lack of boldness
And desire to be the example you have commanded me to be.
Help me. Help me heavenly Father, to do and know thy will.
Grant me unyielding courage to stand against the enemy
And fight the good fight of faith for Jesus' sake.
Oh, Lord God do not abandon me,
(Although I deserve to be abandoned.)
Throughout all my earthly days, stay with me
And have complete control of my mind, body and soul.
Let me not fall short of your blessed will in my life.
How I do love you heavenly Father.
Although my life and actions rarely reveal
The true depth of my heart for you.
You are my passion.
You are my desire.
You are my reason for existence.
You are my true purpose for living.
Teach me to follow you **regardless** of the cost.
Lead me and guide me in truth.
Grant me wisdom, peace, and grace to live in this world
Shine your everlasting light of love and life upon my soul
And live through me
That it might be well with thee.
Beyond the horizon I know you await the souls of those who trust in you
Guard my heart, my soul, my mind, and my tongue
Throughout trial and tribulation
Stay ever near to me.... Amen

Christene Bolte-Luthey

(Amidst Shane's illness)

FEAR

Fear: the ugly beast is bold
Hurling at you things untold
If it could, your heart he'd take
For he knows your faith's at stake.
Fond of playing games he'll feed
On disappointments, doubt and greed.
For he knows where your weaknesses hide
There his strength and power abide.
Once you open up your mind
To worry, fret and thoughts unkind
He will work to gain control
That he may rule your very soul.
This would pleasure him it's true
Therefore friend, I say to you....

Take this wisdom shown to me
Ponder it most carefully
You can break its bonds I know
When to Christ you humbly go.
And prayerfully release your tears
You'll find exchanged is FAITH for fears.
Get on your knees and see you will
God's courage soon begin to fill
The darkened places with his light,
There soon HOPE shines clear and bright.
Once hope dwells inside your mind,
Peace and comfort you will find.
"ASK" God said, and "you'll receive"
Simply "trust" and do "believe."
God your Father knows your pain
Suffer not your cross in vain.
If you let him guide your way
GOLD he'll make of every day!

Chris Luthey

OH, MAGNIFICENT RULER, KING OF KINGS,

My heart lies broken before thee…
I stand shattered amidst Your Holy presence.
THANK YOU for breaking my heart with Your Love!
In YOU, I know that I am made NEW…
In YOU, I feel the hope we all seek so desperately in this world…
In YOU, my search for TRUTH is ended!
For I have found that YOU ALONE—ARE TRUTH!!!
You alone are perfect.
You alone can make whole a soul that is but an empty shell.
Let thy divine hands mold and shape me
Fashion my will to thy pleasure.
Grant mercy when I am weak, for you know my faults and imperfections.
Let my life glorify YOU in each and every circumstance.
Uphold me with thy wisdom
Help me not to displease thee in thought, word or deed.
Keep me Lord from Sin…
Surround and sustain me.
Walk with me daily that I may not grieve thy tender heart.
Cleanse, restore, and renew me.
For you know I long to abide with the Father of ALL CREATION!
The creator of Heaven and Earth…
The sovereign "I AM".
The "Beginning and the end"
Of all that is; or ever shall be!

C. Luthey

"And when those beasts give glory and honor and thanks to him that sat on the throne, who liveth for ever and ever, the four and twenty elders fell down before him…and cast their crowns before the throne, saying, Thou art worthy, O Lord, to receive glory and honor and power: for thou hast created all things, and for thy pleasure they are and were created" Revelation 49-11

Christene Bolte-Luthey

VESSLE OF HONOR

(A Prayer to build Christian Character)

OH GOD MY FATHER,

I feel your magnificent hands molding me
Shaping me—ever so gently.
Working into my soul, LOVE, PEACE, PATIENCE,
JOY STRENGTH, TRUST and FAITH.
All of which come only with time and understanding.
Waiting, wanting, hoping and *feeling* helpless,
Have taught me many things.
In the valley, we are often unaware of the form you are giving us...
For we are not able to dream YOUR wondrous dreams
Nor can we imagine the gift you possess in sculpting our Being...
Yet ever so tenderly you mold throughout our Character
That, which we most desperately lack and need
To become what you created us to be.
Oh, God my heavenly Father
To touch your hands—so full of Love,
I cannot fathom the DEPTH of YOUR SOUL
To hold your hand—so caring and true
And feel the warmth of your spirit
Knowing that you created ALL things.
May I submit MY LIFETIME Lord?
(Each day that You grant me)
To be fashioned according to YOUR perfect will
That by the loving pressure of your wisdom
I may become that which YOU desire?
Take me as a lump of shapeless clay that is my life,
Mold me hour by hour
I thank you—throughout pleasure—or pain
For Your priceless, precious power... Amen

Chris Luthey

WHEN TIME ON EARTH IS THROUGH

The time has come thy "cross" lay down
Receive dear child of God; thy CROWN…
Grieve not as I now call thee near
Where there exists NO PAIN or fear…

Hear MY voice call out to you,
"BE NOT AFRAID, I'LL SEE YOU THROUGH!"
Ride on MY WINGS, of MERCY fair
GLORY in MY PRESENCE; share…

Be not anxious, in thy sorrow
I'll grant you grace and peace to borrow.
Place your fragile hand in MINE
Let thy faith in me now shine!

Close thy eyes, and go to sleep;
By thee always, I shall keep.
Feel me near thee holding tight,
Thy heart and soul with all my might.

Soon for thee my angels come
For thee on "earth" thy work is DONE.
Though many cannot understand
Why I've given THIS command,

I have prepared a place for thee
In PARADISE ETERNALLY!
In it you shall know SWEET PEACE
In which all tears from thee shall cease.

"Yea, though I walk through the valley of the SHADOW OF DEATH, I WILL FEAR NO EVIL; For YOU are with me…Surely goodness and mercy shall follow me all the days of my life; And I will dwell in the house of the Lord Forever"
Psalm 23

Christene Bolte-Luthey

MOST HOLY GOD, HEAVENLY FATHER

It is you who lives and reigns high above all that is—or ever shall be…
Thou art worthy to be praised…
I bow before thee humbly, requesting thy love and boundless mercy—
For I am a poor, wretched sinner
Saved ONLY by the depth of your priceless grace.
Oh, Beloved Master, Redeemer, Savior, Lord,
Accept my humble praise!
Allow me to speak of your wondrous ways…
I have felt the warmth of thy presence
Surrounding me in my darkest hour.
An hour in which I have tasted the emptiness of life
(Without) Your Holy Spirit guiding me,
Keeping me ever safe from death and destruction.
Surely, Thou art the author of Goodness,
Grace Love and Peace…
Thou art the KEEPER of those battered in the storms of life.
Thou art the calm amidst the strongest winds
That beat us with sadness and sorrow.
YOU ONLY are PERFECTION!
YOU—ONLY are LIFE!
YOU ONLY are worthy of ALL I have—
All I Know, all I am…or ever will be Amen

Jesus said, *"Ye shall know the truth, and the truth shall make you free. They answered him, we be Abraham's seed, and were never in bondage to any man; how sayest thou, Ye shall be made free? Jesus answered them.*
Who so ever committeth sin is the servant of sin"
John 8:32-34

"Stand fast therefore in the liberty wherewith Christ hath made us free, and be not entangled again with the yoke of bondage"
Gal. 5:1

ABBA (FATHER):

How I adore thee,
How I long to be in thy presence…
Basking in Your Holiness.
Stay with me always near,
Rest yourself deep within my heart.
For only YOU can know my soul,
My heart, my spirit, and my love for Thee.
I worship, praise and thank you
For all the blessings you have bestowed upon me.
Oh glorious Master and Ruler of my life,
I give glory and honor to you.
Thank you for loving me so much…
Thank you for sending Your Beloved Son
To shed His precious blood on the tree
For the sake of my soul.
(Though I was NOT worthy or Your gift)
I can never thank you enough
For ransoming my soul
From the depths of destruction.
In gratitude I ask Your boundless mercy upon me,
Keep me in Thy wondrous will,
That the days of my life on earth
May be a daily growing experience with YOU.
Feed me with Your Holy Spirit,
Make me into that which you created me to be.
Mold me fashion me,
I surrender in Obedience to Your Pleasure
Grant me wisdom,
Strength and divine truth
That I may be pleasing in Your sight…Amen

"Entreat me not to leave thee…for wither thou goes, I will go; and where thou lodges, I will lodge: thy people shall be my people, and thy God my God: where thou dies, will I die, and there will I be buried: the Lord do so to me, and more also, if ought but death part thee and me"
Ruth 1:16-17

Christene Bolte-Luthey

OH, GOD MY HEAVENLY FATHER,

In YOU I have found The PURPOSE of LIFE…
To hear Thy loving call
And answer it with my whole heart, has granted me SIGHT…
Therefore, I am no longer "blind."
You have given me a voice
To proclaim the GOOD NEWS
Of Salvation in Jesus Christ…
Your blessed word has touched and changed my soul.
You are magnificent in all thy ways
Unto thee I give my heart
And surrender my will.
Lead me Loving Father,
Tenderly throughout the wilderness,
And deliver me unto thyself
At the end of my "earthly" days
That I may dwell in your presence
Throughout eternity! Amen

"How think ye? If a man have a hundred sheep, and one of them be gone astray, does he not leave the ninety and nine and go into the mountains and seek that which has gone astray?" Matt. 18:12

"To the weak became I as weak, that I might gain the weak: I am made all things to all men, that I might by all means save some. And this I do for the gospel's sake, that I might be partaker thereof with you"
1 Cor. 9:22-23

"Wherefore seeing we also are compassed about with so great a cloud of witnesses, let us lay aside every weight, and the sin which does so easily beset us, and let us run with patience the race that is set before us, looking unto Jesus the author and finisher of our faith" Hebrews 12:1-2

BELOVED FATHER,

I praise and bless thee
For thy astounding mercy and compassion upon us.
Thou hast shown, and proven thyself
To my heart in so many ways!
You are:
LOVING…GENTLE…PATIENT…
FAITHFUL…UNDERSTANDING…
COMPASIONATE…CARING…
DEPENDABLE…TRUSTWORTHY…
FULL OF WISDOM,
NOWLEDGE, STRENGTH and POWER!!!
You are: GLORY DEFINED!
You are: like the brightness
That shines from the heavens
Piercing into the soul
With your awesome splendor.
I cannot fathom
The DEPTH of Your LOVE for mankind.
How blessed and fortunate are we,
To have a mighty God
And precious Friend as YOU.

"I saw also the Lord sitting upon a throne, high and lifted up, and his train filled the temple. Above it stood the seraphim: each one had six wings; with twain he covered his face, and with twain he covered his feet, and with twain he did fly. And one cried unto another and said, HOLY, HOLY, HOLY, is the LORD OF HOSTS: the whole earth is full of His glory!" Is. 6:1-3

"And I heard as it were the voice of a great multitude, and as the voice of many waters, and as the voice of mighty thunderings, saying Alleluia! For the Lord God omnipotent reigns" Rev. 19:6

"In Him we live, and move, and have our being" Acts 17:28

Christene Bolte-Luthey

IN CHRIST: MY SOUL IS COMPLETE

The moment is clam the air fresh and sweet
The Spirit surrendered my soul is complete…

No running, nor hiding From God and His hand;
My WILL is submitted to that which He's planned…

Neither bondage nor slavery in this do I find?
The only resistance I carry in mind…

For ONLY my thoughts At times—interfere
But what my heart knows remains crystal clear…

Who better to guide me Than Him whom I love
Who sends me His joy On His Hope from above…

"But Christ as a Son over His own house, whose house we are if we hold fast the confidence and the rejoicing of the hope firm to the end"
Hebrews 3:6

"And now, little children, abide in Him, that when He appears, we may have confidence and not be ashamed before Him at His coming"
1 John 2:28

"Beloved, if our heart does not condemn us, we have confidence toward God"
1 John 3:21

"Now this is the confidence that we have in Him, that if we ask anything according to His will, He hears us" 1 John 5:14

OH GOD MY LOVING FATHER,

You know the inner most depths of my soul
Let me not fail Thee in thought, word or deed...

For you know that I am but a struggling child,
Desperate to serve Thee...

Let me Hear Thy voice,
That I may know beyond a shadow of a doubt,
WHAT I am to do for the sake of Thy Kingdom...

Grant me wisdom Grant me understanding
Help me follow Thee in everything I do
That I may Glorify Thee All the days of my life...

"To love him with all the heart and with all the understanding, and with all the soul, and with all the strength...is more than all whole burnt offerings and sacrifices"
(Mark 12:33)

"I beseech you therefore brethren, by the mercies of God, that you present your bodies a living sacrifice, holy, acceptable unto God"
(Romans 12:1)

"If the blood of bulls and of goats...sanctifies to the purifying of the flesh: how much more shall the blood of Christ, who through the eternal Spirit offered himself without spot to God, purge your conscience from dead works to serve the living God?"
(Hebrews 9:13-14)

"Since you have purified your souls in obeying the truth through the Spirit in sincere love of the brethren, love one another fervently with a pure heart"
(1 Peter 1:22)

Christene Bolte-Luthey

BLESSED FATHER IN HEAVEN,

You are worthy of our praise.
For you have lead us through
The deepest, darkest valleys…
All glory to You in the Highest!
Blessed be Thy Holy name!
You have brought us out of bondage
And set the captives free.
You have delivered us from the devil's snare,
And restored the soul…
All glory, honor and praise are unto you!
You have been my refuge,
My strength, my courage…
You have brought me joy amidst pain,
Peace amidst grief.
Dear precious Master,
Thou hast said in the storm,
"Be still," And, "Do not be afraid."
Your hand has calmed the greatest fears,
Granting my spirit the sweetest peace…
What comfort it is to know that
You shall never leave nor forsake us,
And will guide us all the days of our lives
As a loving Shepherd,
Leading us in paths of Righteousness…
You know our fears you dry our tears,
You are faithful
And true to Your word.
Throughout each and every passing season
You remain the same! Amen

"That He would grant you, according to the riches of His glory, to be strengthened with might through His Spirit in the inner man, that Christ may dwell in your hearts through faith; that you being rooted and grounded in love, may be able to comprehend with all the saints what is the width and length and depth and height to know the love of

Christ which passes knowledge; that you may be filled with all the fullness of God. Now to Him who is able to do exceedingly abundantly above all that we ask or think, according to the power that works in us, to Him be glory in the church by Christ Jesus throughout all ages, world without end"
Eph. 3:16-20

Your Prayer:

Christene Bolte-Luthey

YOU are my ONLY one true peace
Within this world.
Without your life sustaining grace
My faith would be unfurled…
Amidst the strife and all its woes,
I am so very small…
Sometimes overwhelmed it seems—
I'm sometimes saddened by it all.
There are no words that can begin to describe
HOW dear you are to me…
There is no way to measure
What I feel for you
(Can one truly define infinity?)
You are the One that gave me LIFE
And died to pardon my soul.
Therefore, I shall submit my life
And ways
To You and your will forever…Amen

"We are saved by hope: but hope that is seen is not hope: for what a man sees, why does he yet hope for? But if we hope for that we see not, then we with patience wait for it" Romans 8:24-25

"Let the words of my mouth and the meditation of my heart, be acceptable in thy sight. O Lord my strength, and my redeemer" Ps. 19:14

"Be merciful unto me, O God… For my soul trusts in thee: yea, in the shadow of thy wings will I make my refuge" Ps. 57:1

"The peace of God, which passes all understanding, shall keep your hearts and minds through Christ Jesus" Phil. 4:7

MERCIFUL MASTER,

I am not worthy to come before you
Still, I humbly pray,
Please make me white as snow
Cleanse me with the blood of Your righteousness
And sanctify me with Your Holiness,
That I may with grace come boldly to Your throne
Without fear of Your Judgment
And condemnation.

Be not angry with me,
For you know I'm a poor miserable sinner
Saved only by Grace (From damnation…)
Where I would be forever SEPERATED
From your Glory and boundless mercy.

Forget not that I am but a child
Learning and growing each and every day;
In wisdom and knowledge of You…
Be merciful to me oh Lord my God,
And turn not Your face from me…

Let me not forget Thy statutes
Let me not forsake Thy Holy Commandments
But, rather etch them upon my heart
With Your loving hand,
That I may follow Thee… All the days of my life…

I REPENT of my wicked ways,
And plead Your forgiveness,
For each and every SIN
That has displeased, or dishonored you,
Hurt or grieved Your heart.
I am so very unworthy of your love,
Yet I trust that You are forever faithful
To Your promises,
And will guide, keep and protect
Those who take Your hand by Faith…

Christene Bolte-Luthey

BELOVED MASTER,

Redeemer…Lord…
Have mercy upon my soul
For I cannot fathom the depth of thy love.
Neither can I begin to comprehend
The measure of Pain You have endured for me…
You are worthy of all I possess,
And all I seek to gain…
Only YOU have broken
The shackles of sin, death, and hell.
Oh God of LOVE,
You suffered not in vain,
For I honor Your wisdom
And Bless Your heart—
You are TRUE to those You love.
You have taught me to follow that which is right…
And to look beyond what my human eyes can see.
Trusting in YOU,
I know Faith becomes a pure light.
A light that endures—protects—and blesses.
Help me obey Thee, counting not the cost
For it is faith in YOU
That shall spare my Soul
And deliver me upward to the gates of paradise…
That I may look upon thy dear blessed face,
And bask in the Glory of thy Holiness forever! Amen

"He said unto Jesus, Lord, remember me when thou comes into thy kingdom. And Jesus said unto him, Verily I say unto thee, today shall you be with me in paradise"
Luke 23:42-43

"After this manner therefore pray ye: Our Father which art in heaven, Hallowed be thy name, Thy kingdom come, Thy will be done in earth, as it is in heaven"
Matthew 6:9-10

DEAR GOD IN HEAVEN,

Fill my heart with peace…
Comfort me,
For I feel so helpless and confused.

My desire is to serve YOU,
To follow You, And To please You…

Yet I stumble, fail and fall…
I am far from perfect
So very far from "perfection"…

Still, my heart longs to Know Thee
And Thy glorious will…

Therefore, lead me and guide me,
Let me not be tossed about
By the trials of each day.

Keep me standing firmly
In Your righteous ways;
Help me to know Your heart,
And grant me the wisdom to do,
That which is pleasing to You…

You are my HOPE, my PEACE,
My COMFORT, and my JOY
Being that All Salvation,
And eternity rests in YOU.

"Weeping may endure for a night, but joy cometh in the morning…Lord, be thou my helper. Thou hast turned for me in my mourning into dancing, thou hast put off my sackcloth, and girded me with gladness"
Psalm 30:5, 10-11

Christene Bolte-Luthey

LORD GOD IN HEAVEN,

Hear my humble prayer
You know each heart
And the intentions therein…

Search us oh, God
And remove from us
That which pulls us down
Into the pit of despair…

Help us NOT to hold on
To The things of this WORLD
For the weight they possess
Is far more than we can bear…

Oh, God in Heaven; Lord of Hosts
Help free our hands of NEEDLESS waste
Help us to see where our treasures lie
Help us to know what we truly NEED.

You are the keeper of our Souls
(Those who trust in You)
You hold them in Your mighty hand
And grip them tight with Your love.

Help us to understand Life—
Apart from YOU—is VOID!
THERE IS NOTHING IN US
If you abide not in our being…
(Then, we are then destined to hell
Wretched, naked, blind
Floundering aimlessly in darkness and sin).

YOU only are LIGHT in this world
Lead us and guide us,
Take hold of our thoughts,
And control our heart, our ways.
Protect us from Satan (the father of lies)
And Love us through all of our days… Amen

"Godliness with contentment is great gain. For we brought nothing into this world, and it is certain we can carry nothing out"
1 Timothy 6:6-7

Christene Bolte-Luthey

MOST PRECIOUS LOVING FATHER

Who knows ALL things…
I praise and thank You today
For prayers answered—and—unanswered…
Your WISDOM exceeds
All measure of wisdom and knowledge.
Help me serve Thee Help me Follow Thee
Help me Honor and Praise Thee
ALL the days of my life!
Teach me Thy wondrous ways,
And lead me throughout life in TRUTH—
Grant me UNDERSTANDING
Of THY GLORIOUS WILL!
You hold each Tomorrow in Your hand,
And my soul—with every hour…
Take me—HEART, MIND, BODY, and SPIRIT
To do what YOU will…
For I long to be a "vessel" used to Glorify Thee…
Mold me shape me; Love and Guide me
My heart longs so within, to serve and Praise you
For the wondrous things You've done.
You are the PRINCE of PEACE!
A Strong and Mighty Counselor!
One to be Trusted, One that is True
One to be served in ALL that I do!

"For this is the will of God, your sanctification: that you should abstain from sexual immorality; that each of you should know how to possess his own vessel in sanctification and honor"
1 Thes. 4:3-4

"But in a great house there are not only vessels of gold and silver, but also of wood and clay, some for honor, and some for dishonor. Therefore if anyone cleanses himself from the latter, he will be a vessel

for honor, sanctified and useful for the Master, prepared for every good work"
2 Timothy 2:20-21

"But whoever keeps His word, truly the love of God is perfected in him. By this we know that we are in Him"
1 John 2:5

Christene Bolte-Luthey

BLESSED MOST MERCIFUL FATHER,

I FEEL LIKE A TINY SPARROW AT TIMES.
Tossed about on the wind and waves of the sea…
Struggling to endure each gust of anguish that batters my soul.

YOU ONLY ARE MY COMFORT…
My HOPE…
My PEACE…
My PRAYER…
I feel Thy loving hand upon me,
And trust you as a daughter trusts her father
To lead and guide me in the WAYS of WISDOM and TRUTH…

So I may come to know YOU
And Do that which brings pleasure to Your heart.
I place my hand in Yours
Believing that YOU shall never leave nor forsake me
For your LOVE is ENDLESS and shall never fail… Amen

"He who calls you is faithful, who also will do it"
1Thes. 5:23

"He has said, I will never leave thee, nor forsake thee. So that we may boldly say, The lord is my helper, and I will not fear what man shall do unto me"
Hebrews 13:5-6

"Come unto me, all you that labor and are heavy laden, and I will give you rest. Take my yoke upon you, and learn of me; for I am meek and lowly in heart: and you shall find rest unto your souls"
Matthew 11:28-29

DEAREST MOST PRECIOUS FATHER

I write from—and with a most sincere
And grateful heart this day…
Longing with each and every breath
To thank you and praise you
For Your unending faithfulness…
Words have not enough meaning
To express FULLY the depth of all I feel within for YOU…
Words cannot begin to describe
The appreciation that flow in these tears…
Tears brought to my eyes
By, Shame, fear, doubt and sorrow…
All of which were felt BEFORE
You filled me with Your peace, joy, hope and grace.
Saving me from certain death—
Where I would be tormented by Sin's sting.
Sending Thy Beloved sinless Son Jesus Christ
To SUFFER and DIE for ME…
When in all FAIRNESS
I should have endured the weight of the debt
For that which I've done.
Yet before I was even born,
You LOVED ME and PROMISED
Your KINGDOM
When I was yet an "enemy…"
Deserving NOT the slightest glance of your face…
Only You precious Father could LOVE as You have loved…
Understand as only YOU have UNDERSTOOD.
Give as You have GIVEN…
Forgive as You have FORGIVEN…
You are Faithful and true
Throughout joy and pain, laughter and tears.
You are a steady ROCK that remains forever UNSHAKEABLE!

Christene Bolte-Luthey

OH, LORD MY GOD, GLORIOUS MASTER:

Redeemer, King…Thou has taught me to pray
That my Spirit may sing…
All of heaven and earth, shall Bow at Thy Name
For throughout the ages;
You remain the same!
Glory and Honor, Glory and Laud
Worthy of Praise, Thou art oh God.
For Thou doest hold, the WORLD in Thy hand
Possessing ALL power at Thy command.
Righteous and Holy; Wondrous you are;
Shining much brighter…than any known star!
Oh, how Thy Splendor…Fills up the room,
We Lord the "BRIDE," seek YOU, our "GROOM…"
COME Blessed master, Come Glorious King,
Raise up Your church…May we ALL sing…
Waiting to WELCOME Thy sweet return,
Long so for You Lord, our hearts deeply yearn!
Glory in heaven, Glory on earth
The angels proclaim, the JOY of Thy birth.
Hosanna, Hosanna, they sing of You now
Breaking all things But Your precious vow…
To rescue your loved ones from SIN and its sting
Giving NEW meaning to "Let freedom ring."
You are the Savior who sets captives free
Who sits on the throne and forever will be,
The High HOLY Priest in Heaven above
Earning the title, MY PORTRAIT OF LOVE…
Glory and Honor…Thanksgiving and Praise,
I shall with GRACE, submit to THY ways.
That when You come forth with angels to call,
Thou find me Jesus most HUMBLE of all…

"The Spirit and the bride say, come! And let him who hears say, Come! And let him who thirsts come. And whoever desires, let him take the water of life freely"
(Rev. 22:17)

OH, HOLY FATHER,

I pray in the name of Thy Beloved Son Jesus Christ,
Who IS and Evermore shall be…
Grant us this day Lord,
Thy wisdom and grace to walk in OBEDIENCE
According to Thy word.
Let us not stumble in our journey,
That we may—with blameless lives
Greet you on the day of Your glorious return.
Help us to quickly repent
Of ALL that displeases You
And help us to walk in Thy ways…
Protect us from all evil
And sustain us with your awesome power
To fight "the good fight of faith."
Let our hearts be willing to follow Thee
Wherever Thou shall lead
Keep then, our thoughts,
Our will, our goal,
From all that is "likened" to greed…
Lead us and guide us
Near in Thy love
Rocking us gently in Thy tender care
Breathe on us Grace from above…Amen

"But you, O man of God, flee these things and pursue righteousness, godliness, faith, love, patience, gentleness. Fight the good fight of faith, lay hold on eternal life, to which you were also called and have confessed the good confession in the presence of many witnesses" 1 Timothy 6:11-12

Christene Bolte-Luthey

BLESSED FATHER,

To see a world so full of greed
Has broken me oh, Lord,
When I ponder the DEPTH of Your BEING
The LENGTH of Your MERCY
The BREADTH of Your GRACE
Which beacons all weary Lost and floundering souls—
To come unto thee…
Yet, many still care NOT to abide in Thee,

Oh what a priceless treasure they have lost—
What a blessed friend they have forsaken—
What a cherished gift they have left behind—
(All for "things" will surely fade in time)

You, oh God, unlike "earthly" riches
Shall never cease to be…
Your love is endless,
And You shall never come to an end
In strength or power.

Almighty Ruler…
Supreme Judge…
You are like a mountain
That CANNOT be moved.
You are Perfect,
Mighty, and Unchanging—
Steady, True and Firm To Thy will
Thy loving invitation
Is open to all that seek refuge,
Safety, peace and hope—
Amidst a restless, desperate, greedy world…

"How much better it is to get wisdom than gold!"
Pr. 16:16

SWEET SAVIOR, SWEET LORD

Provider of Grace and Life,
You are the Master of ALL living things
The Prince that shall cease all strife...
Lord and redeemer Blessed Sweet Hope
Glory and Honor to Thee
Thou hast forgiven the vilest SIN
Setting all prisoners free...
Thou hast climbed every mountain
And conquered each foe
That sought to kill Thee O, Lord,
Winning each battle in meekness and love
Which is why thou art SO adored...
Thou hast flown like the eagle
And touched so the sky
Unlike any other hast known;
Thou hast humbled thyself like a Lamb to be slain
Revealing the GREATEST LOVE shown...
You only are worthy of honor and praise;
Of Glory and all we hold dear,
For thou hast upheld the righteous with faith
And captured the power of FEAR!

C. Luthey

"Thou shall not be afraid for the terror by night; nor for the arrow that flies by day; nor for the pestilence that walks in darkness...because thou has made the Lord...thy habitation" Ps. 91:5-6, 9

"Ye have not received the spirit of bondage again to fear; but ye have received the Spirit of adoption" Romans 8:1

"Forasmuch then as the children are partakers of flesh and blood, (Jesus)...Likewise took part of the same; that through death he might destroy him that had the power of death, that is, the devil; and deliver them who through fear of death were all their lifetime subject to bondage"
Hebrews 2:14-15

Christene Bolte-Luthey

THE JOURNEY

As I step beyond the shoreline, to embark a distant shore
My heart is ever yearning
For more, and more, and more.
I look at the horizon, and dearest Lord I see,
A vision of a Journey
Unveiling YOU to me.
Afraid that I may falter, I've dwelt upon the land
Forgive me dearest Father, I didn't understand.
I'm ready now to step on board, ready to set sail
Knowing YOU as captain, I know I cannot fail.
No doubt I have been hesitant, to make the journey long
So frightened of the darkened night
But now I'm standing strong.
I'll sail the sea with you aboard, to guide me all the way
It's true you've never faltered, and with me you will stay.
How long will we be sailing? It's only you who know.
I only have to trust in you, wherever we may go.
I thank you for this chance to know, this journey and my guide,
That when we've reached the shoreline, in heaven I'll abide.
And when I step on that great shore, I'll know you, as I should
And feel your presence in my soul, as others never could
Who would not leave the earth's shoreline?
To embark uncharted sea
When that alone is how dear Lord,
A heart encounters Thee…

Chris Luthey

ABOUT THE AUTHOR

Childhood & Adolescent years
- I lived a quaint country life with tight knit family values and love.
- I resided on a picturesque fifty-acre farm, with two loving parents, a sister, and a brother.
- At an early age I began writing poetry with encouragement from several teachers.

At the age of twenty-one I married my husband Scott.
- Nearly twenty years later we live in a small town in Pennsylvania.
- I have two teen-age children (a 17yr.old daughter/15yr. old son).
- I am a full time wife and mother.
- I've continued to write poetry, drawing inspiration from personal experiences, everyday life, family, and friends.
- In 1993 I published my first book of poems titled *Window To My Soul*.
- Since the publishing of my first book, I've spoken to various organizations regarding my near-death experience in the 1985 TORNADO, and the life changing influence it has had on me.
- Today my poems are being used and displayed in hospitals, pregnancy aid centers, nursing homes, bereavement, hospice, and funeral home libraries, organ and tissue donor organizations, fire departments, etc...

Currently
- I am 40 years old (born Dec. 12, 1960).
- Since 1996 I have home schooled our children using a Christian Curriculum.
- In addition to church activities; I write books and poetry.
- I belong to a local Volunteer Fire Department as an Emergency Medical Technician.
- I'm a C.P.R. Instructor and teach E.M.T. courses as a "Secondary Instructor."
- From 1994 to 1999 I served as a HOSPICE volunteer and Bereavement counselor with the Visiting Nurse Association.

- The past two years I've received education in disaster related incidents.
- I am currently a part of the Critical Incident Stress Debriefing Team

Hobbies
- Writing poetry, spending time with my family and friends, photography, golfing, watercolor painting, stained glass projects, gardening/canning, walks along Lake Erie, and hiking through the woods.

9 780759 633063